THE PATRIZI MEMOIRS
A ROMAN FAMILY UNDER NAPOLEON
1796—1815

THE Marchesa Maddalena Patrizi, in compiling these Memoirs, had but one end in view, that of making the subjects of them known to their direct descendants. It was far from her thoughts to give the work to the public ; one hundred copies only were printed. One was offered to our Holy Father, Pius X of Blessed Memory, and in a private audience granted to the writer he expressed the very great pleasure which the perusal of the Memoirs had afforded him.

THE MARCHESA CUNEGONDA PATRIZI

THE
PATRIZI MEMOIRS
A ROMAN FAMILY UNDER NAPOLEON
1796—1815

BY
THE MARCHESA MADDALENA PATRIZI

TRANSLATED BY
MRS. HUGH FRASER
AUTHOR OF "ITALIAN YESTERDAYS" ETC.

WITH AN HISTORICAL INTRODUCTION BY
J. CRAWFORD FRASER

*Seventeen Illustrations
including
A Frontispiece Portrait in Colours*

BRENTANO'S
NEW YORK
1915

PRINTED IN GREAT BRITAIN

AUTHOR'S PREFACE

TO MY CHILDREN

I HAVE collected these Memoirs for your sakes and in response to a wish repeatedly expressed by your father. In calling up the serene and strong personality of your great-great-grandfather, and the very sweet one of her who was his faithful and valiant companion, I have felt that I was affectionately carrying out a task of true filial piety.

It has also been very welcome to me to offer to their memories a homage which was denied in their lifetime, the admiration which their heroic fortitude inspired in a relative of my own mother, that same Count de Tournon, Prefect of Rome, whom they believed to be one of their enemies. Having at my disposal, through the courtesy of his descendants, all his private papers, I have been able to realise how unwillingly he executed the imperial orders and how earnestly he strove to mitigate their severity. I have carefully confronted his documents with our own archives and the very abundant ones furnished to me by the State Papers in France.

As you will see, there is little of my own in the book. I have limited myself to correlating, with scrupulous exactness, the testimony of contemporaries, in the hope of making you love and venerate your ancestors as we have loved and venerated them. My earnest desire is that they may obtain for their descendants that which they possessed—the Faith which no storm of impiety can shake, no suggestion of indifference weaken, and the Strength which maintains, at any cost, the accordance of the principles of conscience with the actions of life, that Strength which I venture to call the point of honour of the Christian's existence.

Your Mother.

December 1911.

TRANSLATOR'S PREFACE

It was towards the mellow end of a June afternoon. We had been out to the " Castello di Constantino " and had sat silently gazing at the wonderful panorama of the ancient city spread out at our feet. New Rome seemed to have vanished, and it was the Rome of the Cæsars that stretched before us, rising in tier upon tier of arches and terraces, with the pines and cypresses of countless gardens serving as dividing-lines and background. The low sunshine lay in a wash of red gold on all the ruined glory, and far away the Sabines were turning to amethyst under the tender blue of the evening sky.

" Let us go now that it is at its best," said Donna Maddalena ; " I have something that I want to show you at home." So we drove down, down through the winding streets that have never changed, to the old Palace opposite the Church of San Luigi dei Francesi. I had not been to the house for many years, and when I was last there the head of the family, my friend's

father-in-law, still reigned autocratically, as his fathers had done before him, according to the traditions of the old régime, and resisted innovations and renovations with the inherited prejudice of centuries. When he died it was tacitly agreed in the family that the old régime was to be buried with him, as a relic no longer in place above ground, though ever to be remembered with respect. Light and air, comfort and convenience, and, above all, that quantum of individual liberty without which thinking people of to-day cannot live—these came flooding into the dark old house, and have made it a dwelling where all seems peace and light. It was very strange to me to be shot upstairs in an automatic lift instead of climbing the long flight of stone steps that I remembered; to find myself walking over polished parquets instead of over the red brick or marble of the older day: and some of the ancestral portraits seemed to me to have taken on a slightly disapproving expression. But the tenets and principles of conduct have not changed. Every member of the family would now fight for them as resolutely as its ancestors did, and, since the story of their most famous fight is one which is being repeated all over the world to-day by parents who insist upon giving their children a Christian education, the relation of their struggle is a matter which will interest many and perhaps inspire courage too.

The opening of the story has another interest, all its own—that of presenting an unusually faithful picture of conditions in Roman social and family life, which have passed away as completely as those of the first ages of Christianity, although but a scant hundred years have elapsed since the Marchese Francesco Patrizi was banished from his home and obliged to report himself once a week to the Police in Paris; since his son, Giovanni, was imprisoned in the Château d'If for refusing to hand over his children to Napoleon to be brought up at the Military School of Prytanée de la Flèche—since Giovanni's royal wife was driven over the Alps with her two little boys and also forced to report herself, like a convict under vigilance, to the police in Paris. It was the royalty that aroused the worst hatred of the Emperor. The cousin of Louis XVI, the gentle lady who had never spoken an unkind word in her life, but who would have gone to the scaffold a hundred times over for her children's salvation, was a thorn in the side of him whom her descendants still call "the parvenu"; and, whereas the persecution of other recalcitrants was left to his officials, Napoleon seems to have made that of the Patrizi family his personal affair. It is a sad and ungrateful task to have to record the baser characteristics of one whom many consider the greatest of men, but the principles at stake on one side, and the guiding motive on the other, enter too largely into modern life to permit of their being glossed over or forgotten.

In preparing this book for the English-speaking Public the translator has kept to the literal text of the letters and diaries. In the narrative portions the material has occasionally been condensed, and some necessary notes and elucidations have been added, as well as an historical introduction. Apart from these details the book is entirely the work of the Marchesa Maddalena Patrizi. The documents cited were collected by her through a long period of industrious research both in France and Italy, and were printed in the " Memorie di Casa Patrizi," for family circulation only, in 1911. In the present work they are offered to the public for the first time.

MARY CRAWFORD FRASER.

CONTENTS

	PAGE
AUTHOR'S PREFACE	v
TRANSLATOR'S PREFACE	vii
HISTORICAL INTRODUCTION	1

CHAPTER I

THE MARRIAGE OF GIOVANNI PATRIZI AND CUNEGONDA OF SAXONY—THE STORY OF THE BRIDE'S FAMILY —HER EARLY YEARS IN FRANCE—DOMESTIC CONDITIONS IN THE LIFE OF THE ROMAN ARISTOCRACY 35

CHAPTER II

PIUS VII AND NAPOLEON—THE EMPEROR'S ASPIRATIONS—THE ABDUCTION OF THE POPE—THE GOLDEN LEVY AND ITS EFFECT ON THE PATRIZI FAMILY 52

CHAPTER III

THE MARCHESE GIOVANNI RESISTS THE DECREE—INEFFECTUAL EFFORTS OF THE PREFECT TO OBTAIN HIS SUBMISSION—HE REFUSES TO GIVE UP HIS CHILDREN 75

CONTENTS

CHAPTER IV

PAGE

THE BLOW FALLS—ARREST AND ABDUCTION OF GIOVANNI PATRIZI—HE IS CONVEYED TO CIVITA VECCHIA AND IMPRISONED IN THE FORT, WHERE HE FINDS MANY FRIENDS AND ACQUAINTANCES . 89

CHAPTER V

EXTRACTS FROM THE MARCHESE'S JOURNAL—HIS EXPERIENCES AT CIVITA VECCHIA—THE BEGINNING OF THE LONG CORRESPONDENCE BETWEEN HIM AND HIS WIFE—HIS DEPARTURE FOR AN UNKNOWN DESTINATION 104

CHAPTER VI

NAPOLEON'S PERSONAL HOSTILITY TO THE PATRIZI FAMILY—HE ORDERS THE SEQUESTRATION OF THEIR REVENUES—GIOVANNI'S JOURNEY TO FENESTRELLE—HOPES AND FEARS IN ROME . . 121

CHAPTER VII

CUNEGONDA LEAVES ROME TO CONDUCT HER CHILDREN TO FRANCE—PIPPO'S DIARY OF THE JOURNEY—THE SOJOURN IN SIENA—THE ORDER OF MALTA AND THE BAILLI RUSPOLI 150

CHAPTER VIII

DIFFICULTIES OF CUNEGONDA'S POSITION—HER CORRESPONDENCE WITH HER HUSBAND IS STRICTLY CENSORED—HER DEPARTURE FROM SIENA—LETTERS FROM THE BOYS TO THEIR FATHER . 171

CONTENTS

CHAPTER IX
CUNEGONDA IN TURIN—HER FRUITLESS EFFORTS TO OBTAIN PERMISSION TO VISIT HER HUSBAND AT FENESTRELLE—A SAD JOURNEY ACROSS THE ALPS . . . 194

CHAPTER X
GIOVANNI'S SECRET CORRESPONDENCE WITH HIS WIFE IS DISCOVERED BY THE POLICE AND RESULTS IN HIS BEING REMOVED TO THE CHÂTEAU D'IF AND PLACED UNDER CLOSE SURVEILLANCE—TREACHERY OF HIS SUPPOSED FRIEND, CARMINATI 207

CHAPTER XI
CUNEGONDA ARRIVES IN PARIS—PIPPO DESCRIBES HIS IMPRESSIONS—THE WHEREABOUTS OF GIOVANNI KEPT SECRET FROM HIS FAMILY—HE IS NOT ALLOWED TO HAVE ANY NEWS OF THEM—CUNEGONDA IS OBLIGED TO TAKE THE BOYS TO LA FLÈCHE UNDER MILITARY ESCORT 224

CHAPTER XII
LIFE AT LA FLÈCHE—THE "NEW CONCORDAT"—THE EMPEROR AND THE POPE—BONAPARTE'S TREACHERY—LETTERS TO GIOVANNI FROM HIS FATHER—DEATH OF THE MARCHESE FRANCESCO PATRIZI . 245

CHAPTER XIII
VISITORS AT LA FLÈCHE—REUNION OF CUNEGONDA AND HER SISTERS—WEARY WAITING—A RAY OF HOPE—THE BEGINNING OF THE END—"ALLELUIA!" 268

CONTENTS

CHAPTER XIV

THE 14TH OF FEBRUARY, 1814, AT THE CHÂTEAU D'IF—
LIBERTY AT LAST—GIOVANNI'S RETURN TO ROME 286

CHAPTER XV

CUNEGONDA AND HER SONS IN PARIS—XAVIER'S DESCRIPTION OF EVENTS—HER HOME-COMING—THE RETURN OF PIUS VII TO ROME—THE DEATH OF GIOVANNI PATRIZI 304

TRANSLATOR'S NOTE 317

INDEX 321

ILLUSTRATIONS

	FACING PAGE
MARCHESA CUNEGONDA PATRIZI (Coloured Plate) *Frontispiece*	
NAPOLEON	4
ROME. CASTLE OF SANT' ANGELO (from an old print)	28
Photo by R. Moscioni.	
TWO SKETCHES FROM THE ALBUM OF CUNEGONDA	38
AN ALMANAC FORMERLY IN THE POSSESSION OF CUNEGONDA	42
MARCHESA PORZIA, WIFE OF FRANCESCO PATRIZI	44
ROME. THE CHURCH OF S. LUIGI DEI FRANCESI, FACING PALAZZO PATRIZI	84
Photo by R. Moscioni.	
MARCHESE GIOVANNI NARO PATRIZI	98
ROME. CASTLE OF SANT' ANGELO (under Pius IX.)	112
Photo by R. Moscioni.	
CIVITA VECCHIA	128
Photo by R. Moscioni.	
SIENA. THE CHAPEL IN THE PIAZZA	150
Photo by R. Moscioni.	
SIENA. THE PIAZZA AND TOWN HALL	164
Photo by R. Moscioni.	
CASTLE OF BARD, ON THE ROAD FROM TURIN TO COURMAYEUR. CUNEGONDA'S JOURNEY OVER THE ALPS	194
Photo by E. Alinari.	
ANCIENT GATEWAY AT SUSA	202
Photo by E. Alinari.	
CHÂTEAU D'IF	222
Photo by Giletta.	
MARCHESE FRANCESCO PATRIZI	262
PIUS VII.	312

HISTORICAL INTRODUCTION

By J. CRAWFORD FRASER

It would seem probable that the earliest actual perception of what he was wont to call his " star " came to Napoleon during the hours immediately following upon the Coup d'État of the eighteenth of Brumaire, Year VII—in the terms of the Gregorian Calendar, the ninth of November, 1799.

For he had just made a first successful, if terrifying experience, in his own person, of the supremacy of deeds over words; that is to say, the supremacy of armed force over the clamour and divided counsels of windbag politicians. For the first time he had dared to measure himself with the constitution of his country; and, after passing through the most momentous hours of his career, had emerged the conqueror by a hair's-breadth— thanks to the superior courage and presence of mind of Lucien Bonaparte in rallying the soldiers to the defence of his elder brother against the enraged representatives of the people. What Napoleon's innermost thoughts were, precisely, during the night which followed in the privacy of his study in the little house that he was occupying in the Rue de la Victoire, will never be known. This much only is certain, that he emerged from his vigil a new man in many respects, a man convinced of his own instrumentality in the designs of Providence for the regeneration of mankind; and one, consequently, not to be hindered in the carrying out of his ideas by any human interference. From that moment "The little Cæsar," as Vaudal styles him, "frail, nervous, impressionable, with his habitual horror of physical contact with the mob," became the ruler indifferent to all opinions except his own.

As he saw it now, all that he had done, hitherto, or that he had it in mind, however vaguely, to do in future, was by the direct inspiration and in conformity with the will of that Heaven which had chosen him from among all the sons of men to be its vicegerent upon earth—a conviction in which he was confirmed by his elevation to the Consulate and the victory of Marengo. At this point, however, it was that he found himself confronted with the greatest of all the problems which had ever presented themselves to him for solution; namely, the reconciliation of what he believed to be his destiny with what, as a Catholic, he never ceased to believe to be the spiritual powers invested in the Catholic Church for the welfare of souls.

In a sense, it seemed to him that this could only be accomplished by taking the Church into partnership with him—a partnership of which the "Concordat" of 1801 was the deed, and in which the share of his partner, Pope Pius VII, was certainly not intended, by the promoter of the scheme, to be the controlling one.

Thenceforth the Church, in Napoleon's eyes, was entitled to no more than the subordinate part of a cog-wheel in the vast machinery of his plans for the betterment of the world; and his subsequent conduct towards the Papacy was the exact measure of his anger at the Pope's rejection of his pretensions to suzerainty over the throne of St. Peter.

The relations to one another of the two partners in the Concordat is shown by a remark of each. "We are willing," said Pius VII, speaking of himself in 1801, "to go as far as the gates of Hell; but we have no intention of going a single step beyond them." And, years later, at the time of his greatest power, in the days after Friedland, Napoleon exclaimed angrily: "The Pope reigns over the souls of men, but I only over their bodies! The Church keeps their souls for itself, and only allows me their carcases!"

Of all his disappointments, none was the equal of that which he suffered on realising his impotency to subjugate the spirit of the Church to the point of accepting him as its overlord upon earth. And, in the bitterness of his failure to bring about the marriage between Church and State—by imposing on the former the obligation of obeying as well as of loving and honouring the latter—Napoleon went so far as to draw down upon himself that ban of excommunication which the good Pope felt compelled to lift from him again in the very hour of its accomplishment as signalised by the retreat of 1812.

This disappointment of Napoleon's, moreover, was the sharper for being that of a proud, self-willed man in love, whose lawful claim (as it seems to him) to complete domination over the object of his affections is rejected with contumely.

In truth, not only was Napoleon an inveterate, natural Catholic, but he was also a mystic; as he once said to one of his Marshals who was attempting to deter him from his project of invading Russia: "Have I yet accomplished the will of Fate? I feel myself driven towards an end of which I am still in ignorance; but, when I shall have attained it, a grain of dust will be sufficient to beat me to the earth." Thus, once a design had taken root in his mind, it followed that, as he actually did so believe it to be an inspiration of Heaven Itself, no means should have appeared to him too outrageous for the execution of it. Similarly, it stands to reason that such designs needed no other justification for Napoleon beyond that of their having been inspired in him.

From the hour in which he had succeeded in

NAPOLEON.
From an engraving by Achille Lefevre.
After a painting by Charles Steuhe.

extorting the Pope's consent to the Concordat in 1801, Napoleon had had only one conviction in regard to Rome—that, in reward for his restoration of the Catholic religion in France, it was the intention of Heaven to entrust him with the temporal overlordship of the Church. This belief was peculiarly easy to him by reason of the years he had spent in France, during which his naturally critical mind had become imbued with the French antipathy to Roman discipline in church matters; in a word, with that " Gallicanism " which has been the scourge of French Catholicism from the days of Henri IV, through those of Louis XIV, Louis XV, and Napoleon III, even to our own. Also, he thought, honestly and weakly enough, that he would the more easily be able to bring the French people back to the Faith—of which the Revolution had deprived it and without which he felt his hold upon the country to be at best but a precarious one—by means of pandering to what he believed to be the national weakness of vanity, not only through establishing its partial independence of Rome, but also by reducing Rome itself to the level of a French department.

In this fixed intention, then, it was that, when the battles of Austerlitz and Jena had made him the master of central Europe, his long-cherished ambition of becoming a second Charlemagne and " Protector of the Holy See " began to take definite shape. The only obstacles in his path were the

Pope and the clergy, with their stronghold in the hearts of the Romans. But even their influence would be of no avail, in Napoleon's eyes, to offer any serious opposition to the power of his glory, of his seductions, and—if need were, as a last resort—of his armies. Of other than moral force, to do him justice, he had no desire to make use in this instance. For the truth was that he was in love with Rome for her own sake, and that he desired all her love in return for himself; so that the idea of sharing it with the Pope was intolerable to him. Indeed, one may say that, so much in love with Rome was Napoleon, that he deemed it derogatory for her to be the handmaid of any less a man (according to his own standpoint in regard to earthly matters) than himself, the Emperor of the West, the new Charlemagne to be.

Having seated his brother Joseph upon the throne of Naples in April 1806 (a necessary strategical preliminary in view of his Roman programme) and having advanced the French outposts to Civita Vecchia in the following month, the Emperor next proceeded to fasten a multiplicity of petty quarrels upon the Pope. These were brought about mainly by the French occupation of the papal territories—on the ground of Pius VII's refusal to depart from his neutrality in the contest between England and France by forbidding the importation of English goods into his dominions—a series of outrages culminating in the seizure, in

October 1807, of the Marches, that part of Italy which lies between the Adriatic and the Apennines, the southern bank of the river Reno and the northern boundary of the kingdom of Naples. Little by little, Pius VII found himself ever more closely hemmed in on all sides by the forces of his relentless adversary.

And then, quite suddenly, came the end. In the dawn of February 2, 1808, a handful of French dragoons, followed by a division of infantry, clattered leisurely out of the fog-bound Campagna across the Ponte Molle, and so on towards the Porta del Popolo, by which, about eight o'clock, they entered the city. They were under the command of General Sixtus de Miollis, who let it be understood that he was on his way with them from Florence to Naples. This fiction, however, deceived no one; more especially when the "visitors" established themselves promptly and methodically in the Castle of Sant' Angelo—which was handed over to them, on their request, by the commandant!—and the neighbouring district. In addition they placed a battery of field-guns in position over against the Quirinal Palace in which the Pope was accustomed to spend the winter months. But when Miollis discovered how this battery had been trained on the Pontiff's own residence, he ordered it to be removed; for violence was not yet a part of his plan.

That same day he asked for an audience of Pius VII, and, on its being accorded to him, explained his presence in the city by representing himself as being merely desirous of paying his respects to the Head of Christendom in passing from Florence to Naples with his troops. To this the defenceless Pope could only reply with what affability he could muster. On leaving the Quirinal, Miollis called at the offices of the papal police and informed the astounded officials whom he found there that, for the future, they would receive their orders from one of his subordinates, a certain General Herbin. At the same time the papal printers were forbidden to print anything whatsoever which might be sent to them from the Quirinal without having first obtained permission to do so from the new Chief of Police.

And so the farce of Miollis' " visit " continued. As the days succeeded one another his real intention became too plain to admit of further pretences, and by the following month he was already sending into exile all who dared to raise their voices against his conduct and the presence of his soldiers in Rome. These rigours he endeavoured to temper by a show of friendship towards the Roman nobility, whom he repeatedly invited to balls and receptions at his headquarters. His attempts at conciliation—albeit, at first, moderately evocative of a response from such patricians as had been led to suppose, from the mildness of the Pope's attitude hitherto in regard to the French invaders, that he would not resent their acceptance of Miollis' advances—were, however, fated to prove a failure. Immediately after the first of his receptions, which had been quite well attended, Pius VII issued a decree peremptorily forbidding his subjects to entertain such social relations with the enemies of their only lawful Sovereign. At the same time he sent a vigorous protest to Paris against the whole business, with no other result than that of determining Napoleon to bring the period of 'precautionary occupation' to a close as soon as possible by substituting for it the formal annexation of Rome, together with the Marches, to the French Empire.

But to do this, all at once, was hardly feasible, mainly by reason of the fact that the Emperor was uncertain as to the effect of the annexation of the Eternal City upon the Government of Austria, with which he was not yet prepared to go to war again. This being so, he confined himself to the incorporation of the Marches with his dominions on April 2, 1808—a foretaste of his quality which was not without effect upon the population both there and in Rome; for, on the reception of the news, there broke out an opposition almost of the dimensions of a revolution. The first sign of this was shown in a recrudescence of brigandage from the Abruzzi westwards, through the Sabines, to the gates of Rome itself. "Brigandage," rather, so called, since the vast majority of "brigands" in this instance were, in all probability, only armed supporters of their rightful ruler, and not by any means thieves or murderers, although there may well have been a certain admixture of bad characters in their ranks.

In order to deal with these bands Miollis, unable to spare any of his own troops for the purpose, endeavoured to organise a small body of Gendarmerie from among the inhabitants of each village in the troubled districts to cope with the menace to his authority. This was the last straw which sufficed to break the Pope's patience—seeing that his own subjects were thus being formed into the nucleus of an army under the orders of foreign and hostile interlopers—and he replied to it by the publication of a decree threatening any one who might participate in it with the lesser excommunication. Within twenty-four hours not a single one of his more decent subjects who had taken service in Miollis' new Gendarmerie but had returned their weapons and their uniforms to the French Chief of Police, from whom they had received them. The only Romans, be it remarked, moreover, who retained their employment under General Herbin were found to be a handful of men, all of whom were known by their criminal antecedents to the Pope's own guardians of the peace ; indeed, a list of them, with their police *dossiers*, had been already forwarded sarcastically by Cardinal Pacca, as Secretary of State, to Herbin as an assistance to his labours.

Simultaneously the Cardinal Secretary made public the fruits of the investigations of his agents into the characters and police-records of such individuals as had been entrusted by Miollis with the duty of recruiting for his local Gendarmerie; he brought them to justice on a charge of high treason before the papal magistrates; and so presented the world at large with such a series of scandalous revelations as completely to discredit the methods both of Miollis himself and his subordinates.

There followed an unsuccessful attempt of the French to kidnap Cardinal Pacca, which was thwarted by the firmness of the Pontiff in person, who concealed his secretary and ordered the fortification of the Quirinal, in which he gave asylum also to three other Cardinals whom Miollis had menaced with transportation if they fell into his hands.

Had Pius VII made use of this moment to give the signal for a general rising against the invaders it would probably have resulted in their overthrow. For six months the Romans had been awaiting some such signal on his part, and all was ready for a revolt. But, for some reason or other, he held back, and nothing happened—to the intense disappointment of his people. Nevertheless, so alarmed had Miollis been by the nearness of the danger that he sent entreaties to Napoleon, begging him to take stronger measures against the opposition of the Pontiff. This was in the September of 1808, the same month in which Murat, the Emperor's brother-in-law, was created by him King of Naples in place of Joseph Bonaparte, who had been lately made King of Spain.

No sooner was Murat seated on the Neapolitan throne than he began to offer his services and those of his army to Napoleon against the " rebellious Romans and their ungrateful Pontiff," as he styled them. But, in truth, the Emperor had no great desire to avail himself of these offers. To begin with, it was no part of his policy to extend his brother-in-law's activities any further beyond the confines of Naples than could be helped. For Rome was still the darling of Napoleon's heart, and he did not intend it to be ravaged. Also, he was never entirely trustful of Murat's ambitions; and this more especially as the latter had given his whole confidence to a man—Count Salicetti—whom Napoleon particularly despised and disliked for his personal cowardice * and his incurable double-dealing. This Salicetti was a Corsican, bilious, sallow of complexion, and with a pair of shifty, chocolate-coloured eyes; a former member of the National Convention of 1793, and a regicide, he had covered himself with obloquy as one of the administrators of the Reign of Terror. A persecutor of religion during his lifetime, when the hour came for him to die, in

* As shown by his inducing two women, a mother and her daughter, to shelter him at the risk of their lives during the Reaction after July 1794—a fact which came to the knowledge of Bonaparte, who, for their sakes alone, abstained from having him arrested.

December 1809, he sent a hasty message to Fra Egidio, the famous lay-brother of the Franciscans in Naples, to pray for him. But, on receiving the summons, the saint replied to it with a shake of the head. "It is too late," he said; "for, as you will find on your return to Palazzo Maresca"— Salicetti's residence off the Chiaja—"he died just after you left there." And so it proved.

Advised, then, by Salicetti, Murat continued to press his offers of interference upon the Emperor throughout the winter and spring of 1808–1809. This did not prevent him from representing himself as a friend in disguise to Pius VII and the Curia at Rome. But, at first, Napoleon would have none of him; until, at long length, worn out by his importunities, and having no one else—on account of the war with Austria that had just broken out— the Emperor sent word to him in the last days of March 1809 that he was to re-enforce Miollis and to place a part of his army for that purpose on the Roman frontier. Murat, however, demurred to the idea of his "beautiful troops being under the orders of a Miollis"; likewise, he insisted that nothing else but only his own nomination to the supreme command in the Roman States "could possibly," as he put it in a letter of April 14, 1809, "disconcert the enemies of the Emperor." These representations, however, were fruitless, Napoleon having no intention of superseding Miollis, whom he liked and trusted both as an aristocrat and a soldier-courtier of the old school of Louis XVI. The only concession which he could be persuaded to make was that Murat might send Salicetti to Rome to represent him among the members of the new Government; but upon the condition that Salicetti, like all the rest, was to be subject to Miollis.

What the Emperor did not know was that Salicetti, without waiting for his permission, had already betaken himself to Rome in order to further the interests of Murat with the Pope and the Curia, as well as to prepare the way for the next step in the affair—that of the imminent, formal annexation of Rome by Murat to the Empire. Arriving thus unexpectedly at Rome early in April, Salicetti informed Miollis of the intended Coup d'État—to the amazement of the General who had been left in ignorance of the Imperial decision—and was told, in exchange, that, come what might, he was to consider himself Miollis' subordinate. This so irritated Salicetti that he returned, forthwith, to Naples; but only to be sent back again at once to Rome. Here he learned that a certain General Lemarrois had been installed as *chargé d'affaires* by Miollis, who had gone to Milan to confer with the Viceroy of Italy, Eugène de Beauharnais, upon the situation, and presumably, to ask his aid towards the subjugation of the Papacy. As a matter of fact, Salicetti did not actually go as far as Rome itself, but broke his journey at Albano, in order not to arouse the suspicions either of the papal authorities or of Miollis' partisans among the French. From Albano "the Corsican Fouché," as Salicetti was nicknamed, was kept in touch with all that was taking place in the city by his indefatigable spies. As he wrote to Murat, if the latter meant to make himself master of Rome in the Emperor's name by proclaiming the annexation before Miollis could return to do so, he must act at once.

Nothing loath, Murat gave orders for his army to advance upon Rome on June 7, Salicetti receiving instructions to meet him there on the tenth of the same month. It appeared to the conspirators that nothing now could prevent them from taking possession of the papal capital.

What was at the bottom of Murat's mind, what astounding designs he may have dared to cherish, must for ever remain a matter for speculation. His secret relations with the Pope, no less than the fact of Napoleon's having at that moment just suffered a serious defeat at Essling, near Vienna, may contribute to something approaching a solution of the problem. Also, his subsequent open defection from Napoleon's cause a few years later may furnish some index to the motives of his conduct on this occasion.

Be that as it may, Salicetti left Albano for the Farnese Palace in Rome, with high hopes, on June 9. His road was that of the Appian Way and the Porta San Giovanni.

Scarcely had he reached his destination, however,

than a post-chaise entered the city at a gallop from the opposite direction, that of the Flaminian Way connecting Rome with Florence and the north. Passing through the Porta del Popolo, the vehicle drew up in the Piazza di Spagna, when there stepped from it three men. The first of these was tall and very thin, and of a pronounced stoop ; a soldier with a uniform of most unmilitary slovenliness ; grey-haired and frightfully disfigured by the scar of a wound in the face—his jaw-bone had been fractured by a British musket-ball in America, where he had served under Lafayette at Yorktown. This was none other than Miollis himself. Of his companions, one was no more than a stripling ; a handsome boy, radiant with the delight of his first political post—Heaven knows, he was destined, soon enough, to have had his fill of such employments !—one Cesare Balbo by name, and of Genoa by extraction.*

The third of the trio was a shorter, stouter man than either of the others, pink-cheeked and smug, whose brown eyes twinkled rapaciously as he glanced around him—a typical lawyer-bureaucrat, Baron Janet, once a barrister of Lons-le-Saulnier, now Solicitor-General of the new Government, and charged with the duty of public prosecutor as well.

To these three were to be added, as soon as they

* Overcome by remorse at his share in the French proceedings in Rome, Balbo fled the city in the June of 1810. Thirty years later, even, in 1839, he was still unable to refer to these transactions without tears of sorrow for his participation in them.

should arrive in Rome, two others: Gerando, a philosopher more interested in Hobbs, Kant, and Descartes than in politics; and a Piedmontese, Dal Pozzo, the bosom friend and "other self" of Janet, whose severities he ardently supported in the councils of the "Consulta," as the new Government appointed to supplant that of Pius VII was to be named. The very differences in character of the five members of it, including Miollis, came eventually, as can easily be understood, to cause its utter failure.

No sooner had Miollis and his friends reached the city than the General, learning of Salicetti's presence at Palazzo Farnese, sent orders to the King of Naples' representative to meet him the next day. In the same hour he resumed the command of his troops from Lemarrois; and so the Neapolitan conspiracy was brought to a halt. Thenceforth the army sent by Murat from Naples under General Pepe was relegated automatically to the position of a mere auxiliary force under the supreme command of Miollis, who by now had procured a corps of gendarmerie as well, under General Radet, from Florence, for his bodyguard. It need hardly be added that, for his timely nipping in the bud of Murat's attempt to make himself master of Rome, he was never forgiven by the ambitious plotter.

On the following morning the Consulta—in which Salicetti was temporarily included by way of placating his master—issued a decree annexing Rome to the Empire in the name of Napoleon.

But, if seriously checked by Miollis's promptitude, Salicetti still persevered in his attempt to discharge the mission with which Murat had entrusted him. During the weeks that followed upon the installation of the Consulta, that body applied itself to the "reforming" of all institutions obnoxious to its theories, in a fury of zealous destruction. Sequestration of church property and the expulsion of monks and nuns from their homes were succeeded by wholesale changes in the life of Rome itself. The setting up of an entirely novel form of legal procedure was accompanied by other radical alterations, such as the abolition of lotteries, privileges, exemption from taxation, and so forth; habits, morals, and even amusements were all in future to be regulated by the codes of Gerando, Janet, and Company. Within an incredibly short space of time some sixty proclamations to this effect in as many departments of daily life had so bewildered and dismayed the unfortunate Romans as almost to make them ask themselves whether their existence were only a perturbing dream, and not a reality at all.

The only thing that now continued to cause the Consulta any disquiet was the steadfastness with which the Pope continued to protest against its usurpation of power. This he did, for the most

HISTORICAL INTRODUCTION

part effectually, so far as the Romans were concerned, by means of placards threatening any adherents of the new order with the severest clerical penalties; so that, as before, the campaign of passive resistance on the part of his subjects came near to paralysing the activities of Miollis and his friends, until it was obvious to them that their sole resource lay in the complete elimination of all papal influence within the circle of their operations. Nevertheless, they hesitated to do this for fear of causing a really serious revolution—at least, this was the constant dread of Miollis, who was supported by the vote of the best-minded of his colleagues, the young Balbo. On the other hand, Janet and Dal Pozzo demanded the arrest and removal of Pius VII in no measured terms. As for Philosopher Gerando, he was against any decisive steps whatsoever.

At this juncture Salicetti, to whom the embarrassments of the Consulta had afforded some considerable consolation for the failure of his attempted seizure of power, was enabled once more to take a hand in Roman affairs in the interests of his master.

Since his disappointment in June he had let slip no opportunity either of keeping Napoleon daily informed both of the mistaken over-zeal of the Consulta and the ever-increasing irritation and confusion among the Romans, or of urging the necessity of Murat's intervention in order to counteract the Consulta's want of determination in regard to the one obstacle to the successful establishment of the Imperial Government—namely, the Pope and the College of Cardinals. Nothing, he had never ceased to insist, but the removal from Rome of Pius VII—that and the breaking-up of the Curia—could bring the Romans to accept the Emperor's reforms in the right spirit.

The hour was an uncertain one for Napoleon. Wagram had not yet been fought, and he was still occupied in making preparations to remedy his all but disastrous defeat at Aspern. Matters were also going against him in Spain. Under these circumstances he was not in a position to decline the offers of assistance at Rome that were being pressed upon him by his brother-in-law and Salicetti. For if, as seemed not at all unlikely, the news of his difficulties in Germany and the Spanish Peninsula were to encourage the Romans to rise and throw off his yoke after the manner of the Spaniards, there were no French forces left in Italy sufficient to prevent them from doing so. Obviously, therefore, there was nothing for it but to call in Murat's help and that of his Neapolitans.

And so, at length, Murat received a hasty line from the Emperor's headquarters bidding him move quickly, so that the thing might be done before it should be too late. Strange to say, it would seem that no intimation to this effect was sent to Miollis, although Radet, who with his Gendarmerie was encamped at a short distance from Rome and to the north of it, got word somehow of what was in the air, and immediately marched into the city, where he reported everything to Miollis.

If the latter was not to be ousted from his command by the King of Naples there was not a moment to be lost. What was to be done must be done before Murat's forces, under Prince Pignatelli, could reach the city and take the conduct of affairs out of the hands of the Consulta. Now or never was the time for Miollis to justify the Emperor's choice of him as Governor of Rome.

"So his Majesty has decided to remove the Pope at last, and has entrusted the job to the King of Naples? Well, then, we will show that we can handle it as well as any one! But we must be careful to keep on the right side."

And, without further ado, Miollis wrote out a warrant for the arrest of "Cardinal Pacca, and, in the event of resistance, that of *every one else* in the Quirinal." Thus he thought to avoid the odium of having actually ordered the arrest of the Pontiff in person. But Radet perfectly understood him, and proceeded, at nine o'clock that night (July 5, 1809), to carry out his instructions. As Pignatelli and the Neapolitans had just arrived from Albano, and were encamped outside the Porta San Giovanni, it was necessary to act with the utmost secrecy to prevent them from discovering and forestalling Miollis's new counterstroke. For, if once Murat were to succeed in his project of assuming the chief part in expelling Pius VII, his position would be unassailable and his influence paramount. Napoleon would be practically compelled to make him Governor of the city, which would thus come *de facto* under a Neapolitan administration. From which Murat might, not unreasonably, hope for developments that should make him, eventually, the chief power in the Peninsula.

This expectation, though, was foiled by Radet's contriving to force the gates of the Quirinal between two and three o'clock in the morning and arresting both the Pope and Cardinal Pacca, whom he then carried off with him at full gallop in a travelling-carriage through Porta Pia towards Tuscany, where they were to be incarcerated in the Carthusian monastery of Ema. So that Miollis had won the second trick against Murat and Salicetti.

None the less, Murat obtained his point to some extent by persuading the Emperor to appoint him Lieutenant-General of the Roman kingdom. In this capacity he made his entry into the city on November 10, 1809, where he remained until the summer of 1810; when, on realising that Napoleon had no thought of allowing him to be anything more than a servant of the Empire, he then abdicated his functions, and was nominally

HISTORICAL INTRODUCTION

succeeded in them by Fouché, the ex-Police Minister and Duke of Otranto—who, however, came no nearer to Rome than Florence.

Nearly four years were to elapse before Murat again tried his hand against Miollis; four years during which the Romans alternately groaned beneath the heel of their French masters and danced in compliance with their decrees. Not until the November of 1812, when the news of Napoleon's first great defeats were brought to Rome, did they begin to believe there might come an end to his dominion over them. But yet another twelve months were to pass by before their hopes received any great encouragement—in the overthrow of the Emperor at Leipzig.

By this time, thanks to the effect of Napoleon's "Continental Blockade" (by which, for seven years, he had prevented all foreign over-seas trade), and of his merciless conscriptions, the country was reduced to a state of anarchy with which the handful of troops under Miollis's orders was utterly unable to cope. Brigandage, fostered by liberalism and want, was everywhere rampant. Bands of marauders wandered throughout Romagna, Campagna, and Umbria, plundering and killing at will. The social order was outwardly crumbling to a fall which not even permanent courts-martial and scores of executions by bullet and rope could long defer. In every open space of Rome, and every day, three or four or more malefactors were shot or hanged as brigands;

but all without any avail. On December 28, 1813, recourse was even had to the erection of the guillotine in Rome under the euphonym of "il nuovo edificio"; but the disorders continued with unabated licence and ferocity.

Already, however, another event of far-reaching import to Miollis and the Consulta had taken place. In the night of November 3–4 Murat had arrived in Rome fresh from the battle-field of Leipzig; he was travelling incognito to his capital of Naples and was only resting for a few hours at an hotel in the Piazza di Spagna. Here Miollis visited him—to be received with an appearance of lassitude and the information that the King of Naples was about to place himself at the head of 30,000 men and to defend Italy along the line of the Po. This was all that he would say; but with Miollis was Count Tournon, the Prefect of Rome,[*] who, as they were passing out through the anteroom, met an acquaintance, an aide-de-camp of Murat's, who whispered to him:

"All is lost. The Emperor has no army any longer, and the Allies must now be on the Rhine." And, with that, he went on to tell of the frightful results of the fighting at Leipzig, and of how, on the next day after the beginning of the retreat from

---

[*] See Madelin, "La Rome de Napoléon," p. 605, an invaluable publication upon the epoch. Tournon, who had succeeded Gerando in the Consulta, was forced, against his will, to be one of the principal tormentors of the Patrizi family.

HISTORICAL INTRODUCTION

Saxony, Murat had left the army for Naples, there "to take certain weighty decisions."

From which, indeed, both Miollis and Tournon, knowing Murat as they did, judged that the worst might now be expected of him; that is to say, that the real reason for his return to Italy was rather to safeguard his own interests by every possible means than to sacrifice himself in the waning cause of Napoleon.

In this surmise they were right. Thenceforth the revolutionary movements among the people seemed to take on a character of daring and of solidarity which they had never before evinced. All classes combined to thwart and harass the luckless Miollis and his colleagues by every conceivable means, from the depredations of patriotic bands to the outspoken pulpit denouncements of the clergy, all of whom derived much of their inspiration to resistance from two of Murat's accredited representatives in Palazzo Farnese, Zuccari and Maghella. By means of these two Murat had contrived to persuade the Romans to look upon him as the Man of Italy and the restorer-to-be of all her former glories and her freedom from foreign enslavement.

His revenge was now about to be accomplished for all bygone disappointments. Already, during the month of October, landing-parties of English troops had disembarked upon the Roman coast at Porto d'Anzio and had put to flight the scanty French garrisons in their path. At any moment they might be expected to advance upon the capital. The city, moreover, was known to be seething with disaffection, and no one could be trusted.

Suddenly, on November 18, the upheaval became an actuality in a rising in the district of Viterbo, headed by an unfrocked priest, Felice Battaglia. After only a few days Battaglia was taken prisoner and brought to Rome, where his true relations with Zuccari were brought to light. The chance of denouncing Murat's complicity in the ex-priest's rebellion was a tempting one; but Miollis was dissuaded from doing so by a letter from Durand, the French Minister at Murat's own Court at Naples, entreating him not to act precipitately for fear of stirring up an even more formidable popular agitation. Also, he was restrained by the arrival in Rome of the Duke of Otranto, Fouché, who had come down from Milan after being turned out of his latest Governor-Generalship—that of Illyria—by the Austrians. What his business might be in Rome none knew but only Fouché himself; but his well-known abilities for sudden tergiversation made it not improbable that he was already acting as an intermediary between the Austrians and Murat.* At any rate, his first act was to save the compromising Battaglia from the executioner by ordering him to be imprisoned indefinitely, and

* The subsequent hospitality extended by the Emperor Francis to Murat's wife and family, as well as the asylum offered by him to Murat—who, however, rejected it in favour of the fatal expedition to Pizzo in 1815—would appear to confirm this belief.

by quashing any further inquiry into his transactions with Zuccari.

On January 5, 1814, after a little more than a fortnight's stay in Rome, Fouché took his departure for Florence—and, with it, the entire contents of Miollis's official treasury, leaving him and the Consulta absolutely denuded of financial means! He had certainly left nothing undone to be of use to the King of Naples, who, on the last day of the old year, had concluded a secret understanding with the Austrian Government. By the terms of this agreement Murat was to become their ally and to clear Central Italy of its French occupants, in return for which his new friends were to do their utmost to obtain the consent of the other European Powers to his retention of the Throne of Naples—an arrangement which was only upset by the refusal of England to ratify it in favour of so dangerous a person.

On the other hand, Miollis was eagerly awaiting his assistance to reduce the unruly Italians to obedience in the name of the Emperor, in accordance with the promise to that effect which Murat had given him on his passage through Rome in the foregoing November. Already, at the end of that same month of November, a detachment of Neapolitan troops had been admitted by Miollis into the city, in this belief. Other detachments of all arms had followed them during the first days of December, until by the 10th there were between 10,000 and 15,000 of Murat's soldiers quartered within the walls. By now the whole of the capital, with the exception of Miollis himself, was convinced that the King of Naples must be about to betray his imperial brother-in-law by adding Rome to his own dominions — a conviction engendered and fostered by the Neapolitan officers themselves, both by their arrogance towards the Romans, whom they treated as a conquered population, as well as by their openly saying that the King was coming to Rome in the character of its master, and with no intention whatever of marching against the Austrians.

Murat, however, had no wish to come face to face with his own compatriots, Miollis and the rest of the French whom his treachery was about to outrage; and so he sent yet another of his agents, the Comte de Vauguyon, to represent him in Rome, together with Zuccari and Maghella. De Vauguyon, who arrived there as a mere tourist, carried with him in his pocket his commission as Governor-General of the Roman States, signed and sealed by Murat. Of this commission, however, he did not make use until the time was come, but remained for a while quietly, and, to all appearances, an unpretentious sight-seer at an hotel in the Piazza di Spagna.

ROME. THE CASTLE OF SANT' ANGELO.
As it was in the lifetime of Giovanni Patrizi.
Photo Moscioni, Rome, after an old print.

By the night of January 18 everything seemed to the conspirators in Palazzo Farnese to be ready for their purpose. On that night, then, Maghella went to dine with Miollis * at the latter's residence in the Doria Palace. Over their wine the talk was led by Maghella on to the subject of antiquities in general, and, in particular, of Miollis's own collection of pictures and statuary in his villa known as the Villa Aldobrandini-Miollis. So disarmed was the General by the astute Maghella's flattery of his views on art, and the ardent expression of Maghella's desire to view his collection, that Miollis offered to show it to him personally, early on the following morning—an offer no sooner made than accepted.

In order, therefore, to be punctually on the spot, Miollis, in lieu of sleeping, as had been his wont for some weeks, in the fortress of Sant' Angelo, whither he had withdrawn his meagre force of artillery and ammunition as a precaution against any attempt upon them by night on the part of the Romans, decided to remain at Palazzo Doria.

No sooner, however, had the two men parted company, than Maghella, returning to his confederate Zuccari, told him of the success of the ruse by which he had not only separated Miollis from his artillery, but had also allayed his suspicions against Murat for the time being. There would never be a better opportunity of achieving their end; and,

* Who, by then, had no illusions left as to the schemes of Murat and his creatures.

at once, the two sent word to Pignatelli—the same as he of Murat's former attempts—to disarm the French garrison as expeditiously as possible under cover of the darkness. Likewise, to their "incognito" chief, de Vauguyon, in Piazza di Spagna, to say that the hour was come for him to reveal himself. This he did, coming at once and in the full uniform of his new rank, to Palazzo Farnese, there to embrace his coadjutors and to draw up with them a suitable proclamation informing the Romans of the latest blessing bestowed upon them by Heaven in response to their prayers for deliverance from their French tormentors.

In this wise, Miollis being surrounded by an army of Neapolitans far outnumbering his own, was obliged to give in—but not until he had been besieged for six weeks in the Castle of Sant' Angelo, whither, in the course of the next day, he was allowed to retreat from Palazzo Doria by the inertia of his foes, who appeared afraid to molest him. Only on March 10, 1814, did he strike his flag, at the dictate, solely, of starvation, and march out with his few "faithfuls," headed by Radet. The honours of war were thankfully accorded to them by order of Vauguyon.

And so ended the French tenure of Romagna, leaving Murat the winner, as he imagined, of the game.

But this was not to be. For Napoleon, perceiving the treachery of Murat, had already written to Pius VII, restoring his dominions to him, on January 18, in the very hour of Maghella's dinner with Miollis ; and the Pope was now preparing to take possession of them once more—and that with the whole of Europe at his back. It was at Bologna that they met, the Pontiff and Murat,* on which occasion it is said that the soldier of fortune, in his endeavour to persuade Pius VII of the desire of the Romans to come under his, Murat's, own rule, showed him a petition signed by the heads of many noble families, in which they testified their preference ; and that the other, refusing even to glance at the list of traitors to himself, their only rightful Sovereign, tore it up and threw the fragments into the fire.

And so they separated, the Pope on his way to Rome, and Murat on that leading to his defeat at the hands of the Austrians at Occhiobello, by which he was to be made an outcast and an adventurer during the little time that remained to him on earth.

In the meanwhile, General Sixtus de Miollis, followed by the remnant of his army, was sorrowfully retracing his steps towards the place whence he had formerly set out so full of belief in the irresistible power of his Emperor. The violation of the papal neutrality in the European struggle, from which he had hoped so much, had utterly failed of

* Then on the march against Austria in consequence of the failure of the attempted treaty.

its purpose, and Rome was once more the capital of its lawful monarch—just as one looks forward soon to see another capital, that of Belgium, wrested from the condition to which it was recently subjected by another General Sixtus—Sixtus von Arnim—in this present year of 1914.

The six years during which the Romans had lived under their French masters had been a severe test of character. All that was best and worst had been sifted to its foundations and had come out on one side or the other. If many, alas! of the nobility had been found wanting both in loyalty to their religious inheritance and their Sovereign, others, again, had proved their right indisputably to the title of " the Faithful."

Among the latter there is no more striking example than that of the House of Patrizi in the person of its eldest son, Don Giovanni, the hero of these " Memoirs." Jeered at in softer times for his devotion to the Catholic Church, by lesser men, Don Giovanni yet showed himself in the hour of danger to be a Man—to the manifest confusion of his detractors who, themselves, offered little or no resistance to Napoleon's blandishments and threats. In truth, so impressed by Don Giovanni's fearlessness were even his adversaries that he had no more sincere admirers than the very men whose unsuccessful mission it was to coerce him. Both Miollis and Tournon have testified their appreciation of his unflinching courage. For they were neither of them cowards—and, to brave men, a brave man, albeit an opponent, is ever of their common brotherhood.

THE PATRIZI MEMOIRS

CHAPTER I

ON January 3, 1796, the Palazzo della Consulta on the Quirinal hill was the scene of a very brilliant assembly gathered to celebrate the betrothal of Marchese Giovanni Naro Patrizi to the Princess Cunegonda of Saxony. The host was Cardinal Braschi, the nephew of the reigning Pope, and some of the greatest names in Europe were included in the list of his guests, among whom was Prince Augustus of England. But the interest of all was centred on the bride, her father, Prince Xavier of Saxony, and her brother, Prince Joseph. Of the three, perhaps Prince Joseph excited the most curiosity, not only because he had not been seen in Rome before, but on account of an adventure of his at the Court of Russia two years earlier. The connection with Russian affairs was of long standing, for Prince Xavier, the father of Joseph and Cunegonda, was the second son of Frederic Augustus II of Poland, and for several years regent for his young nephew, Frederic Augustus III, who became the first King of Saxony. The young Prince Joseph had been taken into great affection by the Empress Catharine, a favour which had apparently excited jealousy in her Court, for he was drawn into a violent quarrel with a Russian nobleman who instantly challenged him to fight a duel. Before the affair could come off the Empress was informed of what had taken place, and her fury knew no bounds on hearing that Joseph's adversary had dared to challenge a Prince of the Blood. She punished her subject's audacity by condemning him to Siberia for eight years. Two of these were over when the Prince assisted at his sister's betrothal. Six years afterwards Count ———, having worked out the term of his imprisonment, was set at liberty, and his first act was to call out Prince Joseph again. The duel, postponed for eight years, was fought to a finish this time; the Russian's eye and hand, as also his vindictiveness, had not weakened in captivity, and he killed his man.

Although the bride was called Cunegonda of Saxony, she was really half Italian—a fact which accounts in part for her complete mastery of the language, and perhaps also for the readiness with which she adapted herself to the Roman modes of life, at that time rather different from those of the French Court, where her childhood was passed. Her father, the brother of the "Grande Dauphine," the mother of Louis XVI, had departed from the traditions of his class and married for love. While he was acting as Regent for his nephew, he was constantly obliged to confer with the boy's mother, and thus made the acquaintance of her lady-in-waiting, a beautiful Italian girl, the Contessina Chiara Spinelli of Fermo.

We first hear of the young lady as having been introduced, with her uncle and her brother, at the Court of Vienna by the poet Metastasio. The reasons for their visit are not explained, but we gather that they were cordially welcomed, and, when they wished to travel further, warmly recommended to the mother of the King of Saxony, for not only was Chiara at once attached to the royal lady's household, but honourable employments were found for her father and her brother as well.

Prince Xavier fell madly in love with her, and a secret marriage took place. But it was not possible to keep the secret long. The Prince, learning that his relations with the maid of honour had become the subject, first of gossip and then of scandal, at once declared the fact of his marriage, and turned all his energies to obtaining the recognition of his beautiful young wife as a Princess of the Blood. He met, naturally, with violent opposition from all the related royalties, but such was his determination and persistence that he succeeded in the end, and all the privileges of his own rank were formally granted to his wife. This victory of affection was only gained when they had been married for twelve years, and in the meanwhile, the young King having come of age, Prince Xavier wisely changed his residence and took up his abode in France, where, as the uncle of the reigning monarch, he was made exceedingly welcome.

He had great wealth, and, having bought the château of Pont-sur-Seine from the Rohans, he fitted it up very magnificently and made it, as he fondly believed, his home and that of his children after him. Here most of them were born, two sons and five daughters, of whom Gondina, as she was usually called, was the youngest but one. Although the château was at some distance from Paris, there seems to have been much pleasant coming and going between it and Versailles, for the Saxon Princesses were constantly with the children of France, and there is in Palazzo Patrizi a delightful little old album, in which Gondina tried her small hand at drawing. There are sketches of flowers and scenery, and portraits, childish but quite recognisable, of Louis XVI, Marie Antoinette, and the Dauphin. Also a distinctly malicious sketch of a prim, elderly woman with a most disagreeable expression, a governess she-dragon of some kind, who was evidently not popular in the royal nurseries.

The relics of Gondina's happy childhood have an almost tragic charm, for the clouds of the Revolution were already heavy on the horizon when she wrote her careful exercises in history and poetry in those yellow old copy-books, she and all around her in the hot-house of the Court so utterly unconscious of the impending cataclysm. Among her things is a tiny

TWO SKETCHES FROM THE ALBUM OF CUNEGONDA.

almanac bound in brown leather, "Etrennes mignones (*sic*) curieuses et utiles pour l'année 1790," published by the Court Printer, Guillot. Stamped in gold, on the cover, is a picture of the storming of the Bastille! In the letterpress is given an account, carefully edited for royal ears, of the events of the preceding year.

The eldest of Gondina's sisters was happily married, before the storm broke, to the Duc d'Esclignac. The King made a very grand affair of her wedding, both he and the Queen assisting in person at the ceremony. Unlike many others of their class, the d'Esclignacs succeeded in making good their escape, and taking refuge in Saxony. The young Duchess's father and mother fled with their other children to Italy, but the splendid home at Pont-sur-Seine was sacked from top to bottom by the revolutionists, who, however, overlooked the family archives and the valuable library, both of which properties are now preserved in the State Library at Troyes.

Prince Xavier brought his family to Fermo, in the hope that her native air would restore his wife's health, which had suffered severely from the terrifying shocks of the past few months. She revived wonderfully at first, and in the autumn of 1792 seemed so much better that he ventured to leave her with her relations in Fermo and to take his four young daughters for a journey to Augsburg, where he seems to have had some affairs to settle. To his great grief, however, his beloved wife grew suddenly worse and died before he could return to Fermo.

Princess Chiara's death was a terrible blow to her husband. He felt that without her sweet presence family life was no longer possible. His eldest son died just as he was about to enter the Church; whilst the younger, Prince Joseph, entered the army and was attached to the Russian service; so that there were left only the four daughters, and poor Prince Xavier, realising his inability to superintend their education himself, brought them to Rome and confided them to his good friend, the Princess Cornelia Barberini.

What the poor children thought of the transfer is not recorded. No one in those days took any notice of young people's feelings, and we may be sure that these were only expressed to each other. It would have been considered outrageous for them to dispute the rulings of their omnipotent and supposedly all-wise elders; but it is more than probable that many bitter tears were shed in the big bedroom in the Barberini palace when the rushlight burnt low and their attendants were asleep. The gay untrammelled life at Pont-sur-Seine and Versailles, for all the terrors and storms in which it had closed, must have looked wonderfully sweet and kind compared to their present existence. The loss of their mother was naturally an ever-present grief; now, in a manner of speaking, their father was lost to them too, and they were probably very much afraid of Princess Barberini, who seems to have been rather a stern person, if one may judge by the steps she took to carrry out the charge laid upon her.

She had not the slightest idea of being daily and hourly responsible for four beautiful heiresses brought up on far less Spartan lines than those of Roman noble families; and so, without a moment's hesitation, she shut the young Princesses up in the convent of the Oblates of Tor de' Specchi, there to be kept under lock and key till they were of marriageable age, and suitable marriages had been arranged for them! * The whole arrangement looks very cruel to us, and one's heart aches over what the subjects of it must have suffered day after day and month after month—the wearisome confinement of young minds and bodies in the dull convent precincts, the longing for air and fun and freedom that must have consumed those poor little hearts!

It took four years to liberate them all. One by one they were brought out to meet the husbands chosen for them—to promise and vow all that a woman can give, to a complete stranger, and, what seems most wonderful, to live up to the vows! Gondina was the third to emerge from the convent, and the history of her life with Giovanni Naro Patrizi is the history of an ideal love-marriage unshadowed by a cloud, warm and

* In quite recent years a curiously similar incident occurred. Four young heiresses, sisters, were confided to these distinguished Religious, to be taken care of till they should reach a marriageable age.

tender and faithful to the very end, a union where perfect trust and perfect affection hallowed and illuminated every thought and action of husband and wife. Both, it is true, were profoundly religious at heart, and, regarding their union as a supremely sacred matter, brought every sense and faculty to fulfilling the obligations it imposed; one can only feel that their crystal purity of intention received its fitting reward. There is something to be said, too, for the atmosphere in which they found themselves, an atmosphere where virtue and faith and sweetness were expected as matters of course, and where the modern theory of individual rights, irrespective of family obligations, would have been regarded as the blackest of heresies.

Princess Gondina had always put her whole heart into whatever she undertook; her little copybooks are full of a clear, strong handwriting, and testify to a great deal of intelligence as well as good-will even when she was very young. That her intelligence was much above the average is shown by her later correspondence. Her views are always sensible as well as elevated, and they are expressed with commendable clearness and concentration. Her husband's complete trust in her judgment is shown again and again during the enforced separation which events induced. After writing to express his own wishes and feelings on the burning questions which arose,

THE COVER OF AN ALMANAC.
Formerly in the possession of Cunegonda.

he always wound up by saying, "Nevertheless, I leave everything in your hands. Use your own judgment—it will certainly be right."

The most important years of Gondina's development had been passed in the close seclusion of the convent, where, judged by modern standards, the education must have been anything but liberal; yet when she came out to be married she at once took her place in an exceedingly critical, and, to her, quite unknown society, with perfect grace and dignity, and learned men pronounced her to be a very cultivated woman. A letter written before her marriage describes her as "so beautiful, so white, so diaphanous, that she is enchanting to behold. Her hands are miraculous. . . . She is very gentle and very cultured."

When she married Giovanni Patrizi, his father, Francesco, was a man of only middle age, and in every sense the head of the family. His son could own no property during his father's life-time, and the latter ruled, in theory, as autocratically as any oriental potentate. But, in fact, he was not particularly interested in ruling; his own tastes and aspirations were literary and artistic, and he gladly left the management of his many affairs to his wife Porzia, and his eldest son. The former was a very notable woman, and the administration could not have fallen into more capable hands. Judged from her own letters alone, of which there are great numbers in the Patrizi archives, she appears as the most practical and the most resolute of business women. Her handwriting is vigorously masculine, and her orders as short and incisive as military commands. But in the private diaries and letters of her children Porzia Patrizi appears in quite a different light, tenderly affectionate and warm-hearted, scrupulously considerate of the feelings of others, and a pillar of strength in time of trouble. The only portrait of " Marchesa Porzia" in the Patrizi gallery was painted very soon after her marriage, and one finds it difficult to connect the smiling, rather mischievous, but extremely pretty young woman, dressed in the richest of Pompadour costumes—all gold lace and rosebuds—with the mother and grandmother of later life, who (like a certain gentleman of Irish fame) was loved as much as she was feared, and feared as much as she was loved.

Marchesa Porzia and Cunegonda of Saxony understood each other at once, and the tie between them only strengthened with the passing of years. Yet, to our modern eyes, the relation would seem a very hazardous one at first sight, for the etiquette of the time did not grant the young couple even a day of privacy after their wedding. This took place on January 7, at the Church of St. Philip Neri, a saint for whom Giovanni Patrizi had a special devotion. There was a grand feast and reception afterwards at the Patrizi Palace, and when this was over the bride and bridegroom drove out to Albano, accompanied by the latter's father and

MARCHESA PORZIA.
The wife of Francesco Patrizi.

mother and his uncle, Monsignor Naro. The next day all the other relations and many friends went out to Albano, and were entertained at dinner; then the whole party returned to Rome together, and Giovanni and his Gondina began their married life as a couple of grown-up children always under the eyes of their elders. That such was the prevailing custom in all the patrician Roman families we know; but there can have been few, if any, where the system worked with such absolute smoothness and harmony as in Palazzo Patrizi. In the immensely voluminous archives of that time (they were all great letter-writers and diarists) there is not a hint of a disagreement on any subject; not a shadow or suspicion of discord ever darkens a single page. The keenest interest and sympathy in one another's joys and sorrows, the glow of perfect trust and understanding, illuminate every record of the family from the time of Giovanni's marriage, and the heavy trials that fell upon them some years later seem only to have drawn them all more closely together.

There were no clouds on the horizon when Princess Cunegonda came to gladden the rather elderly and serious circle of Casa Patrizi. Her mother-in-law was as eminent, if we may use the word, in social gifts as in practical ones, and she exercised a great influence over the society of Rome at that time. She had, like all the other great ladies of her day, a kind of court composed of admirers and friends; but those admitted to Marchesa Porzia's intimacy were all men of marked distinction in one way or another, and the faithfulness with which they passed their evenings in her *salon* showed clearly enough the high estimation in which they held her. The list of names is imposing—Cardinal Consalvi, Cardinal Albani, and many other Eminences and Monsignori, the Grand Master of the (temporarily suppressed) Knights of Malta, the Governor of Rome, and more of the same stamp. It strikes one as a somewhat sombre society this, into which the young girl fresh from her convent was suddenly introduced. But the good fairies who had hovered over her cradle had dowered her with some subtle and exquisite power by which she drew all hearts, young or old, to love her and rejoice over her. She at once became the acknowledged queen and idol of the Patrizi household and the Patrizi *salon*. Her father-in-law wrote her the tenderest verses; the prelates and men of letters vied with one another in the court they paid her; and it says much for both her character and that of her mother-in-law that the latter, although a comparatively young woman herself, never seemed to feel the slightest jealousy of the blooming girl who had thus come to share her throne. On the contrary, the Marchesa Porzia seemed to take pleasure in the popularity of her charming daughter-in-law. When the nursery of the Palace began to fill she took upon herself the chief care of the children, their young mother being rather delicate, but at the same time she deferred in all things regarding them to their mother's wishes. To us, who happen to remember the reign of a recent grandmother in that same house, it seems an unheard-of marvel that Marchesa Porzia, eighty or ninety years nearer the patriarchal days, should ever have deferred to anybody at all.

One detail of Cunegonda's marriage strikes one curiously as affording a remarkable contrast to the practice of later times. Her father, Prince Xavier, wished to give each of his daughters a dowry of fifty thousand dollars; but a special permission had to be obtained for this large-handedness from the Pope, the cash dowry of any bride of a noble house being limited by statute to the sum of thirty thousand dollars. As usual, even in our own day, only a small portion of the income was settled upon the bride for her pin-money—in Cunegonda's case seven hundred dollars a year—the remainder passing entirely under the control of her husband's family, to be used and administered for the general benefit. One reads so often in the ancient chronicles of heiresses bringing enormous properties to their husbands that the mention of the old statute strikes a rather surprising note.

One great pleasure Cunegonda must have had was in finding in her new home a wee sister-in-law of three years old, with whom she could fancy herself a child again, until her own children came to fill her heart. Her sisters, it is true, were living in Rome, one married to the eldest son of Prince Altieri, one to the Duca Riario, and one, the youngest, to Marchese Massimo ; but as each had, like herself, been absorbed into the husband's family and taken up with his interests, Gondina depended almost entirely on the Patrizi circle for sociability and cheer. Any friends whom she introduced there were, however, cordially received, and one, the sculptor Canova, taken into the little ring of intimates who constantly met in Marchesa Porzia's drawing-room. For Gondina he executed a charming marble head of the Madonna, which is still a treasured possession of her descendants.

Her first boy was born in June 1797, and named, after his great-grandfather, Xavier; the second, Constantine, came in the following year, and the last, Filippo, who seems to have been a most quaint and vivacious child, five years later, in 1803. He and Xavier were born Romans, but Constantine's birth took place in Siena, which was the original cradle of the Patrizis, and where they owned—and still own —a large palace. In this connection it should be said that there have been three acknowledged saints in the family, the last of which, he of Siena, had a rather curious history. Some five hundred years ago the gilded youth of the city had entered into a league to see who could ruin himself first in the race for pleasure. Terrible scandals ensued, but neither threats nor prayers availed to bring them to better ways. Among these young profligates the Patrizi boy was distinguished for the wildest misdeeds, the maddest course of dissipation, until something—what, precisely, is unknown to this day—arrested, terrified, and converted him all in a moment. He embraced a life of constant prayer and severe penance, and, at the end of no more than a single year, died in the odour of sanctity. His body is preserved incorrupt, but much mummified, at Siena, where he is greatly venerated, though not by his baptismal name. Strangers are naturally puzzled when the good "Sanesi" refer casually to their "Beato Tarlato," the "Blessed Moth-eaten One"; but the poor saint is never called anything else, because his face is all pitted with tiny indentations such as one sees in worm-eaten wood. When a small "Sanese" is born into the world he is carried to the Duomo to be baptized, and before returning home is always taken to pay his respects to the "Beato Tarlato." It happened that one of the present generation of Patrizi children was born in Siena, but the heads of the family had forgotten all about the expected visit to the "saint," and the baby, who was rather delicate, was brought straight back from the Duomo to the palace. Then there broke forth a storm of shocked protest—the town fairly hummed with indignation. What, a child of the Patrizi, born in Siena, had not been taken to salute the holy ancestor and receive his blessing? What an affront to the good patron! What was the world coming to when such things could happen?

All of which, being faithfully reported to the child's mother, she hastened to allay the tempest by causing it to be proclaimed that she wished to take the infant herself, and that as soon as she was sufficiently recovered to go out her first visit should be made in state to the " Beato." The townspeople, good souls, saw in this an unusual zeal for their protector's honour, and declared themselves satisfied; but insisted on receiving due notice beforehand of the day and hour arranged for the expedition. This was of course conceded, and when at last the Marchesa drove out, with the baby in her arms, the whole city was *en fête*. All the church bells were ringing together, garlands and tapestries decorated the streets, fireworks blazed, and the shrine of the " Beato Tarlato " was more gorgeously illuminated with fine wax candles than it had ever been before. He seems to have smiled on the delicate baby, for it grew up as strong and vigorous as all its brothers and sisters!

It is a responsibility, as well as a benediction, to have saints in the family. One of the Gonzagas was heard to say that he hoped their own list of holy ones was by this time complete, since one more canonisation would bankrupt his line! Where there are wealthy descendants, they are naturally expected to contribute to the many expenses connected with the long anterior examination of facts and the great ceremonies of the crowning function itself when this is decided upon.

In another town in Tuscany there is a Patrizi saint whose tomb is opened once every hundred years. Then from all over Italy the devout gather to honour and invoke him, bringing many rich offerings to the church where his body reposes. In the palace in Rome there is a painting showing the portraits of the three holy ancestors on the same canvas, but without distinguishing them by name. The central head in the picture had always passed for that of this collateral ancestor until a short time since, when, his centenary recurring, the young Marchese (who succeeded his father some eight years ago) was deputed by his mother to represent the family at the celebrations. It sounds like a trying ordeal for youthful nerves to preside at the opening of a coffin five or six hundred years old, but on each preceding occasion the body had been found absolutely incorrupt, and there was no reason to expect that any change should have taken place in the last intervening century. Nor had it. The saint lay as if just fallen asleep, so bland and lifelike that it seemed as if he must open his eyes when the unaccustomed daylight struck them. His limbs and joints were supple as those of a slumbering child, and so little had five hundred years changed his features that the young Marchese, on returning home, pointed out his real portrait, saying: "We have been quite mistaken. *This* is he—not the one we have always called by his name!"

CHAPTER II

IN order to make clear the condition of things in Rome during the closing years of the Napoleonic supremacy it is necessary to touch briefly on facts some of which have been alluded to in a preceding work of the translator, "Italian Yesterdays." The First Consul, from a variety of motives, some doubtless sincere, some purely political, had undertaken the re-establishment of religion in France, and had won great applause for his pious intentions; but the high hopes founded on his proclamations and promises soon faded away. The illusions which Pius VII had nourished were rudely dispelled, and the detailed account of the Concordat of 1801 is the record of a veritable Via Crucis of sorrow and pain. Nevertheless, officially, the First Consul figured as the benefactor and protector of the Church, and, once seated on the Imperial Throne, traded very largely on what he considered a valuable asset to his credit.

When he insisted on the Pope's presence at his coronation, Pius consented to attend, in the hope that by personal intercourse it would be possible to do much for the reorganisation and improvement of church matters both in France and Italy, the kingdom which had permitted Napoleon to don the iron crown of the Lombard Sovereigns before setting himself to attain the imperial one which had been worn by Charlemagne. The incidents of the coronation in Notre Dame showed with brutal frankness that the Emperor intended the Pope to be regarded actually as his Head Chaplain. After keeping the venerable Pontiff waiting in the cathedral for an hour and a half, he crowned himself and then his wife—an act more eloquent of his real intentions than any explicit programme could possibly have been. Henceforth Rome was to be merely the second capital of the Empire.

Pius VII returned thither after an absence of six months in great grief of mind. No further illusions were possible, and the Emperor barely took the trouble to find pretexts for his systematic encroachments on the papal territories and for the persecution of papal subjects. His demands were so arrogant that not even he could have imagined they would be granted, and they became more insulting every day. He was furious because the Pope refused to annul the marriage of Jerome with the American Protestant, Miss Patterson; he demanded that the representatives of Powers hostile to France should be banished from Rome, and the ports of the papal dominions closed to their vessels; he insisted that the Pope should instal Joseph Bonaparte on the throne of Ferdinand in Naples; and his last pretension was that France should have the management of ecclesiastical affairs. He knew that he was demanding the impossible; his own plans were clearly defined in his mind, and he was simply inventing pretexts for carrying them out in the belief that, although the nobles were opposed to him, the mass of the people would receive him with acclamation.

By February 1808 the French troops were in possession of Rome and all the Roman territories; the Pope's flag had been removed, whilst the French tricolor was raised on Castel Sant' Angelo, and eight cannon were planted before the Quirinal Palace, the Pope's residence. All prelates and ecclesiastics not Roman-born were banished from the city. By March 31 General Herbin had reviewed the pontifical troops, and despatched them to Naples to be incorporated in the French army. Several subjects of the Holy Father, and an officer of King Ferdinand IV of Naples, had been shot by order of General de Miollis. Pius VII, while always adjuring his subjects to avoid bloodshed, protested indignantly but in vain against all these outrages. All the public offices were filled with French functionaries; the clergy were required to take the oath of allegiance to the usurper, which most of them refused to do and were deported. To crown all, it was ordered that Te Deums should be sung in every church of the city in thanksgiving for the "Liberation of Rome."

These measures naturally met with the most stubborn resistance. For some time the French authorities had to turn their whole attention to capturing and disposing of the recalcitrants. The entire corps of the Noble Guards was put under arrest; its commander, Prince Altieri, was imprisoned in Castel Sant' Angelo; priests and officials by hundreds were deported to prisons in the north of Italy and in France. The invaders had broken up the Pope's immediate household some months earlier, when Cardinal Gabrielli, his Secretary of State, had been sent into banishment, his place being filled (September 1808) by Cardinal Pacca, the wisest and most faithful of all the Pontiff's adherents. Cardinal Pacca's removal being now needed, in order that his beloved master might be deprived of even moral support, his rooms at the Quirinal were suddenly invaded one day by a company of French soldiers, and he was told that he must leave Rome within the hour.

The Holy Father, informed by his attendants of what was taking place, forgot his age and infirmities, forgot his personal danger, and flew to the Cardinal's rescue in such a storm of indignation that his adversaries seem to have been momentarily paralysed into inaction, for Pius VII took bodily possession of his friend and carried him off to his own apartments, where they were both kept close prisoners for ten long months, cut off from communication with the outside world, and not knowing from one day to another what new blow would be struck at them.

The blow was long in falling, for, in spite of all that his rigours could bring to bear, Napoleon was still afraid that if he laid hands on the Pope the result might be a revolution in the city. So, many months were allowed to pass in order to dispel any apprehensions that might be afloat as to the Sovereign's personal safety, and, when his abduction had been decided upon, every precaution was taken to insure secrecy and despatch. In the dead of night, on July 5, 1809, scaling-ladders were set up against the windows of his rooms, and the kidnapping party under General Radet forced an entrance. The process, though, was neither so silent nor so rapid as was hoped, for the inmates (who had doubtless learnt to be very light sleepers by that time!) immediately became aware of what was going on. The Pope realised that he was about to be carried away, and in those last precious moments of liberty, while his assailants were scraping their ladders against his windows, he thought only of his people, and wrote, with complete concentration and calmness, the famous proclamation which, confided then and there to some trusty hand, was printed and posted all over Rome by the next morning. Torn down a hundred times, a hundred times it reappeared, to the rage of the French authorities, until every Roman could almost repeat it by heart. For nobility and simplicity, as

THE ARREST OF PIUS VII

well as for profound Christian feeling, it is worthy to rank in the archives of humanity with the prayer in which Pius IX poured out his heart on the Scala Santa on September 19, 1870.

Pius VII had been taken unawares in material things, so that he had but one small piece of silver money in his possession that night. But if fate was trying to surprise him into showing fear or anger she must have been grievously disappointed. By the time Radet's ruffians broke into the Pontiff's room he was kneeling at his *prie-dieu*, fully dressed, and he scarcely looked round at their entrance. Dragged roughly to his feet, he bade farewell to his weeping attendants, gave them the blessing which they knelt to implore, and then he was hurried downstairs, pushed into a carriage, of which the blinds were already fastened down; the doors were locked as soon as he was inside, and then, surrounded by mounted guards, he was driven away at full speed across the Campagna, towards the north.

It is not necessary to follow Pius VII on this sad journey. Some of the incidents of his captivity have been described in a former volume,* and for us the chief interest lies in the sequence of events in Rome after his departure. For it was then that Napoleon began to put into effect the measures which, he believed, would result in the Gallicising of Italy, an end which he looked upon

* "Italian Yesterdays," vol. i.

as absolutely necessary to the stability of his rule over his new subjects. With this object in view, the heads of the great houses, to the number of thirty, were "invited" to form a municipal council for the government of the city. Various lures in the way of pay and distinction were held out, but of thirty only four so far fell from grace as to accept the degrading favour. Twenty-one never condescended to answer the communication at all; but five, in an outburst of generous indignation, refused it categorically and with contumely. These were Altieri, Massimo, Barberini, Rospigliosi, and Francesco Patrizi, the father-in-law of Cunegonda of Saxony. Prince Altieri had already drawn upon himself the imperial disfavour not only on account of his violently anti-French opinions, but also by what the French police reports called his "ridiculous devotion to his wife, the Princess of Saxony." Massimo had married another of the royal sisters whom Napoleon so much disliked, and he was able to strike at three of them with one blow when he gave the order to have the five nobles above mentioned brought to Paris and detained as prisoners for a year and a half, during which period they were ordered to report themselves to the police once a week.

But this was only the beginning. The conqueror's most cherished design was to possess himself of the rising generation in Italy and completely denationalise it. For this purpose he directed that a census should be taken of all the noble families of the country, from the highest to the least considerable, with the statistics of their incomes and the number and names and ages of their male children. Those who were grown up, whether married or single, were to be drafted into the Garde Impériale or employed in various offices at Court. Those whose education was not yet completed were to be sent to different military schools established in France, to be trained for service in the army—at the expense of their parents, although the latter were to renounce all authority over their children and all right of interference in the education to be meted out to them. The "Golden Levy," as it was called, was to include all nobly born boys, except those of delicate constitution, from the age of eight upwards.

Every possible detail had to be furnished regarding the subjects chosen. Their age, health, aptitudes, and general disposition, together with the exact rank and fortune of their parents, were all subjects of the strictest inquiry; so that the scheme took a long time to organise, and the Marchese Francesco Patrizi had been set at liberty and had returned to his home when the first shot was fired, so to speak, at his own family, in the shape of an intimation to his son Giovanni, announcing that General de Miollis had graciously nominated him to have the honour of serving "at the feet of H.I. Majesty" in the Imperial Guard in Paris.

Needless to say, the "honour" was refused, and

the next mention of the Patrizi occurs in a secret report from the head of the police in Rome to the Duc de Rovigo, the Minister of Police in Paris. The report describes, with almost hysterical alarm, a pious society known as the "Forty Hours," just founded in Rome for the perpetual adoration of the Blessed Sacrament. It was composed of four hundred gentlemen who, in companies of four, took turns in praying all night in whichever church was designated for the devotion of the "Forty Hours." This struck the French police as such an inexplicable fancy that they decided the arrangement must cloak a dangerous conspiracy, and they sent the account of it to Paris in duplicate, by special couriers, one in April and one in May 1810. The Marchese Patrizi (meaning the elder) was named as one of the chief leaders and organisers of the evidently evil-intentioned band of plotters.

All the prayers that were being put up in Rome could not avert the next blow which fell upon it and which convulsed society to its base. The census for the "Golden Levy" had been taken with great precautions, and the whole scheme kept a profound secret until it was ripe for execution. Then, in one day, a score of families were notified that the Emperor, in his great kindness and clemency, had named their boys as pupils in his military schools, a favour for which the parents were to show their gratitude by sending the children to France with the least possible delay.

It had never been the habit of the nobles to send their sons away from home for their education. This was carried on by a private tutor under their parents' very watchful eyes, and even those who were attending the University Courses lived at home. The system continues to this day. The Emperor's so-called favours elicited a tempest of protest, and the office of the Count de Tournon, the Prefect of Rome, was stormed by distracted mothers imploring him to intervene and not permit their children to be taken away from them. Theirs was not merely selfish grief, or maternal fear that their sons would not be kindly treated; their despair was only too well justified by the irreligion and immorality of the French establishments. The Emperor's decree, if carried out, would mean that every attempt would be made to wean the young souls from Faith as well as patriotism—and in those simple times people thought as much about their children's souls as they did about their brains and bodies.

Count de Tournon, a wise and kind-hearted man, opposed the new ordinance with all his might; but he was powerless to prevent it from being carried out. He had been tormented for information of the most intimate kind as to the families involved, and in his Memoirs,* he says:

* M. Louis Madelin had access to Count de Tournon's Memoirs, and drew upon them largely for " La Rome de Napoléon;" but they are still unpublished, as are all other documents referred to in this connection except the Memoirs of Cardinal Pacca.

"I was overwhelmed with fresh questions. Then, all at once, I received through the Governor the nomination of a multitude of young men and boys to be sub-lieutenants, to be pupils in military schools, to be pages, etc. The dismay was overwhelming, and one cry came from the heart of every mother.

"I was appalled by this act, which was only calculated to estrange the parents without giving any solid guarantees to France by taking possession of a few children. The policy of M. de Rovigo was carrying us back to the most barbarous times. I had nothing to do with the execution of the measure, which was confided to the Government and the Chief of Police; but I received all the complaints, I heard the lamentations of the families, and I suffered for them and for my country, upon which all the hatred must fall. I attempted to intervene, and did obtain a few exemptions, but the greater number had to submit."

Poor Count Tournon was regarded by the Romans as a hard man entirely devoted to the interests of Napoleon. They believed he could have averted their misfortunes had he so desired; his position for some years was a peculiarly odious one, for it was seldom that he could obtain any leniency for people whom he pitied from the bottom of his heart, and, though he never failed to make the attempt, yet his communications with the afflicted families were chiefly confined to exhorting them to submit with patience rather than draw further disfavour on themselves by useless rebellion. It was not until the Marchesa Patrizi obtained access to his private papers that justice was done to his memory in Rome.

In spite of the zeal of M. Roederer, the French Prefect of Spoleto, and his subordinates, it was found impossible to supply the two hundred names requisitioned from Rome and Trasimène (the new name for Umbria) for the French military schools. The limit of age—eight to twelve—applying to that of the Prytanée de la Flèche caused the number designated for that institution to fall short of fifteen, although, as the lists show, the Roman families had been sifted unsparingly. Among the children chosen for La Flèche were two sons of Giovanni and Cunegonda Patrizi, described as follows in the list still preserved in Paris:

"Patrizi, Xavier; twelve years old; family of the ancient nobility. Parents' revenues, ten thousand 'scudi romani.' *Observation:* in good health and of good constitution; the eldest of the children.

"Patrizi, Philip; eight years old, brother of the above-mentioned. Good health. There is another son, aged ten, who has delicate health."

The first summonses in obedience to the Emperor's order were issued on July 9, 1811, when Alessandro

Chigi and Urbano Barberini were called by imperial decree to the school at St. Germain, two Ruspoli boys, an Altieri, a Spada, a Sacchetti, and seventeen others to Saint-Cyr, and thirty-four noble children from Rome and Trasimène to the Prytanée de la Flèche. On the same day the Emperor named a Doria, a Santa Croce, a Pallavicini, an Odescalchi, a Caetani, a Potenziani, and a Baglioni, as Councillors of State. Resistance was attempted, but it was soon recognised that reason was of no avail when opposed to force, and it resolved itself for the most part into more subtle attempts to evade the odious enactment. Tournon in Rome and Roederer in Trasimène were besieged with petitions from parents, furnishing every imaginable excuse, including medical certificates, to demonstrate the absolute necessity of delaying the departure of their children for France.

Roederer, who feared above all things to appear wanting in zeal in carrying out the orders of his imperial master, had a really genial inspiration. He invited the recalcitrant parents of his district and their children to a great dinner in his residence at Spoleto. The invitation was gladly accepted, in the hope of softening the Prefect's heart and of persuading him to convince his Government of the cruel injustice of the ordinance. The feast went forward with every appearance of cordiality till the moment for the toasts arrived, when Roederer, rising with his glass in his hand, made a speech in which he wished the boys a pleasant journey, the greatest profit from their studies, and, when the time should come, the honour of acquiring world-wide fame in the service of His Imperial and Royal Majesty. Then, addressing the parents, he added that, in order to spare them every inconvenience, he had ordered for the following morning as many coaches as would be required to convey their sons to France.

Roederer was in no way averse to his task, but the Prefect of Rome, as we have seen, carried out the one assigned to him with the greatest repugnance. He could scarcely bring himself to lend his aid to General de Miollis, and, when obliged to send out the brevets, generally left the disagreeable task to his secretary. The brevets were distributed anyhow, at intervals of a few days, perhaps to minimise the force of the general resistance and to allay excitement. Tournon was personally acquainted with all the families designated for the "Leva dorata," and when the turn of the Casa Patrizi came he foresaw the most obstinate resistance. Convinced that this would seriously affect the prestige of the Imperial Government in Rome, he employed every argument he could think of to turn the tempest aside, insisting almost violently to General de Miollis upon the prudence of withdrawing the peremptory order, and on the other hand using all his influence with the Marchese Patrizi to persuade him to submit to it quietly.

Here is the exact text of the Decree:

"PALACE OF SAINT-CLOUD,
"*July* 9, 1811.

"Napoleon Emperor of the French, King of Italy, Protector of the Confederation of the Rhine, Mediator of the Swiss Confederation, etc., etc.
"We have decreed and decree the following:
"Are named pupils and pensioners of our Prytanée * de la Flèche. . . .
"Patrizi Xavier and Patrizi Philip. . . .
"Our Ministers of War and of General Police are charged with that which concerns them respectively for the execution of this decree.
"*Signed*,
"N."

On August 30, 1811, the following intimation was sent to Palazzo Patrizi:

"The Auditor of the Council of State, Prefect of the Department of Rome,
"To the Marchese Patrizi.
"Sir,
"I have the honour to inform you that H.I. and R.M. has deigned to name your sons Messrs. Xavier and Philip to be pupils at the military school of La Flèche.

---

* The name is derived from the building reserved for the fifty senators, who for a tenth part of the year, together with the "Archons," directed the Government of Athens. They were called "Prytanes." The word "Prytanée" was usually employed in France to designate a military school.

"I enclose herewith the brevets of admission, from which you can derive all necessary information as to outfit, payments, and other details.

"I am persuaded that you will appreciate above all the benevolent intentions shown by H.M. in deigning to select your family before others.

"As the brevets explain that your sons are to reach their destination without delay, I beg that you will inform me of the precise day of their departure, which must take place during the first fortnight of September, and at the same time to furnish me with their certificates of baptism made out in due and legal form."

The communication is signed by a deputy of the Prefect, who evidently disliked the thought of appending his own name to the unlucky document. With it came the brevets for the two boys, signed in Paris by the Minister for War, the Duc de Feltre.

"Io più non credo che di dolor si muoia!" *

It was with this cry of pain that the Marchese Giovanni Patrizi began the writing of his memoirs a few months before his death. Some years had passed since the day when he was ordered to send away his boys, but time could never obliterate

* "No more believe I men can die of grief!"

the memory of the despair which then filled his mind.

"I can declare from my own experience," he writes, "that only a father, a Christian father, can conceive of what I felt when, on August 7, 1811, I received the ominous news that a large number of the sons of our Roman nobility had been summoned by an imperial decree to be educated in French military schools. I pitied the fate of the children no less than that of their parents, and I was chilled with the fear that I should all too soon be added to the number, overtaken by the same misfortune. From day to day I expected to receive the fatal announcement, but I never ceased to offer fervent prayers to Almighty God and the most Blessed Virgin that I might become childless rather than renounce my sacred right to give my sons a Christian education.

"We are always ready to believe in what we desire; when a few days had passed without bringing the dreaded announcement there sprang up in my heart the hope that, by a singular favour of Heaven, my sons were not included in the dreadful decree. And, as day followed day, this hope naturally became stronger, and I began to sleep more tranquilly.

"On the twenty-ninth of August a note from the Prefecture was brought to our house, addressed to the Marchese Patrizi. It was, of course, intended for my father; but, as at that time his health was not good, and I had taken over the management of domestic affairs to relieve him, I felt authorised to open the missive. I learnt that the Prefect, or rather his deputy (he being away on leave) desired to speak with the Marchese that very morning, and for this purpose requested him to call upon him at the hour he named. I imagined that the business had to do with agricultural matters, the extirpation of the locusts, or something of the kind, matters for the discussion of which we had, till then, sent one of our stewards. Having no desire to visit the Bureaux personally, I decided to follow precedent, and sent on the note to the person who had hitherto represented the family on these occasions. But I was informed, in reply to my message, that this person was very ill—as indeed was the case, for he died three weeks later.

"Feeling the strongest repulsion myself to setting foot in the offices of the Prefecture, yet not wishing to appear uncivil, I wrote to the Magistrate to say that the Marchese Patrizi, being indisposed, could not do as he was requested, but would attend to the business, whatever it might be, in his own house, if some one could be sent to him there.

"I had dismissed the trifling matter from my mind, when, on the afternoon of the same day, I happened to be with a friend, who asked me if anything new had taken place in regard to my sons.

"'Nothing, Heaven be praised!' I replied. He congratulated me on this, and then went on to say that, during the forenoon, a great number of parents had been summoned to the Prefecture, and there informed of the Decree by which one or more of their children were ordered to military schools in France.

"Great God! only Thou knowest the pang that went through my heart at my friend's words—for now I understood the object of the intimation received that morning. I turned pale, a deadly chill came over me, and I left my friend abruptly and staggered trembling along the streets without knowing where I was going. The thought of returning home and beholding my children again filled me with dread; I sought for some ray of solace in my trouble, and found none. Nay, Religion itself, to which Christians turn for consolation in the heaviest sorrows, served only, as it were, to increase my distress. I already saw my children handed over to irreligious teachers, deprived of all means of preserving the seeds of piety implanted in their tender hearts, seduced by pernicious discourses, by wicked examples—already vacillating in their faith, corrupted in their lives, changed in a short time from innocent lambs into ravening wolves! I hoped, it is true, that the fatherly Providence of the Almighty would renew in their favour the miracle of the Furnace of Babylon; but at the same time I recognised that I could not reasonably hope for such a prodigy unless I were obliged to give up my little ones by irresistibly superior force.

"These miserable reflections remained with me all through that evening, through the sleepless night which followed it, and all the next very sad day. I only spoke to a few friends of the burden which was oppressing me, and was careful not to breathe a word of it to my parents or my wife. I did not wish them to share my affliction a moment sooner than should be necessary. But, at the same time, it was beyond my powers of deception to conceal altogether the anxiety which was wringing my heart, and as in such circumstances imagination is apt to be active, I fancied, in looking at my dear ones, who were sad and silent because of my own unexplained depression, that they had heard of the Decree and were doing their best, through pure pity, to keep me in ignorance of it!

"When the next day dawned—the thirty-first of August, for ever memorable as the most unfortunate of my whole life—my father sent for me very early to come to his apartment. I hastened thither and found the good old man, his face profoundly sad, his voice trembling and half inaudible as he told me that what I had feared was true. 'Son,' he said, 'in order to spare you a troubled night I would not impart to you, last evening, the distressing news which you can, alas! too easily divine, and which was brought for you yesterday afternoon in these papers.'

"So speaking, he handed me a letter. My hand shook as I took it. It contained the brevets by which my sons Xavier and Philip, under the imperial decree, were named as pupils at the Prytanée de la Flèche, a military school about two days' journey from Paris. The middle of September was the time set for their departure. A note from the deputy who was acting during the Prefect's absence was enclosed with the brevets, and in it the official congratulated me—ah, what an insult!—on the honour conferred upon me by the Emperor.

* * * * *

"And now I was under the hard necessity of acquainting the mother with the destiny of her children. I went to her, all my grief depicted in my countenance. My excellent wife had no prevision of its cause, and reproached me gently with the melancholy of my bearing. . . . I replied that it was not unfounded. In an instant she understood, and asked, 'Is it about the children?'

"I showed her the brevets. She began to read them, but half-way through she burst into a storm of weeping.

"At that moment, it being the hour when they always came to see their mother, the boys and their tutor entered the room. At sight of them she cried, 'Oh, my sons, they want you in Paris.' The little fellows rushed into her arms, sobbing pitifully. The good tutor, utterly overcome, added his own no less passionate tears and lamentations. I prayed for courage, and it was granted me; I was in extremest need of consolation myself, but I had to impart consolation, not receive it. I caught hold of my good little Constantine—whose tears, like those of the others, were raining on his beloved mother's face—and told him that he was not included in the barbarous order.

"At that announcement the innocent little soul gave a great gasp of relief, as if a burden were lifted from his heart; his face brightened, his tears ceased —but only for a moment. Then he was weeping again with his brothers and his mother over their coming separation. I made an effort to awake in their Christian hearts the warmest trust in the mercy of God and the protection of the Blessed Virgin, and instantly they all began to pray, brokenly and with sobs, yet with entire earnestness. The devoted mother solemnly offered to God all that she had suffered to bring her children into the world, beseeching Him to recall them to Himself in that very hour and leave her bereft rather than permit them to be exposed to the perils of a corrupt education. The boys endorsed the sacrifice of their lives, and I, in the silence of my heart, confirmed it.

"But fresh weeping followed, and I went in search of aid to stem this flood of grief—went to fetch my own dearest mother, upon whose heart I had never called in vain. I found with her my cousin Spada, and our friend Giustiniani. I called upon her and upon them for help. . . . My mother, as if she had had wings to her feet, flew to my apartment, and reached it while I, worn out, was following, supported in the arms of those two heavenly-minded friends who sought every means to comfort me.

"On re-entering my wife's room I saw that my mother was holding her to her heart and inspiring her with the faith and resignation in which her own was so rich . . . and so these two, grieving, yet submitting to the will of God, laid their sorrow before Him.

CHAPTER III

THE Memoirs continue :

"Prince Tommaso Corsini happened to be in Rome at that time, employed on a mission for the Emperor. Himself a Roman, and the father of a family, he could not view with indifference this barbarous measure, involving such a number of the children of his fellow-citizens, and it was rumoured that he had made remonstrances against it in Paris. Some of the mothers, relying on the credit which the Prince enjoyed at the Imperial Court, hastened to visit him to implore his help. My wife, unwilling to miss any possible chances of help, decided to do the same. We went together to see the Prince. He told us that it was hopeless to look for entire exemption from the Decree, but that a modification of it might easily be obtained. He advised us to petition that one of our sons should be taken as a page and the other one be allowed to remain at home !

"This suggestion filled us with horror. We were to voluntarily sacrifice one of our boys ! Never could we have made such a choice, for both were equally dear to us. We explained to the Prince that we could not accept his plan, and we proposed, with his approval, to send a petition direct to the Emperor, asking that both children might be exempt, or, if that could not be, that at least their departure might be delayed until the following spring. Corsini very kindly promised to see that the petition should reach its destination, and, as soon as it was written, I took it to him myself."

Here ensues the text of the letter to the Emperor. It furnishes such a searching light on the downtrodden attitude of even the proudest Romans under Napoleon's rule, that it is worth giving entire:

"SIRE,

"The honour which Your Majesty has deigned to confer on Xavier and Philip, the sons of the undersigned, by naming them as pupils at the Prytanée de la Flèche, lays upon their parents the duty of expressing to Your Majesty their most respectful gratitude, but paternal affection, of which Your Majesty knows so well the strength, as well as the peculiar circumstances of the case, oblige them to lay before the Throne the following reasons for granting the exemption which is hereby humbly implored.

"The delicate constitutions of the children would certainly suffer from the novel system of life. The hopes founded on the eldest son by his parents, not only in the study of belles-lettres, in which he is well advanced, in regard to his assistance in family

PETITION TO NAPOLEON

affairs, but also in view of a suitable marriage which may be arranged for him from one day to another, would all be rendered vain. The health of the children's mother has been very delicate for years past, and, being unable to undertake a long journey, she would suffer a great shock in the separation.

"Should Your Majesty not see fit to give ear to these humble remonstrances, then the undersigned, submitting to Your orders, still find courage to implore, at least, permission to delay the children's journey to the Military School until the coming spring. Their father, desiring to escort them, and being obliged to put the affairs of his house in order, could not undertake the journey before the end of October. At that date the season is too severe to permit of risking the health of two delicate boys by a long journey. For this reason their parents ask Your Majesty for the postponement which they confidently hope to obtain from Your clemency. . . . "

The recollection of our own early carriage journeys across the yet untunnelled Alps (one, I remember, precisely in the month of October, occupied three days of violent snow-storm!) makes the last excuse seem a very reasonable one; but, as the Marchesa Patrizi remarks, one experiences something like amazement on finding the "possibility of soon arranging a suitable marriage" for a boy of twelve put forward as a serious argument against removing him from home. For the distracted parents it must be pleaded that the threatened exile would consume all the best years of their sons' youth, and thus mar all plans for their future, and the case was sufficiently desperate to justify any argument that could be brought to bear upon it.

Looking at it all now, a hundred years later, one wonders that Giovanni and Cunegonda Patrizi should have hoped for a single moment that Napoleon would hearken to their appeal. They were representatives of the old stiff-necked aristocracy which disdained to recognise his supremacy in anything but overwhelming force, and they were closely connected with the Bourbons, whom he was teaching the world to forget. On September 17 a note from the Director-General of Police was sent to the Palazzo, asking that the Marchese Patrizi would call at the Prefecture that morning. Without saying anything to his son, Giovanni's father obeyed the summons, for in his journal Giovanni writes: "When I came to table that day I saw that my mother was inwardly disturbed, and that my father's expression was even sadder than usual. I did not divine the cause, but this melancholy of the elders rendered the meal silent and mournful. When it was ended my father turned to me and told me that a note had come which was intended for me, but that, wishing to spare me the pain of an interview with the Director of Police, he had taken upon himself to go to the Prefecture in my stead. He went on to relate how the Director had urged him to send his grandchildren away at once, to which he had replied that the matter was in the hands of their father, who alone had the right to dispose of them. The official had insisted that their grandfather, as head of the family, was equally responsible, and represented that, as our house was by no means in the good graces of the Government, it would be only prudent to refrain from any exhibition of repugnance to obeying the imperial orders, lest such sentiments should bring serious trouble upon us.

"To this my father replied that he could not understand what the Government found to complain of in our conduct, since we kept ourselves entirely apart from public affairs and lived like quiet, respectable citizens in the retirement of our own home. The Director condescended to say that our respectability at least left nothing to complain of (what benignity!) But he then went on to insist so strongly on the necessity of submission that my good father, unable to resist such pressure, and perhaps alarmed by the other's threats, was reduced to asking a postponement only till the end of September, to which the Director replied gaily, 'A la bonne heure!' and granted the enormous favour of thirteen days' grace!"

The young Marchese was by no means pleased with this new turn of affairs, which bore the appearance of his implied consent to parting with his children; he at once set every machinery to hand in motion to obtain at least sufficient delay for him to receive an answer to the petition he had sent to the Emperor in Paris. Through a Frenchman named Gérard, who was high in favour with General de Miollis, and who had already rendered friendly service to the Patrizis, the Marchese Giovanni obtained a kind of unofficial permission to absent himself on his estates (where his presence was urgently needed at this season of the year) and was further told by the friendly Gérard not to disturb himself if further efforts were made to hasten the departure of his children, but at once to notify Gérard himself of anything of the kind.

Thus a couple of weeks passed quietly, and then with the return of Count Tournon to Rome, came another summons to the Prefecture. It was October 2, and the anxious father went thither, recommending his children's cause to the Blessed Angel Guardians, whose Feast it was. This was the beginning of the real battle: a long and bitter one for Patrizi, in which his personal liberty, family ties, home, and revenues were destined to be sacrificed for years, and, as many would have said, in vain.

Count Tournon received his visitor with the greatest urbanity, but begged him to name a day for the children's departure, since he was himself being pressed by General de Miollis to furnish him with the precise date on which they would be sent away from Rome.

"I replied," the Marchese writes, "that I was still waiting for the answer to the petition I had sent to the Emperor. I also represented that, as I had received the orders quite twenty days later than many others who had not yet sent their sons to France, it appeared just that mine should not be forced to precede them. Also that I was absolutely obliged to be away from Rome and on my father's estates for business matters all through the month of October, by which epoch I could not expose my boys to the cold of a journey across the Alps; all which considerations made it impossible for me to take them to France before the spring.

"The Prefect showed great alarm at this proposition, and assured me it was useless to hope for any result from my petition. He said that I could easily find a reliable escort for my children if I could not accompany them myself; but that, after all, the winter would not be so far advanced as to render a journey impossible. He told me he thought I might obtain permission to delay it till the end of November, or even of December—but till the spring? No, that was out of the question!

"He then entreated me to name an early date for the fulfilment of the order, holding out hopes that promptness in this might gain entire exemption for one child at least. But, as I was not dazzled by the prospects he held out, I repeated that I had already named the earliest date possible for the journey, adding that . . . nothing would induce me to deprive myself of my natural right to direct the education of my children."

To this the Prefect replied that the measure was intended as a correction to the ultra-clerical education given to boys in Rome; whereupon the Marchese retorted that that education was adapted to their individual needs; that those who wished to embrace the ecclesiastical life were assisted to do so, and those whose careers were to lie in the world enjoyed every facility for following the necessary studies.

But this assertion the Prefect combated hotly, insisting that there was " too much Church " in the whole programme, and that, although that might be advantageous for the next life, it was of very little use in this. Then, apparently wishing to soften the impression he had made, he went on to say that it was no order, but an invitation which the Emperor had sent, and that, if some parents chose to decline it, they need not fear that the gendarmes would be sent to their houses to enforce it—this was not a conscription!

The Marchese, now thoroughly angry, said that, if it was merely an invitation, he was free to accept or refuse as seemed good to him; but the diplomatic Prefect reminded him that royal invitations differed greatly from private ones, and that to refuse this would certainly involve the family in further misfortune. Having already shown itself adverse to the new order of things, it was not looked upon with favour.

The Marchese replied: "No misfortune that could happen to a father could be worse than that of losing his children."

"And how can you say you are losing them," exclaimed the Prefect, " in sending them where the Emperor wishes?"

"I consider them lost when I cannot bring them up according to my principles," was the answer.

The Prefect protested that Patrizi must be regarding France as another Turkey, and enlarged on the flourishing condition of religion there, more flourishing, he declared, than it was in Rome!

"I am willing to believe it—and am glad to learn that it is so," replied the Marchese, very politely; "but permit me to say that I can perceive no intention of benevolence in the act of the Emperor, but, on the contrary, a very clear one of inflicting a heavy punishment on our family."

"You are quite mistaken," Count Tournon declared. "The children of nobles who have given in their adhesion and are actually holding employment under the Government have been sent for as well as yours." And with much kindness he begged Patrizi to regard him now as a friend and not as an official, since he was really trying to persuade him to give in solely for his own good.

But the other was not to be shaken. With calm obstinacy he repeated his assertions that he could fix no earlier date than the following spring for carrying out the mandate, and the Prefect, between the desire to help his friends and the necessity of obeying orders, accused the Patrizis of making open war on the new Government and the Emperor; on being told that people who lived apart from public affairs in the retirement of their own homes could scarcely be accused of "making war," the Prefect made the startling assertion that war was of two kinds, positive and negative, and, after describing the positive sort, declared that the conduct of the Patrizis in refusing every offer of public employment fully justified the accusation of making war in the negative fashion!

The Marchese replying that he and his father had followed what they considered their duty, his opponent pointed out that such ideas were vastly displeasing to the authorities; that history was full of the disasters people had brought upon themselves by similar conduct; and he attempted once more to dazzle the Marchese by enumerating the distinguished posts he might yet fill if he would be reasonable.

Patrizi's curt reply that nothing would ever induce him to alter his decision in that regard evoked a sharp speech from Count Tournon to the

ROME. THE CHURCH OF S. LUIGI DEI FRANCESI.
Facing The Palazzo Patrizi.
Photo Moscioni, Rome.

effect that, the new order of things being firmly and completely established, it was useless for the Marchese to permit regrets for his old Sovereign to prevent him from accepting engagement under the Emperor. Patrizi was too proud to reply to this almost taunt, but in his heart he cried: "If ever I forget you, Holy Father, may my right hand forget her cunning!"

The Prefect understood that, in the face of such obstinacy, there was no more to be done; with a return of his charming manner, he affected to wipe the whole preceding conversation out of existence by saying that the next morning he would send to Palazzo Patrizi to know the day decided upon for the children's journey to Paris, and dismissed his visitor with smiling cordiality.

"And so," continues the Marchese in his Memoirs, "I came away, grateful to the Prefect for all his politeness, but more grateful to Heaven for having given me strength to reply as I had done, and also more determined than ever to combat the Emperor's designs on those who were dearest to me."

Punctually the next morning the Prefect's message arrived, and the Marchese replied to it, as he tells us, with joyful malice, in terms so ambiguous that they left his intentions as to moving, even in the following spring, shrouded in uncertainty.

On October 7 the patient Prefect issued another invitation to an interview, which seems to have had no effect, for on the 10th of the same month we find the Marchese leaving Rome to attend to affairs in two of his father's fiefs, Castel Giuliano and Sasso, where his presence was peremptorily required, several leases having expired, and new tenants being installed on the farms. Patrizi had feared that, during his absence, heavy pressure might be brought to bear on his father, and that the latter, less resolute in nature than his son, might yield some point which would compromise future action; so he gave instructions that all communications of whatever kind should be taken straight to his wife, who promised, for her part, to answer nothing until his own return to the city. Nevertheless, he says it was with a heavy heart that he went through all the wearisome business of inventories, and so forth, and that all his thoughts turned to what might be taking place at home; although he felt a great unwillingness to go back, having a presentiment that his reappearance would be the signal for some new and unexpected stroke of ill-fortune.

He remained away until October 29. When he reached home he found that his forebodings were not without justification. An imperious and very ill-written letter (some of the employés of the Government were distinctly illiterate) had arrived for him on October 23. It was signed by a deputy of the Prefect, and mentioned November 15 as the latest date allowed for the departure of his sons.

A few days later came another, from de Miollis himself, addressed to Cunegonda, he having understood that she was now in charge of the boys. In amazingly bad French he told her that, if her own health did not permit of her accompanying her sons to France, she had better at once find some responsible person to take them, adding that promptness in the matter might have some favourable influence on the position of " M. Patrizi."

It was a veiled threat, but Patrizi was there to answer for himself. The proud Roman's blood was up; weary of attempting to pacify his persecutors by speaking of a possible departure in the spring, he haughtily refused to have his children taken away from himself and their mother, adding sarcastically that, since he was told to regard the Emperor's order as a " favour," he could not imagine that the favour was to be forced upon him against his will. He wound up by saying once more that nothing should shake his determination to superintend the education of his sons himself.

This called forth an intimation from the Director of the Police, on November 10, to the effect that, unless the young Patrizis had left Rome by the 25th, their father would be "obliged" to accompany them to Paris and remain there under surveillance himself. The Marchese wrote a reply which, by this time, both he and the authorities must have known by heart. Repeating all the reasons already adduced for his decision, he absolutely refused to give up his children, and added that, as nothing could shake his resolution, he awaited with resignation such measures as the authorities might see fit to take in regard to himself.

CHAPTER IV

"On the morning of the twenty-fourth of November," Giovanni writes, "I had been to the Church of the Holy Name of Mary to assist at the Office of the day. When this was over I was coming out of the Oratory by way of the sacristy when I met one of my servants, and saw by his face that he was no bearer of good news. He handed me a note which proved to be a police order to leave Rome with my sons the next day. The charming intimation closed with threats of very stern measures should I persist in my resistance, and I was informed that the necessary passports were being forwarded to me. My servant told me that these had been brought by Signor Pelucchi, a Commissary of Police, who was now waiting for me in my house.

"I remained to hear Mass, God knows in what agitation of mind, and then hurried home, pondering by the way on what action I was to take, upon what answers I should give. I felt that now the question of resistance or submission would turn on the strength or weakness of my wife. My own heart would have inclined to resistance, but I realised that prudence might counsel differently.

"On reaching home I went to my wife's room, and my first words were: 'Well, what ought I to do?' Without hesitation she replied that we must resist to the very last, and her courage rekindled my own. Invoking the aid of the Blessed Virgin, I hastened to where the Commissary was waiting for me on the floor above. He had the passports in his hands. I told him that I had repeatedly explained to the authorities my firm intention of remaining where I was, and that, in consequence, the passports were useless to me, and I would not receive them. Much surprised, Signor Pelucchi exclaimed, 'You will not accept them?' 'No,' I said. He then represented that he ought to make a *procès verbal* of my refusal, and I asked if a personal note from me to the Director of Police would answer the purpose. On his affirmation I returned to my wife's room to write it, and she came to meet me, asking anxiously about the result of the colloquy upstairs. Her eyes bore traces of the tears she had been shedding at the foot of the crucifix while praying that I might be strengthened in this struggle. When I related what had occurred she was filled with consternation. I wrote the note and took it to the Commissary, who, on receiving it, exhorted me in whispers to give way in order to avoid the distress which my obstinacy would draw down upon me. . . . At last he withdrew.

. . . . .

"After these events I expected to be arrested and

THE GATHERING STORM

carried away with my children that same night, which was anything but a tranquil one, although by a special grace of Heaven I could anticipate the coming blow with imperturbability. On the morning of the twenty-fifth I arose, and, nothing new having happened, went out very early to church in order that those who, as I foresaw, might enter my room and force me to leave at any moment should not have to send out into the city to seek me, as had happened the day before. Hours passed . . . towards midday I went out again, sure that, on returning to the house, I would find it full of armed men. But I was quite mistaken. All was quiet. We sat down to table, and I confess that I dined with a very good appetite.

. . . .

"The meal was scarcely over when a servant, evidently much frightened, informed me that a French officer was in the ante-room asking to speak with me. Every one was alarmed except myself. Again praying to the Blessed Virgin, I went out to see what was wanted of me, and found the captain of the gendarmes, De Filippi, who, with the greatest courtesy and, as he explained, to his own profound regret, said that the Director had ordered him to tell me that, if I insisted any further in refusing to leave Rome, forcible measures would be applied to me in person. I replied that I could not reconsider my decision, and was prepared for everything.

"'But I have terrible orders,' De Filippi said.

"'I am in their hands,' I replied; 'they can shoot or guillotine me, but they cannot make me change my mind.'

"'You and your sons will be deported this very night,' said he.

"'I really trust that I shall be granted a few hours in which to make my arrangements,' I protested.

"De Filippi continued, with all kindness, to insist on his point, and then, feeling that he had better understand me once for all, I spoke in a prouder tone and told him that I should not recede from my decision even in the face of death; that Almighty God, as well as Nature, had given me the undeniable right to direct the education of my children; that I would show there were still Romans in Rome, and would demonstrate to the whole of Italy that the pretended honour conferred by the Government was in reality a monstrous infliction. I confess that it would have been perhaps better not to say all this, as it was quite useless; but in the heat of passion it is not possible to measure every word one speaks.

"Then the honest soldier relinquished his attempt in despair, and I thanked him most sincerely for the gentleness and consideration with which he had carried out his most unpleasant commission.

"I cannot describe how quiet, almost happy, I felt after this i terview. I went into the next room where my parents, my wife, and some faithful friends were anxiously awaiting its result; and I turned all my efforts towards calming and encouraging them. I made sure that my arrest and deportation would take place that night; but nothing came to disturb us, and when the twenty-sixth of November dawned I was still safe in my own house.

. . . . .

"The day passed without incident, and when the evening came I bade good-night to my wife, who was preparing to retire, and told her to sleep peacefully, since I was sure nothing untoward would happen that night. The event, however, unfortunately, did not justify my prophecy.

"Having parted from my wife, I repaired to my mother's apartment, where supper was about to be served. To this I sat down with my parents, my sister, the Rev. Stefano Monticelli, and our friend, Parisani. The Chevalier Don Lorenzo Giustiniani and Signor Carlo Collicola were also with us. The meal had scarcely begun when a servant informed me that a French official wished to speak with me. I rose from the table, but before I could reach the door I saw, standing in the doorway, a 'Maréchal de Logis' of gendarmes, who said that the Governor wished to see the Marchese Patrizi. At these words my beloved father, full of eagerness to suffer in my stead, pretended to think the summons was for him, as no Christian name had been mentioned, and rose from the table, intending to answer it in person. I had instantly understood its meaning, and forestalled him by preparing to follow the officer at once. He, however, was amiable enough to let me finish my supper first, and meanwhile I thought of ordering my carriage, so as not to keep the Governor waiting. But the gendarme said that was unnecessary, the Governor's carriage having been sent to fetch me. A profound gloom had fallen on the whole party. I kissed the hands of my dear parents, whom I hoped to see again within an hour, took leave of my sister and our friends, and, accompanied by my new guardian, started out to meet my destiny."

It was two years before Giovanni Patrizi beheld those loved faces again!

"A little way down the stairs," he relates, "I found another gendarme posted as sentry, and two or three more below, when I reached the front door. Emerging from the house with this novel variety of escort, I was surprised to see that the promised carriage was not there. The Marshal explained that it was waiting a little way off, and then led me to the right, a movement which led me to suspect that it was not the Governor's palace, but the Castel Sant' Angelo, that was my destination. In this I was wrong, for a vehicle which had been waiting at a little distance drew up to the steps of San Luigi dei Francesi. It proved to be a 'carretella' (a kind of buggy) to which three horses were harnessed, a clear indication of a long journey in prospect. I was not left any longer in doubt when my guardian told the driver to take the road to Civita Vecchia.

"I entreated the gendarme to send up word to my family that they must not expect me back that night. They would hear my real fate soon enough next day!

"I flattered myself that the gendarme had complied with my request, for he muttered something to one of his comrades. Of his words I caught but one distinctly, 'children.' At once I was filled with fear that, after capturing me, the next step would be to take possession of those innocent ones."

Here follows a characteristically Italian remark to the effect that those who read the journal will imagine that at this point the writer "shed floods of tears, and, in a voice broken with sobs and sighs, called on the beloved names of country, parents, wife and sons, from whom I was being barbarously torn away! Such would indeed have been the case had not Heaven come to my assistance, causing me to become like an immovable rock under the fierce blows of persecution. I can honestly say that I did not lose my tranquillity. On the contrary, in that terrible moment a supreme peace and serenity reigned in my heart, so that when we had gone a little way I began to joke with my keeper about the stratagem he had employed to seize me. But one cloud darkened my sky: my painful anxiety about the fate of my children. My imagination fixed on the word I thought I had heard, depicted the terrible tragedy which might at that very hour be taking place in my house; I heard in fancy the cries and laments of my wife, of my sons, of my father and mother in the stress of that cruel moment. I imagined these tender little beings confided for the journey to the care of a stranger, perhaps of a rough soldier. At one moment I thought they might be following me on the road to Civita Vecchia, at another that they were perhaps even now being hurried along the Via Flaminia, so as to meet me and my gaoler at Viterbo or some other point on the road to France. . . ."

Giovanni Patrizi's message was never delivered to his family. The little circle, anxious to know the result of the interview with General de Miollis, waited in vain for his return. At last it was decided to send to the Governor's residence to inquire for him, and the good Signor Collicola offered to act as messenger. He hastened to the Palazzo Doria only to be told that the Governor was at the theatre. At the theatre he learnt that the Governor had left, and so returned to Palazzo Doria. After trying to track him for some time, he was curtly informed that the Marchese Patrizi was "travelling." At once grasping the meaning of this information, he resolved to keep it to himself, for that night at least, and on his return to Palazzo Patrizi his depressed and mysterious demeanour led the family to suppose that Giovanni had been taken to Sant' Angelo, a mistake which Collicola did not correct. That was bad enough, but the truth—that Giovanni was being spirited away to some unknown prison—was so much worse that his friend had not the heart to disclose it.

By some means, however, it became known in the house next morning, first to his parents, and then, through her mother-in-law, to Cunegonda. The blow was as terrible as it was unexpected, and it required all their fortitude to meet it in a manner worthy of their faith and race. The poor little boys, realising that they were the cause of the trouble, were terribly afflicted, but tried in their childish way to follow the example of their elders' patience and resignation.

It was a bitterly cold night. The light buggy with its three horses rattled and bumped through the darkness for some five or six hours without a halt, and the unfortunate prisoner, called from his supper to pay an evening visit, and quite unprovided with extra wraps, suffered horribly from the cold before the first halt was called at Monterone towards three o'clock in the morning. The place was but a tiny hamlet serving as a posting-station about half-way between Rome and Civita Vecchia. " Here," says the Marchese, " I imagined that we should change horses, but it turned out that the halt was intended merely to rest those we had. I alighted from the carriage, and we entered a room contiguous to the stable; here a roaring fire was burning, and nine or ten peasants were sleeping on the floor around it, their feet all turned to the flame. Others, who probably considered themselves too distinguished for such a position, were sleeping in bunks against the wall. The fire was most consoling, for I was chilled to the bone. Still imagining we should get fresh horses, I was somewhat surprised at the long halt we were making, and I began to fancy that we were waiting to permit my sons and their captors to rejoin us here. The thought, though it had caused me painful anxiety hitherto, now brought comfort; it would have been most sweet to have those dear little companions on my journey, however alarming the goal! Already I pictured their arrival at this dark den; their tears and their fears, and the joy with which I would take them into my arms to comfort and sustain them with all the authority of a father!"

Giovanni Patrizi, although the most sincere and warm-hearted of men, had a distinct sense of dramatic fitness, and in every circumstance he shows himself naively anxious to extract all the aroma possible from every situation. It is a characteristic of the Latin races which has drawn forth much adverse comment from Northerners, who are loud in asserting that it denotes shallowness of feeling.

MARCHESE GIOVANNI NARO PATRIZI.
In the Robes of the Senator of Rome.

Nothing could be more unjust. The Latins live in the fullest light of family publicity, comparing their thoughts and sentiments on every subject that comes up with a frankness that, among us, would result in angry discussion, but that serves their more expansive temperament in good stead. They do feel, deeply, and consider it no reproach to have it known. They enjoy drama, it is true; they seem to be born for it; but they have no self-consciousness, and the Englishman's nervous terror of "looking like a fool" if he betrays the slightest emotion is incomprehensible to them. *En passant* I must remark that the everlasting repression of all demonstration of feeling with us has resulted, in many circles, in the killing of feeling altogether! We are nothing like so loving or so faithful to family and friends as are the Latins. Nowhere in these times is the tie between parents and children, brothers and sisters, so strong, so tender, so enduring as among the people of southern Europe.

This little digression is meant to explain why Giovanni Patrizi so carefully notes down his own words and actions on all important occasions, as if to assure himself, when looking back on them, that his deportment throughout has been unassailable. Even while waiting in the miserable posting-house at Monterone, torn with anxiety about his boys, he was careful to !make the right impression, and tell us that he began to walk about the waiting-room with brisk, free steps, humming softly to himself, in order that all might understand that prisoners of his stamp knew as little of cowardly discouragement as they knew of guilt.

After a long delay, during which the Marchese seems to have given up his hopes and fears of being rejoined by his sons, the journey was resumed, the gendarme having thoughtfully filled all the bottom of the carriage with hay to keep their feet a little warmer than they had been on the way down. The moon had set; the night, though still, was intensely dark; and the road onwards from Monterone was notoriously infested with brigands and malefactors of all kinds. Only two mounted guards had accompanied the carriage so far, and one of them was now ordered to ride on quickly and notify the authorities at Civita Vecchia of the approach of the prisoner. His companion, on leaving Monterone, tied his horse to the back of the carriage and climbed up beside the driver, his loaded carbine ready for use. The Marchese frankly acknowledges that the idea of finding himself the central figure under a rain of bullets did not add to the charm of the journey, and he decided, if a skirmish should take place, to declare himself a prisoner, an announcement which he evidently thought should secure for him the sympathies of the attacking party.

He and his guards were not molested, however, and in the grey of the dawn Civita Vecchia loomed up in the distance. By eight o'clock on that cold November 27 Napoleon's supremacy had, for the time, no more to fear from Giovanni Naro Patrizi, he being under lock and key in the fort. The dangerous rebel was longing for an hour of rest and privacy after the fatigues and emotions of the night. He had to walk up and down on the drill-ground for some time before obtaining it, but then, to his great satisfaction, he found that he was to have the turnkey's comfortable room, all the others being crowded already. In order to reach it he had passed another of which the door stood open, and there he recognised several Roman friends who had vanished more or less recently from their accustomed haunts in town. Rejoiced at his luck, he attempted to leave his room to greet them, but the Concierge stopped him, saying that orders had been issued forbidding him to have communication with other prisoners. This was a great disappointment, but the Marchese took it philosophically, and only asked permission to write to his family and also to send a note to one Bucci, the steward of the palace which his mother owned in Civita Vecchia.

So a long letter was despatched to Rome, and in it, to his infinite credit, Patrizi gave quite a roseate account of his experiences, dilated on the comfort of his quarters—in fact, said everything possible to cheer and comfort the anxious ones at home, winding up, quaintly enough, by asking for "some linen to provide for the cleanliness of the body, and some books of devotion to comfort the spirit." The letter was despatched by the returning gendarme, and a note was conveyed to Bucci instructing him to supply the prisoner with food and other necessaries, including a bed.

"I was quite resigned to the decrees of Heaven," Giovanni writes, "and was congratulating myself on being so well lodged, close to the family of the Concierge, who was only anxious to serve me in every way, when the good man entered my room, with downcast countenance and evident reluctance, to inform me that another apartment, very different from this one, had been assigned to me. This amazed me a good deal. The Concierge said the change would be made that afternoon.

"At the appointed hour I was conducted thither . . . and found it to be a tiny cell, one of a series looking out on a covered loggia. The window was about twenty inches broad and thirty high, filled with a frame of glazed cotton—which, however, admitted a certain amount of light. A broken fireplace, bare walls, smeared with smoke and oil, and ornamented with scrawls of charcoal and impressions of filthy fingers—and, hanging from the blackened ceiling, cobwebs which I calculated must date from the days of Numa and Ancus Martius! In this lurid den I found a beautifully arranged bed, which the excellent Bucci had brought from the Palazzo Montoro, and by the end of the second day the tiny room was supplied with every comfort it could contain, from the same source. It suggested the idea of a rough peasant dressed in the elegant garments of a Parisian dandy!"

CHAPTER V

THE Marchese's Journal continues:

"When the Concierge had transferred me to my new room he locked me in, and a sentinel was stationed outside the door, with orders to keep a strict watch night and day so that no one should approach to speak to me. In looking around on my new dwelling-place and comparing my so-called crime with the punishment it had drawn down upon me, I could not refrain from amused laughter!

"In order not to forget that I was a Christian I asked for the loan of some book of devotion pending the arrival of such provision from Rome. In answer to my request, the golden book of St. Ignatius' Spiritual Exercises was put into my hands, and at once I conceived the idea of turning my imprisonment to advantage by making a spiritual Retreat. I resolved to begin the next day, and to that end I mapped out a careful schedule for the regulation of my time. Would that I had indeed profited by this grace of Heaven for the good of my soul!

"On the twenty-eighth of November, while I was occupied in these spiritual exercises, I heard the grating of the prison gates and was honoured by a visit from the Mayor of Civita Vecchia, Signor Capotti, who was accompanied by the Commissary of Police and by Signor Guglielmi, to whom we had rented the Montoro Palace in the town. The courteous Mayor did everything possible to show his consideration, and begged me to tell him if there were anything that I desired. The only request I proffered was that I might be put into another room. The visit, though most polite, was an extremely brief one, probably because the Mayor, a man of elegance and refinement, could not bring himself to sit down in such a room—and, in that, I could sympathise with him!

"Although, by the favour of Heaven, I still enjoyed my accustomed interior tranquillity during my imprisonment, the thought of my children was never absent from my mind, and my uncertainty as to their immediate destiny kept me in much suspense. Hence it is impossible to express my relief when, on November the twenty-eighth, I received, together with a valise full of necessaries, a letter from my wife, in which she informed me that, so far, nothing new had transpired in regard to the beloved objects of my solicitude. My first act was to render profound thanks to the Almighty for this precious favour, and then I offered up my own life to perpetual imprisonment if by such a sacrifice I could save those innocent young souls from the education we so much dreaded for them.

"During the first two days of my incarceration, writing materials were doled out to me for a few moments at a time, as the orders were that I was not to be allowed to write letters at all. Permission was accorded, however, for a few letters to my own family, and an occasional note to our good Bucci at the Palazzo Montoro; but all these communications I had to leave open, to be read by the authorities. When the letter or the note was written, the pen and ink were instantly removed! After three days I managed to retain firm possession of them, but the rigours of the censorship continued unabated. The thing which I found most hard to bear in my new mode of life was the complete deprivation of the comforts of religion. On December the 1st, the First Sunday of Advent, I heard repeated salvoes of artillery, which announced the anniversary of the Emperor's coronation; but I could not hear Mass either on that day or any other during my detention at Civita Vecchia, as the Holy Sacrifice had been prohibited in the fortress.

"Another trouble, and not a light one, was caused from the situation of my room. It was surrounded by others filled with a goodly number of refractory conscripts awaiting in Civita Vecchia their departure to Sicily. It was not wronging these young fellows to say that their training left much to be desired; from the break of day till late in the evening they filled all that part of the building with shouting, singing, and quarrelling, and the heavy tramping of their feet never ceased outside my door.

"On December the 2nd Signor Giulio Guglielmi,

our tenant, who had already paid me several visits, brought me the welcome news that he had obtained permission from the commander of the fort for my transfer to another room. So I returned to the one I had first occupied, and found great pleasure in looking out once more at earth and sky after having had barely a glimpse of the latter for four days. Guglielmi promised also to procure permission for me to take a little exercise, a thing which was absolutely necessary for my health.

"Although in my new quarters I was not so closely guarded as before, still I was forbidden to hold communication with any one except my jailers, and the Concierge was made responsible for the carrying out of the order."

And here we must transcribe the first letter of the Marchesa Cunegonda to her husband; it is written on a tiny piece of paper, yellow now with age, and bears the marks of having been folded into the smallest possible space. It was the first of hundreds that the loving wife was to write before she saw Giovanni's face again, and it was more successful in reaching its destination than the greater part of those that followed it. From the family correspondence it appears that Bucci, the Patrizi steward at Civita Vecchia, managed to convey, though with great difficulty, several missives to his master, with such secrecy that they escaped the observation of his lynx-eyed guardians, and great was the comfort they brought to the lonely prisoner. This first one, folded to almost infinitesimal size, was probably concealed within a loaf of bread, all the food for the Marchese being furnished from Palazzo Montoro. It is pathetic in its almost incoherent simplicity and tenderness.

"What can I say to you, Giovanni, my dear?" writes Cunegonda on November 27. "You know me well enough to understand all that I want to express. My greatest trouble is the thought that you are suffering anxiety about the children and me; I entreat you, as a favour, to set your mind at rest. The blow has fallen on you—God will give you strength and will not permit us to be tempted above our strength. I am in a frenzy to have news of you, and I hope that you will be able to give it yourself. Assure me that you are well, that you are tranquil; courage, my dear, courage! God is for us, our Mother" (*Mamma nostra*, the Blessed Virgin) "is for us; what have we to fear? The children weep, and that is natural; but they are well, and they understand how greatly they are beholden to you; do not think of me. God will help me; I am thinking only of you, and when I can be assured that you have not lost your calmness and courage I shall be satisfied; remember that all my happiness depends on you. Already Maria Agnese* knows all, let that suffice you. Farewell,

---

* She appears to have been Giovanni's sister, a religious in the Dominican convent at Magnanapoli, spoken of earlier as "Maria Vincenza."

my dearest Giovanni, I glory in being the wife of a Confessor of Christ ; this will tell you all that I have in my heart."

This letter was followed by another written in the same tone of calm fortitude, but the next after that brought news which filled the Marchese with grief and apprehension. It was written in duplicate, one copy intended for the eyes of the censor of the fortress, the other, long and confidential, reached him secretly. His fears for his children were to be confirmed at last ; the hope that his own imprisonment might buy their safety was now proved to be vain.

On December 2 his wife writes :

"My dear Giovanni,
"On Saturday afternoon the Commissary, Pepe, came to me, and, in the name of the Minister-General of Police, informed me that I must send away our two boys on the 8th inst. I replied that I was merely the guardian, not the master of my sons, and that, in the absence of their father, I could not dispose of them. This morning the Commissary returned, bringing word from the Director-General that it was quite true that I was not the master of the children so long as my husband was in Rome ; but that, he being away, it was my duty to dispose of them, and that, if I refused to do so, the 'Mairie' would be responsible for naming a person to accompany them. The

Commissary is to return to-morrow at midday for my answer. Giovanni mine, I have sought counsel, particularly with the two persons for whom you have such a great esteem, S—— and L——. They were unanimous in their opinion that forcible measures have been decided upon, and will be put into operation; that, by permitting the children to go away with a stranger, we should be voluntarily renouncing the right and the power which God has given us over them, a thing that conscience forbids us to do. So, to-morrow, I shall tell Pepe that I cannot consent to confide the children to another person; but, also, that I do not wish to take a journey without my husband, and that I request that he should be brought back to Rome with the same force with which he was taken to the fortress; and I also request that the Director-General will see that my husband receives the letter in which I have manifested to him my resolution. I am exceedingly anxious that this (the private one) should reach you before that other which you will receive through the police, in order that you may be fully informed of everything, and be tranquil in mind, for these are wise counsels, given according to God, and thus you will perhaps be able to answer me freely and fully. Not so, however, in regard to the letter you will receive through the police; on the contrary, I pray you to respond to that in as few words as possible. Good-bye, my Giovanni; I have no time to write more. I hope to see you again, soon, and then we can talk with more ease. What days ! God be blessed ! "

Here is the official letter intended for the eyes of the Police :

"MY DEAR HUSBAND,   ROME, *December* 3.

"Last Saturday the Signor Commissario came to inform me that I was to arrange to send the children to Paris; I replied that I had no authority save that of a guardian, and could decide on nothing during your absence. Yesterday the same Commissary returned to tell me, from the Director-General, that I was to accompany them myself; otherwise the 'Mairie' would designate some other person for that charge. True to our maxim of never confiding our children to others, I replied this morning that I was ready to go with them, but that I wished the Director-General would kindly put yesterday's message in writing, so that I might send it to you. Also I asked for your return, in order that you also might accompany the children. In this moment I learn that the Director-General refuses to put the message in writing, as I had requested; but says that I am to tell you to write to him asking that you may be brought back here in order to accompany the boys. He promises that this letter shall reach you. This much I communicate in haste, and am, with all attachment,

"Your most affectionate wife,
"CUNEGONDA OF SAXONY PATRIZI."

The Marchese received both his wife's letters, the private one reaching him first, as she intended. The news caused him great distress. "This unexpected blow," he says in his diary, "struck me to the heart, and my hand trembled as I wrote, in few words, to my wife, that I was ready to carry out her wise and Christian counsels. Besides, the thought of having her companionship on the journey mitigated my sorrow, for until now she had hesitated to undertake it, on account of her variable health. On that same day the Commandant of the fort, M. Callo, a Piedmontese, came into my room to give me permission to enjoy, for two hours every day, a promenade on the bastions of the fortress, excluding the parade-ground, however; forbidding me to speak with any one, and adding that I should always be under the vigilance of a sentinel. At once I took advantage of the grace accorded me, but the letter I had received in the morning prevented my feeling the pleasure which I should otherwise have had in this solace.

"On the 5th I received, through the Roman police, the official letter of my wife, in which she begged me to ask the Director-General that I might be brought back to Rome in order to travel with her and our children. I carried out her wishes in a letter to the Director, written on the 6th.

"Towards dusk of that day I heard proclaimed in the rooms next to mine the arrival of a number

ROME. THE CASTLE OF SANT' ANGELO.
Photo Moscioni, Rome.

of new inmates, all men of the best society. They were the 'Curiali' of Rome" (here follows a long list of names of lawyers who, having refused to take the required oath of allegiance to the Emperor, had been detained for several months in the Castle of Sant' Angelo and were now brought to Civita Vecchia, to be sent from there to the Island of Corsica). "I felt the greatest desire to embrace such of my friends as were among the new prisoners, but the vigilance with which I was guarded gave me no hope of doing so. Very soon I perceived that supper was being prepared for them in the next room, and, hearing them so near, I came close to the door of my cell to have the consolation at least of seeing through the cracks these true Christian heroes" (our famous compromisers of to-day would call them at the very least foolish intransigeants), "since I could not press them to my heart. The first whom I saw enter was the excellent Belli, with whom I was particularly acquainted. With him were others, but not all the party, since the table was too small to accommodate them all at a time. The sight of them made me more than ever anxious to greet them. The good Concierge must have divined my wish, for soon afterwards he entered my room, saying that he would allow me to go into the other one to show myself to my colleagues.

"On the instant I left my retreat and threw myself on the neck of my friend Belli and that of the excellent Ceccacci. The vivacious Gasparri was there also, with Benedetti and others. . . . After the first greetings they told me that they had not expected to find me still in Civita Vecchia, but had hoped to meet me on the road returning to Rome, a Commissary of Police having informed them that my affair was all arranged, and that probably that very day I should be able to return home. This announcement gave me the greatest pleasure. . . .

"When our short interview was over I returned to my own room. I learnt later, to my horror, that those twelve ornaments of the Roman Curia, on account of the late hour of their arrival, had not been able to procure beds from their acquaintances in the town (who, however, furnished them the next day), and had been obliged to sleep on straw in two miserable ground-floor rooms from which they were not transferred for some days. The morning after their arrival, distressed at the thought of the horrible night those incomparable men must have passed, I should have wished to bring them all into my own room had such a thing been possible. If not altogether, I was at least consoled in part, for the obliging Concierge allowed me to take in Belli and Giorgi. In order to keep up the appearance of my being in solitary confinement, my guests' beds had to be returned to their own prison in the morning, to be brought back to mine at night after the fortress was closed. To tell the truth, after the advent of these legal captives, my solitary con-

finement was reduced to a mere farce, one or the
other being constantly in my apartment, although
always on the alert for fear of getting the poor
Concierge into trouble should some one of the
authorities pay us an unexpected visit. But when
once night had fallen, and, the fortress being closed,
there was no danger of any one's coming to disturb
our peace, then all or most of the councillors as-
sembled in my room; one or two tables of 'ombre'
or 'bézique' were organised, and very pleasant
hours were passed.

"A few days later, the order for my solitary
confinement, which from the constant infractions
had become purely imaginary, was officially rescinded,
and I received permission to move about and speak
with whom I pleased. The only person who had
great difficulty in approaching me was my Bucci"
(the steward). "The assiduous and charitable assistance he always rendered to the prisoners, particularly
if they were ecclesiastics, caused the new Government
to suspect him of too strong an attachment for the
old one, a state of things which rendered access to
the fortress very difficult for him. During all my
stay in Civita Vecchia I only succeeded in seeing
him five or six times, and his wife, whom the Mayor
was kind enough to bring, once.

"Following the letter I had sent to the Director-
General of Police in Rome, I expected every day
to be recalled to the Seven Hills, and the Mayor,
who favoured me with many visits, always told me

that my return was close at hand—that he was expecting the notification of the order with every courier who arrived. On December the 8th this anticipation had become so confident that not only did the Mayor assure me that I should be set at liberty on that day, without fail, not only did the Commissary of Police announce the fact publicly, but my excellent Bucci had made all his arrangements and prepared a bed for me in his house. In any case I would not have availed myself of his hospitality, having promised to stay with Signor Giulio Guglielmi. He himself had to leave for Monte Romano on the 8th on private business, but he had charged his wife to have everything in readiness for me, and had asked a friend of his to conduct me to the house. But the 8th passed by; the 9th found me still in the fortress; also the 10th and 11th, and several days more, and I continued to carry on my quiet and cheerful existence in the good company of my amiable fellow prisoners.

"Several days had passed without bringing me any news from home, when, on the morning of the 16th, just as I had sat down to write to my wife, and had written but a word or two, there entered my room the same man who had twice before been sent to me from Rome. He handed me a letter, but I perceived from his expression that it could contain no good news. It was written in the name of my wife, but the handwriting was that of my friend Parisani. At the beginning were a few words inscribed by the trembling hand of my father:

'I embrace you and I bless you! Your most loving father!' The date was of December the 15th, and the contents informed me that our Maestro di Casa (steward) had that morning been summoned by the Director-General of Police, who ordered him to send me that very evening a coach and five hundred scudi in money; the Director added that a gendarme would go with the carriage to escort me to Lyons. The letter mentioned that the Director had advised that I should take warm clothes with me, on account of the cold at Lyons, and that this led my family to suppose that I was to be detained in that place.

"The letter had been sent on in haste in order that I might not be taken by surprise on the arrival of the gendarme. My good wife concluded it with a few words in her own writing, as trembling and convulsed as that of my father: 'Farewell, my Giovannino. Your most loving wife, Gondina.' Even our friend's writing betrayed his agitation. I cannot deny that this blow struck me very heavily. As soon as I had read the sad epistle I was convinced that my ultimate destination was not Lyons, but Fenestrelle or some other state prison. My own hand shook as I wrote in reply a few words which showed clearly enough my distress; the only request I made was that my old valet, Bennini, might be sent to accompany me. Then I hastened to find Giorgi, one of my room companions, to tell him of the new turn in my affairs. He was horrified, as were all his worthy colleagues. But our good and merciful Father did not permit my distress to be of long duration. He gave me grace to raise my eyes to Him, to bow my head to His adorable will, and very soon I became perfectly tranquil once more.

"That afternoon, while I was walking with my friends on the bastions, whence we could see the road to Rome, I fancied that every coach I saw was the one which was to convey me to my new destination; but when the evening came, and the fort was closed, I assured myself that there was nothing to fear for that night, and so, with the usual quiet and gaiety, I sat down to enjoy over a game of 'ombre' the amiable society of my dear fellow prisoners.

"Having passed the night a little less tranquilly than usual, I rose in the morning to perform my religious exercises, and suddenly became aware that the Concierge (till then ignorant of the coming changes) was speaking in the next room about my immediate departure. From this I understood all, and, in fact, a few moments later the Mayor appeared, accompanied by the gendarme who was to act as my escort. This man was a Brigadier named Collia, and he had orders to go with me as far as Turin, where the further dispositions in regard to my destination would be made known.

"This confirmed me in my conviction that not Lyons, but Fenestrelle, was the spot which the *clemency* of the Emperor had selected for me.

The Mayor counted out to me the five hundred scudi (which my father repaid to the police in Rome), and I received the order, from the same source, to pay the above-mentioned gendarme three hundred francs, a sum which, according to military estimates of distance, would allow him five francs (one scudo) a day for the journey from Rome to Turin, and from Turin back to Rome. The said sum I instantly counted out to my new guardian. I was told that the journey was to be made by post (that is to say, changing horses at the ordinary posting-stations), and that from Civita Vecchia I was to go that same day to Viterbo, where we could strike the main road to the north.

"As soon as the Mayor and the gendarme had withdrawn another person entered the room—Filippo Appolloni, my own *maestro di casa*, who had come from Rome with the gendarme in order to see me once more. He brought me a letter from my wife. When I asked him which of my servants was to accompany me, he replied that it would be the groom, Mariano. I was not much pleased with the arrangement, having only small confidence in the fellow, who, besides being very young, had only been a few months in my service. But I had to resign myself. I thought it as well, before leaving, to write a letter intended for my parents, my wife, my children, and my sisters, in which I manifested all the emotions that a son, a husband, a father, a brother could not but feel in such circumstances. Then the Brigadier, my guard, reappeared, informing me that all was ready for our departure. I tenderly embraced all my beloved comrades, who almost all had tears in their eyes. Among them Belli, after having embraced me, threw himself on the bed and wept openly. This sight touched me deeply, but did not disturb the inner peace of my heart, and I went calmly whither God was calling me."

CHAPTER VI

THE curious rancour which Napoleon nourished in regard to the Patrizi family showed itself at this point in a step which excited the indignation of the Emperor's own employés. The Marchese Giovanni was a close prisoner; his sons, with their mother, were already on their way to France; but their enemy was not appeased by these forced submissions. He ordered the sequestration of the entire revenues of the Patrizi family. Count Tournon, the Governor of Rome, was appalled at this arbitrary and cruel decree, and at once wrote confidentially to his friend, M. Angèles, the Director of Police in Paris, to ask for its repeal. The letter is dated January 23, 1812.

"A month since," the Count writes, "he (General de Miollis) instructed me to immediately sequestrate the property of M. Jean Patrizi. To this I promptly replied, informing him that, as M. Jean Patrizi's father and mother are still living, it is unlikely that the property has been divided, and I ask him for further instructions. The answer was a renewed order to put the seal on all M. Jean Patrizi's property, and nothing was said in reply to my request for explanations.

"I took out an order in conformity with the General's letter and sent it on to the Director of the Domains; two days later he sent me a certificate proving that all the Patrizi property belonged to the father. This document I transmitted to M. Miollis; he sent for the Director of Domains and for me, and in my presence ordered the Director to sequestrate all property pertaining to the Patrizi family. The Director demanded to have the order in writing, but this M. Miollis obstinately refused to give. At last, after a long scene, the Director consented to place the seals, and this has been done.

"So, while Madame Patrizi is on the way to take her sons to La Flèche, while her husband is at Fenestrelle, the goods of the father are sequestrated, although the order speaks only of Jean Patrizi. I beseech you to give orders for removing a sequestration so unjust and so little in accord with the commands of the Minister. . . .

(*Signea*) "TOURNON."

In his Memoirs Count Tournon writes thus of that critical moment:

"The Marquis Patrizi refused to consent to the departure of his children; he was carried off, himself, and shut up in Fenestrelle, so harsh had the methods become. His poor wife, born Princess of Saxony, an angel of piety, is sadly accompanying her children in order to preserve them from the contagion of French impiety."

The reason of this incredible vexation—a reason of which Tournon was probably ignorant—is to be found in a marginal note on a report of General de Miollis, in which he gave an account of the Marchese Patrizi's resistance to the Decree of July 9. This note, in the Emperor's own handwriting, says :

"Let this individual be arrested, sent to Fenestrelle, and all his goods sequestrated.

"NAPOLEON."

In the state archives of Paris there exists the following report to His Majesty, the Emperor and King :

"SIRE,
"The Prefect of the Department of the Ombronne" (Umbria) "informs me that, in consequence of a decree of the Prefect of Rome, issued in conformity with instructions from Your Majesty communicated by the Vicegerent of the Governor-General, an order of sequestration is to be placed on *all the goods, without exception*, belonging to Sieur Jean Patrizi, a proprietor in Rome.

"The Sieur Patrizi possesses in the city of Siena a palace and lands producing approximately an annual revenue of 2,000 francs. The Prefect of the Ombronne inquires whether these properties are to be included in the order for sequestration, like those which the Sieur Patrizi possesses in the Department of Rome.

"Not knowing what decision Your Majesty has taken on this subject, I beg that I may receive Your Majesty's orders.

"The Minister of Finance,
"THE DUKE OF GAETA."

The answer to this inquiry was short and to the point. The Emperor wrote on the margin of the Duke's letter:

"Yes!
"NAPOLEON.
"ST. CLOUD PALACE OF THE TUILERIES,
"*January* 30, 1812."

When orders were given in this form they were not discussed; indeed, they were not spoken of. They were fulfilled, and that was all. The Patrizi family would have been reduced to destitution had not the tenants, respecting its misfortunes, animated by the same principles, and confident of better things in the future, continued, secretly, and in spite of the menaces of the Government, to offer small loans of money to their landlord.

And when these means of assistance, on which, from delicacy of feeling, the Patrizis were very loth to trespass, came to an end, the family sacrificed jewels and plate rather than recede from the attitude they had taken in the conflict with injustice and violence. They even attempted to keep the bad news from the Marchese Giovanni, but it was imparted to him at Bologna by Monsignor Naro, his mother's uncle, as he relates in his Memoirs.

Of his departure from Civita Vecchia, he writes:

"At the gate of the fortress I found the travelling-carriage and got into it, with my escort. The sea at that moment was tossed by a violent storm which seemed to threaten even the vessels inside the harbour. This extravagance of the weather, however, did not penetrate inland, and, as we left the sea behind, the sky cleared. Having left Civita Vecchia after ten in the morning, it was impossible to reach Viterbo without travelling during a great part of the night—and that over roads that were anything but good. Therefore I proposed to the gendarme that we should pass the night at Monte Romano, a place belonging to the Arch-hospital of Santo Spirito, where I knew that we should find the oft-mentioned Signor Guglielmi, who would certainly receive us with pleasure.

"The gendarme accepted my proposal, but on

arriving at Monte Romano I learnt, to my regret, that Guglielmi had had an accident and was laid up at Corneto. There were there, however, Messrs. Francesco Bruschi and Vincenzo Calabrini, co-tenants with him of the estate, and they received me and treated me with every courtesy at the Palazzo S. Spirito, which they had rented.

"On the morning of the 18th of December, at the break of day, I left Monte Romano and towards noon reached Viterbo, where I stopped for dinner at the Palazzo Chigi Montoro, belonging to my mother. Here I had the consolation of embracing again the excellent Monsignore de Bonneval, formerly Bishop of Seney in France, whom I immediately notified of my arrival, since, according to the instructions my guard had received from the police in Rome, I was forbidden to pay any visits and was to be allowed to receive very few.

"The noble, incomparable prelate had the goodness to come to me at once, and, embracing me with tears, said that his eyes must speak for his tongue, as the Italian language was not very familiar to him. He communicated to me a letter from our mutual friend, Cavaliere Bassi, in which the writer drew a sad picture of the present situation of my family.

"The next night I stopped at S. Lorenzo Nuovo, and on the 19th, at ten o'clock in the evening, I reached Siena, where I went to rest at my own house. Here there was no lack of good friends to visit me, for I have many in this second home-country. As it was impossible for me, in my situation, to go and pay my respects in person to the Very Rev. Archbishop Zondadari,* I sent him word at least of my wishes, and of my regret that I was not permitted to carry them out. The venerable and gracious prelate, full of kind feelings towards myself and my family, would not allow me to leave Siena without having had the happiness of saluting him, and on the morning of the 20th, a few minutes before my departure, he condescended to come to my house and honour me with a visit.

"I cannot express the confusion which overwhelmed me at this mark of goodness from the saintly pastor, a confusion immeasurably increased by the rudeness of my guard, who hurried my departure to such an extent that I was, as it were, forced to dismiss the illustrious personage who had bestowed on me such a mark of favour. On that morning I had the consolation of assisting, in my private chapel, at Holy Mass, of which I had been deprived ever since the 25th of November.

"That evening I reached Florence and put up at the Hotel New York. The next morning, having heard Mass, as was my duty, in honour of St.

* This good prelate is described in a French police report, 1808, as "a tiger, the enemy of France and of humanity, who must be muzzled by a severe police."

Thomas, whose feast it was, I continued my journey and stopped for the night at Covigliano, a village situated high up in the Apennines. Leaving that place on the 22nd, I fulfilled my religious duties for the Sunday at Loiano, and was there, in the quality of a prisoner, presented to the Commissary of Police. Some one had made my guard believe that this functionary wished to see me; but I at once perceived, from his manner, that nothing was further from his desires. Some malicious wag had wished to inflict this little inconvenience on us both, and on me the very slight mortification it involved, not realising that in these days it is not a disgrace, but an honour, to be a prisoner.

"On the same day, towards two in the afternoon, I reached Bologna. I had asked, as a favour, of my mentor, to be allowed to lodge in Palazzo Spada with my uncle, Monsignor Naro, Majordomo of St. Peter's, who for the last eighteen months had been exiled to Bologna for having refused to take the oath required of him in his character of a Canon of the Vatican. The desired favour was granted, and we drew up at the door of the palace. My good uncle was glad to see me again, but his joy was sadly tempered by beholding me in such a position. After the first exchange of greetings he gave me a letter which he had received from my mother but a few moments earlier, enclosing one that I myself had written to him from Civita Vecchia.

"Who can describe my tender mother's laments

CIVITAVECCHIA.
Photo Moscioni, Rome.

over my destination? She declared herself convinced that I was being taken to Fenestrelle,* she described the uncontrollable grief of the whole family when my farewell letter from Civita Vecchia was read; and finally she narrated how an imperial usher had presented himself at the house to sequestrate all my effects. She went on to say they hoped to avert the execution of the order by showing a certificate which my father had already exhibited to the authorities, declaring that I had no property whatever in the house, it all belonging to my father, including even the furniture of the rooms assigned to me. This new blow was as heavy as it was unexpected, and depressed me much, since it was an indication of the extreme rigour which was being adopted in the proceedings against me.

"Now, while I was having a conversation the reverse of cheerful with my uncle, and he was making the necessary dispositions for my stay that night, my gendarme discovered that some comrades of his were lodging in the palace, and he confided to me his fears that they would get him into trouble with his superiors for having brought me there against the orders he had received, forbidding him to let me visit any private house. Since in Viterbo and in Siena he had taken upon himself to disregard these orders simply to oblige me, I saw the reasonableness of his present protest. My uncle agreed

* This distant prison fortress had an evil name for rigour and discomfort.

with me, and in consequence I asked to be transferred from Palazzo Spada to the Hotel del Pellegrino.

"Truth constrains me to say that my custodian appeared genuinely grateful for my consideration in this matter, and also very sorry to have had to deprive me of the pleasure of being with my uncle . . . but I enjoyed the same pleasure at the hotel, where he came and remained with me for some hours, prolonging his visit till after we had supped. Then we separated, sadly uncertain of the time and place where we should be permitted to embrace each other again.

"I also received the kind visit of my cousin, Donna Prudenza Spada, and her husband, the Marchese Valerio Boschi. Two other friends came as well, Canon Bolognetti of the Vatican and Canon De Rossi of Sta. Maria in Cosmedin, both under sentence of exile for the same cause as my uncle.

"On the 23rd we slept at Parma, and on the 24th at Voghera, where I was cheered on that most holy night by the joyous sound of the church bells ringing for the Nativity of the Divine Redeemer. On the morning of Christmas Day we left Voghera, heard Mass at Tortona, dined at Alessandria, and at ten that night we reached Turin, where we put up at the Hotel de Londres. So here I was at last in Delphi, where the Oracle would pronounce decisively on my fate! I longed for the daylight to come, so that I could go and consult the venerated tripod and hear my sentence, for my guardian had told me that he was the bearer of a letter from the Director-General of Police in Rome to the corresponding functionary in Turin, from whom fresh orders were to be expected as to my now interesting self. So, having assisted at the Divine Sacrifice on the morning of the 26th at the elegant church of S. Lorenzo, where only the feast of the Proto-martyr (Saint Stephen) was commemorated, we repaired to the Palace of Police, but found that M. Danzer, the Director, was absent.

"The High-priest being away, the awe-inspiring curtain was not raised, and the oracle was dumb. We returned at two o'clock, when my guard was admitted to the audience first, and I was left to wait in the anteroom. I was then introduced into the presence of the Augur, and inquired of him as to my fate. He replied mysteriously that it was hidden from him, and that he must get his orders from His Serene Highness the Prince-Governor; that is to say, of my fellow-citizen, Prince Camillo Borghese.* Who would have believed, a few years ago, that my fate was to depend on this creature—or, to put it more clearly, on this automaton, the loyal executor of the harsh orders of his reigning brother-in-law?

"The Director asked me whether I was accom-

---

* "A fool, odious and despised, whose connection with Napoleon robbed him of all prestige in the eyes of his fellow-countrymen."—Madelin, "La Rome de Napoleon."

panied by a servant, and, on my replying in the affirmative, he remarked that, as the man would have to share my fortunes, it would be well to find out whether he was disposed to follow whithersoever they might lead. I promised to do this, and then made bold to ask the official whether I might go about the city with my guide while waiting for the final oracle to issue from the Napoleon-Borghese tripod. He replied politely, no; on the contrary, I was told to hold myself in readiness for the departure, which would probably take place that same night. Obedient to these commands, I returned to the hotel, and spent the rest of the day, and about half of the night, sitting by the fire.

"The 27th dawned, the feast of the beloved disciple whose name I am privileged to bear. When the sun was high in the heavens, I was still uncertain of my fate. Towards noon a gendarme, sent by the police, came to inform me that I was to leave Turin in two hours. Here humour entered into the situation, for the herald of bad news, in making this pleasant announcement, displayed before my eyes a paper containing the order for my deportation to Fenestrelle with an escort of two gendarmes, to each of whom I was to pay five francs a day, as well as the money for their return journey! I really believe that the man was ashamed to pronounce this sentence, and showed me the paper to let me find it out for myself. The first word

I saw was 'Fenistrelle.' Not in the least cast down by this new trait of imperial *benevolence*, of which I had had such striking proofs, I proceeded to inquire of the herald as to the distance to Fenestrelle, and the best means of making the journey.

"He pretended to be surprised at my having learnt the name of my destination . . . and indeed I felt grateful to him for the courtesy which had allowed me to read it rather than hear it actually pronounced. . . . But now there arrived on the scene the two gendarmes who were to take this great criminal in charge, to carry him into the recesses of the Alps; the other, who had brought me to Turin, was free from that moment.

"And here I must say something about the character of this soldier. From the first moment when I had the misfortune to make his acquaintance he declared himself anxious to fall in with my wishes in every way that should be possible to him; but it appeared that very little was possible, since he did next to nothing in that way. Under a mask of moderation he concealed extreme rigour. He was always at my side, like a ferocious mastiff, and never, so to speak, lost sight of me. On two nights only, and that because the lodging permitted of no other arrangement, had he been induced to sleep in a room separate from mine; but close to it. The fear of compromising himself prevented him from letting me pay any visit to friends or relations in the cities through which we passed, and it was with difficulty that he was persuaded to let me receive them. Having been induced to let me lodge with my uncle in Bologna, he was afraid of the gendarmes in the palace, and the pleasure had to be renounced. His conduct in Siena, obliging me actually to dismiss the Archbishop, showed that he was wanting in all good manners, and I really travelled as fast as I could to be quit of his unwelcome company!

"In the two satellites assigned to me in Turin I found more gentleness and refinement. It was on the 27th of December, towards three in the afternoon, that I left that place with my new guards. We passed the night at Pinerolo, and on the 28th, the Feast of the Holy Innocents, an hour after midday, we reached the village of Fenestrelle.

"My guards stopped at the village inn, evidently hoping that I would order dinner there for them and myself; but I requested to be taken at once to the Commandant. The snow was falling as I climbed the *giogo* and entered the fortress of S. Carlo, where the excellent official, M. Bernard David, and his worthy wife gave me the kindest of welcomes. But the most cordial demonstrations of friendship awaited me from Count Andrea Baccili of Fermo and the Abbé Domenico Sala, my fellow citizen. As soon as they heard of my arrival they left their dinner and hastened to the apartment of the Commandant, where they embraced me with all the warmth of their kind hearts.

"The first of these gentlemen had, three months earlier, completed the third year of his imprisonment in the fortress; the second had been there nearly ten months. Count Baccili I knew only by reputation, with the Abbé I was well acquainted; but from that moment, recognising in them fellow-victims of the *bipenne* (double-headed axe) that was attacking me, I began to feel for them a very tender friendship. It was from them that I received the welcome information that I was not to be condemned to solitary confinement, a measure which I had been led to apprehend from the rigour with which I had been treated at Civita Vecchia and on my journey. And then, understanding my great need of food at that moment, they invited me to their table, and on my asking if they would accept my company regularly at meals, most kindly consented to the arrangement. I was indeed glad to find that the wish (for congenial companions) which I had formed as soon as I suspected that I was being sent to Fenestrelle, was to be so fully gratified.

"Some of the prisoners, for the most part ecclesiastics and very distinguished, came to greet their new colleague, and the good Commendatore of San Lorenzo, whom I knew well and who, being confined to his bed, could not come in person, sent his servant to make a thousand obliging offers in his name. But inexpressible was my joy when my friend Baccili led me to where I could present my homage to His Eminence Cardinal Pacca, and I could imprint an affectionate kiss on the sacred purple * which he so worthily wears, and which is surely adorned with a new gem for every one of the insults and sorrows he has so intrepidly endured in defence of the inalienable rights of the Holy See.

"It was then the end of the twenty-ninth month that this incomparable prelate, Prime Minister, and fellow-sufferer in the abduction of the great and immortal Pius VII, my true and only Sovereign, had passed in this fortress under rigorous guard. He received me with the graciousness which is a part of his angelic character, condescended to press me to his heart, and then and there began to overwhelm me with favours, which have never ceased to the present day.

"I was then conducted to the room assigned to me, which, thanks to the kindness of my friends, I should in any case have found prepared for my arrival; but in this the Cardinal had most graciously forestalled them. The room was an excellent one, but unfortunately very distant from that of the good comrades who had made me free of their table; and so, in consequence of the many representations made by my friend Baccili to the wife of the Commandant, I was soon transferred to another much better apartment . . . next to his own.

* "Baciar la sacra porpora," a form of words still employed when speaking of saluting a prelate,

"On the day of my arrival at Fenestrelle I thought it wise to dismiss my servant, who, as I clearly perceived, would not have been contented to remain with me there, although he declared himself willing to do so should I command him. . . . After two or three days I was admitted, in company with the Cardinal and my friend Baccili, to the society of the Châtelaine, with whom we have kept up our friendly relations to this day.

"Ever adoring the eternally loving and just dispositions of Heaven, I could contemplate with a quiet mind my new situation, rendered so much less irksome by the society of the good priests, by the abundance of religious consolations, by the permanent presence of the August Sacrament in the chapel of the fort, thus affording every facility for the exercise of our holy religion, the privation of which I had felt so deeply in my unhappy sojourn at Civita Vecchia."

The accomplished compiler of the Memoirs is careful to note here that the poor servant Mariano did not abandon his master from motives of cowardice. In a letter written by the Marchesa Cunegonda to her husband in the month of November 1812, she says : " I hear that Mariano, who left you at Fenestrelle, has got married. He was thinking of this before, and this was probably the reason why he was frightened at the idea of a state prison."

And now the correspondence between husband and wife became more active, the poor lady still believing her spouse to be at Civita Vecchia. On December 16 she writes:

"My dearest Giovanni,—

"Two lines before your departure. I wish to know, and I pray you to tell the Signor Filippo" (evidently her messenger), "whether you are quiet and resigned. I pray God with all my heart that it may be so.

"I received word this morning that, when it is desired that I should leave" (for France), "the passports will be sent to me, but that meanwhile I am merely to continue my preparations. This, as I perceive, is for fear I should meet you on the road. Well, I shall start as soon as I have permission. Don Lorenzo" (Giustiniani) "insists that I ought to travel slowly. I wished to hasten to reach Paris in order to procure your liberation; but he says that you will be quite at peace in your new lodging, and that you would prefer my travelling easily. This seems to accord with all you have said and written, so I will follow his counsel. Meanwhile Cristina" (Cunegonda's sister, married to the Marchese Massimo) "is writing to-day to Marianna to intercede for you." (Marianna was another sister, married to Prince Altieri, who had accepted office under the new Government and was believed to have strong influence at Court.) "How many things I long to say to you, my dear Gio, but I have no time, and you understand it all. I hope we shall see one another soon; but till then be sure that no moment passes without my thinking of you.

"Pray for me, and take care of yourself. Farewell."

"ROME, *December* 21*st*, 1811.

" MY DEAREST GIOVANNI,

"In the confusion and bewilderment caused us by your unexpected departure we did not think of arranging for you to have direct news of us in the course of your journey; I am trying to remedy this involuntary oversight to-day by sending this letter to Turin, to a faithful person, so that it may be delivered into your own hands. I think with grief, my dear, that every moment now takes you farther away from us, and even now we are not certain of your destination; greatly I fear it may be Fenestrelle. That which consoles me in the midst of so many afflictions is the certainty that our Good Father is with you, and that He will never forsake you; on the contrary, that He will bestow all the spiritual consolations which can sustain and encourage you in your solitude. The prayers being put up for you are without number, even by persons who do not know you, but who take deep interest in all that concerns you. We got news of you from Viterbo, and it was a great pleasure to me to hear that you were so calm; and indeed, how should you be otherwise? . . . I can give you good news of all here at home, your father being about as usual; the children are all well, and nothing more has been said about my departure as yet; I wrote you that I was told to wait until they should send the passports, and I obey. It is not Parisani who will accompany me; it would have been too great a privation to your father to be separated from him just now; so our excellent friend Don Lorenzo has offered himself (as escort), and you may believe how gladly I accepted, knowing how welcome to you would be this new proof of his friendship.

"So be reassured as to what regards me, for I shall travel in good company. I will be very careful of myself and will travel slowly, according to your wish.

"The last letter, which you wrote to the whole family before leaving Civita Vecchia, touched us all to the last degree. Mariuccia* was very pleased with the one you wrote her a few days earlier. Your twelve fellow prisoners are inconsolable for your absence.

"Farewell, my Giovanni, dear; I must not prolong this letter as I should miss the hour of the post. Write to me if you can; do not send the letter through the police, but simply by post as

* Giovanni's younger sister.

every one does. Your father and mother, your children, your sister, your friends, send you a thousand loving messages. Good-bye, my dearest, good-bye!"

Both Cunegonda and her husband, as well as the rest of the circle in Palazzo Patrizi, firmly believed that as soon as the little boys should have been brought to France their father would be set at liberty, and it was in this assurance that Cunegonda showed herself now so willing and even anxious to undertake the journey. In those days of rough and often dangerous journeying, it would have been considered unsafe as well as improper for a woman of her rank to travel without a male escort of her own class, and we see that first Signor Parisani, and then Don Lorenzo Giustiniani, came forward to fill the part of protector and guide in Giovanni's absence. His satisfaction at the arrangement is taken for granted, and the Memoirs, as they go on, show the (to our more sophisticated eyes) strange spectacle of a young and beautiful lady and her children entrusted unhesitatingly to the care of a popular society man—not only for the journey to France, but for the whole period of her sojourn in that country, when, the boys being interned at the military school, the Marchesa and her husband's friend, faithful as a watch-dog to his charge, are constrained to keep house together for nearly two years! And this without the faintest suspicion of scandal having ever been suggested! *Autre temps, autres mœurs!*

Cunegonda's two letters only reached her husband at Fenestrelle. Giovanni was a good deal troubled at the news that his brother-in-law, Prince Altieri, had undertaken to plead his cause with the Emperor. To the proud Roman the act seemed as if it might be regarded in the light of a capitulation on his part, and he wrote very frankly to his wife on the subject. The letter is dated from Fenestrelle, on New Year's Day, 1812:

"DEAREST GONDINA MIA,

"Here I come to give you news of myself for the first time from my latest place of exile—news such as you wish, I am sure, for they are excellent! I am quite well and completely tranquil. Nothing is wanting here either for the soul or the body. For the soul, we are so happy as to have our Lord, Who condescends to be a prisoner with us—for we have Masses in abundance and every facility for frequenting the Sacraments. For the body, I am enjoying excellent health and have a fine appetite and surprisingly good digestion! And I need not tell you how delightful is the company of my friends, who load me with kindnesses. Altogether, Gondina mine, I must say in all sincerity that so far it has required no great virtue on my part to resign myself to stay at Fenestrelle, and if it were not for the separation from those whom I love as my own self, I could regard this sojourn more as a *villeggiatura* than an imprisonment. I think you must already have heard that I am allowed to walk all over the fort, and to converse with those of my fellow prisoners who are not condemned to solitary confinement. In this way I have been a great deal with the Canonico Bacchi and the Abbé Sala, from whom I receive many kind attentions. The one thing that lies heavy on my heart and causes me anxiety is the fate of our dear children, and for this cause I am going to write you very frankly all I feel, leaving you, however, in perfect freedom to act as shall seem best to you, taking counsel of your Crucifix, of your own conscience, and of the incomparable friend of my heart who now accompanies you.

"In the first place, I must say that I was a little sorry about what you wrote me in the last letter addressed to Civita Vecchia—that you had written to your sister, Altieri, to try to obtain my liberation. If this step was taken with a view to effecting the possibility of my accompanying you on your journey, I have nothing to say against it; but if it tended to remove me from my present situation by making it appear that I regret the position I have maintained hitherto, I cannot approve of it, since, far from regretting my actions, I am prepared to remain a prisoner for life if, by such imprisonment, I could save my sons. Nor do I feel that we should let them be taken from us save by actual force, or at any rate where it should appear certain that such force would be used. I believe that those who, in Paris or in Rome, have interested themselves to have me set at liberty, have made me appear what I was *not*—changed; and this afflicts me. . . . It is true that I consented to have you go to Paris with the children, but this was solely to avoid the danger of their being confided to a stranger; in granting this consent I had no intention of signifying that I withdrew my opposition to giving them up, an act to which we could only be brought by compulsion.

"I will tell you now how I would wish you to act when you reach Paris; but let it be clearly understood that in this I do not imply any obligation which compromises yourself or our excellent friend, for I do not wish you to be compelled to pay me a visit among these smiling hills! In the first place, I exhort you not to think of me at all; on no account let the fear of added severity towards me deter you from doing frankly whatever you judge to be right. So, then, you must not think of me at all.

"When you reach Paris you should use every possible means to obtain the exemption of the boys from the Prytanée. The attempts will probably be in vain, and it will be well to make inquiries as to the kind of education given in the schools existing in Paris, in one of which your nephew, d'Esclignac, was placed. And if the reports are not unfavourable you might obtain the transference of our boys from the Prytanée to such a school. If even this is not to be obtained, and it is absolutely insisted upon that they should go to the Prytanée de la Flèche, then I advise you to go in person to the Director of Police and represent to him that I sanctioned your going to Paris so as not to give the children into the hands of a stranger, but that this does not in any way mean that I have authorised you to give them up. Say that you know my character, and that you are convinced I should fly into the most furious passion with you if I learnt that you had voluntarily, and without my explicit consent, let the children go, and that, for your own peace of mind and to preserve peace in the family, you wish to be allowed to write and ask me what is to be done. If you can only obtain this I know very well what I shall reply; but it will be hard to obtain, and I fear that, after all, you will be obliged to submit to the will of the authorities.

"So now recommend yourself earnestly to God and to the Blessed Virgin, and act as your conscience and your prudence shall dictate. I shall be apprised of all either before or after you have handed over the children, a thing of which the thought fills me with horror. Beware of taking any steps to obtain my liberation. That will come when it shall please God, and when he who oppresses us shall be satiated.

"Try, meanwhile, to protract as much as possible

the remainder of your journey to Paris. On this account I should prefer to have you travel by post rather than by " (private) " carriage, so that you could go more slowly and with less expense. If you have started in the carriage it might be well, if possible, to leave it, and continue the journey by post. Do whatever seems best to you, and remember, Gondina mine, that time is precious."

The maxim was not quoted in its usual sense. To gain time by every available means and excuse was the object just then, and it is pathetic to read the Marchese's suggestions for creating occasions of delay. When he gives minute directions for one proceeding after another, even going so far as to tell his wife to describe him as an irascible creature whose fury she dreaded, he knows that unless Heaven intervenes the oppressor will have to be obeyed in the end. But his faith in the power of prayer inspires him with the strongest hope that Heaven will intervene, that if he and his wife hold out to the last moment the cup of the usurper's iniquities will be full, and that the divine vengeance will deprive him of further power for evil. But the time was not yet, and Giovanni's faith was to be perfected by a long and searching trial before it was finally triumphantly justified. The Memoirs show him sometimes in a very human light, anxious for approbation, not incapable of harmless vanity, disturbed by discomforts, and very sensible of material alleviations in his lot. But all these little flaws, which would not be noticed in a less exalted character, are forgotten in presence of the man's splendid, unwavering faith in God and the ultimate victory of Right over Wrong, the faith that never faltered and gave him strength to contemplate that which he would gladly have suffered martyrdom to prevent—the imperilling of his children's souls by the insensate tyranny of Napoleon. In his later years, as will presently be shown, he reproached himself for having taken life so easily, and often expressed profound contrition for what he called his sins. From the dawn of reason to the day of his death, his life, and that of all dependent on him, was regulated by the most scrupulous Christian standards, and a voluntary offence against God was a misfortune to be contemplated with extreme horror; so that it is hard for us, with the diminished sensitiveness of a laxer day, to see in what his sinfulness consisted.

One most attractive quality in Giovanni Patrizi was his warm love of his friends. Friendship, a hundred years ago, still retained the sacredness of a tie only less binding than blood-relationship. The family friends were called into its councils, threw themselves into its interests, and sacrificed time and means as well as personal comfort in its service—good offices so deeply appreciated that they were returned with loving interest whenever the opportunity arose.

At the end of the long letter to his wife, just quoted, Giovanni adds, speaking of Don Lorenzo Giustiniani:

"What, then, can you say in my name to the incomparable friend? Tell him that I do not know how even to begin to express the infinite gratitude I feel towards him. Tell him that my friendship for him will be eternal, and that, although we may be separated in the body, we shall never be separated in spirit, either in this life or in the next, as I trust in the Divine Infinite Mercy. Tell him that to him I recommend the boys and you—but these are needless words! Tell him that he must recommend me earnestly to the Lord —and do you and the children the same—as I unworthily do for you all, and embrace you all in the Adorable Hearts of Jesus and Mary. Gondina mine, for pity's sake be careful of your health. I entreat you to understand that in all I have suggested I have no intention of binding you in any way, but that I leave you in full, fullest liberty to do whatever you think best. I wish that, if you find it possible, you will send me a reply by the same channel which conveys this letter to you. Gondina mine, who would have thought, sixteen years ago to-day, that I should be writing to you from this place? Such is this world!

"Love me always, and believe me, with the greatest tenderness, you most affectionate husband,

"GIOVANNI."

On the same day, January 7, 1812, the anniversary of their wedding, Gondina echoes her husband's exclamation :

"If any one had told us, sixteen years ago, that on this day I should be writing to you from so far away, I wandering about and you shut up in a fortress, we should have refused to believe him—and yet so it is! May God be blessed for it nevertheless, and I thank Him from my heart for the tranquillity of mind He gives you and which, certainly, can only come from Him."

CHAPTER VII

THE irregularity of the postal arrangements, as well as the irritating supervision of the police, left Giovanni Patrizi for some time in ignorance of what was taking place in Rome. It was only when his wife and children had travelled as far as Siena and were resting there that Cunegonda was able to write to him in detail, and the letter was long in reaching him in the seclusion of Fenestrelle. Cunegonda could not overcome her dislike to writing letters which had to pass under the eyes of the authorities, and in her first short note from Siena announces joyfully that she has found a means of communicating her news by private hand. On January 3, 1812, she writes:

"Dearest Giovanni mine, I have had the great good fortune to find in this city a way of letting you have news of us, and I am immediately taking advantage of it. We received your letter from Bologna, and are hoping very soon to get one from you in Turin, but you must be anxious about us, having heard nothing in such a critical moment. You must know, then, that after repeated intima-

SIENA. THE CHAPEL IN THE PIAZZA.
Photo Moscioni, Rome.

tions, each more pressing than the last, and after various menaces, I was forced to leave Rome on December 26, with the two boys, a manservant, my maid, and, instead of Parisani, our good friend Don Lorenzo, as I wrote you to Turin. I arrived here" (at Siena) "on the 30th, and, as I was worn out with so many fatigues, I am staying for some days. I have a bad cold and really need to rest in order to find strength to continue the long journey; but the thought of it at this season alarms me greatly, and I am going to try to obtain permission to remain here at least until the worst of the winter has passed; I trust that this grace will not be refused me. . . . I am intensely anxious to get some detailed news of you, and I am hoping that you will be able to send them to me through M. Gazan, who, I am told, is very amiable, and full of cordiality towards the prisoners.

"So I beg of you to answer this letter of mine at once, for, even if I am not allowed to stay here as long as I should like, I will certainly remain long enough to receive your letter. I have good news of your mother, and also of your father— at least his health is not worse—Costantino too is well, and is being very good."

Costantino, it will be remembered, was the Patrizis' second son, ten years old at this time, and, on account of his rather delicate health exempted from the general kidnapping scheme which had involved his family in so much trouble.

This seems to be the place to explain that the amiable Monsieur Gazan, spoken of in the Marchesa's letter to her husband, was a French officer acting as adjutant in the garrison of Fenestrelle. He still kept up a close friendship with a former prisoner there, a certain Luigi Custode, who was now living in Siena. The correspondence between the two was constant and intimate, the officer, who was afterwards denounced to the authorities, giving his friend minute detailed accounts of everything that occurred in the prison and interesting himself in facilitating the correspondence of the inmates with their friends and relatives in the outside world. The Commandant of Fenestrelle, Monsieur David, was also suspected of favouring the communications of the prisoners with their friends, and was, apparently, replaced a little later by an official of the Gendarmerie.

Meanwhile Cunegonda, joyfully availing herself of the chance to write *à cœur ouvert* to her husband, sends him, on the "29 of 1812," a long letter finally describing all the details of her enforced departure from Rome.

"Dear Giovanni mine,

"In my last letter I told you that I had received your answer to mine of the 3rd. I cannot express the consolation it was to me to see your handwriting, and more especially to receive the assurance of the peace and tranquillity of spirit that you enjoy, as well as the good news about your health. Already from Rome I wrote you that I knew of all this from others, but I was ardently desiring to have it confirmed by yourself.

"How I thank God, my dear Giovanni, for all the graces He bestows upon you, and how many things I would like to say to you on this subject; but I reserve them for the time when it shall please Him that we can see one another again, and meanwhile I pray from my heart that He will preserve you in your present peace and give you ever greater courage, poor Giovanni!

"What anxiety you must have been in at receiving no news from home—and at such an exciting time! I am glad I was the first to set your mind more at ease, but I cannot understand how it was that the letters from Rome did not reach you, since your mother writes me that the first she wrote you from there" (after the Marchesa's departure with the boys) "was sent on the 28th of December. . . . Before this correspondence of ours is well established" (in good working order) "a certain time will doubtless have to pass, and I hope that before then it will be no longer necessary for us to write to each other at all!

"So you cannot reconcile all those threats and

orders driving me away from Rome with the refusal to send me the passports ? I, to whom it happened, cannot understand it either. It is true that I was told to continue my preparations for departure, but you know how it is that, for a journey of this kind, there are many things that cannot be done or decided until the day is fixed. On Sunday, the 22nd of December, towards the Ave Maria" (half an hour after sunset) "the same Commissary Pepe"* (who had so often brought disagreeable messages before) "presented himself and informed me that the Director of Police had given the strictest orders that I was to leave Rome that same night; but that he, Pepe, had obtained for me the grace of waiting till Monday" (the next) " morning.

"I replied that it was perfectly impossible for me to be ready in such a short time, and that I begged to be granted at least until the day after Christmas. Pepe went off to transmit this request, and returned on Monday morning to say that unless I started that moment the children would be taken away without me. I had instant recourse to Christina" (Cunegonda's sister married to Massimo), "to whom I was already so deeply indebted and who showed me her affection once more on this occasion. She went to the Director, and, after entreating him for three-quarters of an hour, extorted permission for me to wait until the 26th, as I had asked. There, in a few

* Domenico Pepe, a Neapolitan who stood high in the police. Not to be confounded with Guglielmo Pepe, Murat's general.

words, is the story of my vicissitudes! When I can describe them to you in detail you will be astonished.

"You make me laugh when you tell me you are leading a life of ease and that you fear you are gaining no merit thereby. Do you think you have suffered so little hitherto? Now you have a little rest, and it is my turn to carry the burden, but do not worry yourself about that; you know I have good shoulders, and that I am well helped—so, courage—forward!

"I am not surprised that you never received the letter I wrote you to Turin. In the first place, it did not arrive in time, and, secondly, the person to whom I had confided it—the sister of a friend of mine—was so afraid of getting compromised that she had not the courage to send it to you, and it still reposes in her possession. This is the sixth that I have written to you. . . ."

Here follow greetings from friends in Siena, the announcement that Cunegonda had written to her mother-in-law to be indulgent with Mariano who had deserted his master in order to get married, and a list of names which at least show that the sojourn in Siena was a fairly pleasant one for the Marchesa and her children. The letter closes with a postscript from Don Lorenzo Giustiniani.

"Never speak of thanking me. It is I who must give God thanks, for I have ever in my heart the words of St. Paul: 'Communicating to the necessities of the saints.' Let us look forward to thanking our God with one heart and one voice for the benefits which He daily bestows upon us."

One seems to hear the language of the Christians in apostolic times, when faith inspired their every action, and to this faith they added the courage that attains to heroism, without being in the least conscious of it !

The Marchesa Cunegonda had drawn from that source, and from the inexhaustible one of maternal love, the strength to accompany her children, notwithstanding the dangers which she must confront on the way. During the previous winter she had been violently ill with pleurisy, and when she spoke of her contemplated journey to the family physician, Dottor Bomba, he had energetically opposed such a step, on the ground that it was sheer madness for her to undertake it. Finding he could not shake her resolve, he tried to take matters into his own hands, and appealed to the authorities to forbid the journey, saying that the Marchesa was so troubled with contractions of the lungs, difficulty in breathing, and palpitation of the heart, that to undertake a journey now would in all probability bring on a return of her illness.

The only reply the good doctor's expostulations called forth was the suggestion that another escort should be found for the Patrizi children—a suggestion which only served to strengthen her decision never to give them up to strangers.

The stages of the journey were naively described by Filippo, the youngest of the two boys, in a careful little diary, most queerly spelt, which he kept during the whole journey. This feat, on the part of a child only eight years old, is a crushing contradiction of the assertion, so often made, that education was at a very low ebb in Rome, particularly among the aristocratic classes. It is doubtful whether a child of that age, in any country, with all the so-called advantages of modern schooling, could do better to-day than little Pippo Patrizi a hundred years ago.

The journal opens with a grandiose inscription, written as large as the small hand could make it, to this effect:

" Diary of the journey from Rome to Paris made by Philip Patrizi in company with his mother, the Chevalier Giustiniani, his brother Saverio, a maid, and a man-servant.

" First day of the journey (Thursday).

" *From Rome to Ronciglione.* This morning, the 26th of December, we left home at 8.15 by French time, with our own carriage, with 6 mules belonging to Pollastri, and a coachman named Tommato Giusti of excellent quality (!), and another who was also good, but I do not know his name. *Storto.* At 10 o'clock we arrived at Storto; stayed there a little and continued our journey towards *Baccano.* At half-past one we reached Baccano, where, having restored ourselves at a fire, we had dinner, and dinner was a soup with paste, a piece of roast veal, a fry of calves' brains, a plate of *regaglie*, larks, sheeps'-milk cheese, and wine of Oriolo and also of Campagnano." (Pippo takes great interest in his dinner, and always gives full details of the menu.)

"Second day of the journey (Friday).

"*From Ronciglione to Viterbo.*

"At half-past five in the morning we got up, then we had breakfast, then we went to the church of St. Sebastiano, where we heard Mass, and then at 8 o'clock we left for Viterbo. Just beyond Ronciglione we passed over the mountain of Viterbo, where from a certain spot you can see the lake of Vico.

"*Viterbo.* At twelve we arrived at Viterbo and went to stop at Casa Chigi, where, when we had warmed ourselves, we had dinner." (Here follows the menu, of course.) "After dinner we went out, Saverio and I, with M. le Chevalier Giustiniani, and we went to the church of San Bernardo, and then to the church of Santa Rosa, where we saw the saint's body, the which is so preserved that it looks as if she had died this very day; and then we went to see the Porta Fiorentina and the Road of the Oak outside that same gate; at a quarter past four we returned to the house, where we found Monsignore the Bishop of Serrey and the Russian Minister, who both went away at five o'clock, and we remained in conversation with Signor Giacomo Chiuchiulini" (there must have been a struggle over the spelling of this name), "the steward of Casa Chigi. Then, being at liberty, we wrote our journals, had supper, and went to bed at 8 1/4.

"Third day (Saturday).

"*From Viterbo to Acquapendente.**

"*Acquapendente.* Thus called on account of a waterfall named the Fifth Moon. Immediately on entering the city we saw a pretty little church. The streets of this city are narrow, but well paved. The Post Hotel, where we stopped, is exceedingly bad. It is enough to say that there were only two rooms, with two beds in each, which rooms were close next to those of the *vetturini*; the beds were also bad; but I will cease to abuse the hotel and tell about the supper. First I must say that the maid at the hotel tried to force us to eat meat, this being a fast day."

Here follows a scornful account of the improvised "maigre" menu.

"After supper we did not go to bed, for the reasons I have explained, but I slept on a bench and the Chevalier Giustiniani before the fire. We got up an hour afterwards, that is to say, at two in the morning, and came away from Acquapendente and the horrid hotel.

* "Hanging water."

"Fourth day of the journey (Sunday) :

"*From Acquapendente to S. Quirico.* After leaving Acquapendente we crossed the Georgian Bridge which is upon the river Paglia, and then we went five times through the Rigo torrent, and then we stopped at Ponte Centino, the last posting-station of the Papal States, where four horses were attached to pull us up the mountain of Radicofani, the which is as steep as it can be and very stony; when one reaches a certain point one sees Radicofani, and you think you have arrived there, but in reality you have to wind round and round for a long time before getting to it. We arrived about half-past eight at Radicofani, which is 100 miles distant from Rome; there we heard Mass, and, having restored ourselves at the fire, had dinner, and while we were dining the maid told us that the room in which the Holy Father Pius VII slept when he was being carried away from Rome had burnt up on account of the huge fire that some French soldiers made. The end of a beam caught fire, and then the whole room got burnt.

"At half-past twelve we left Raditofani to go to S. Quirico in Tuscany; before arriving there, there is the river Oricia; we reached S. Quirico at half-past five, and went to lodge in the Palazzo Chigi, where they made a good fire for us. Then we had supper, and were well treated at that. Then we went to bed; the beds were all covered with red damask, with the canopies all of red damask too.

"Fifth day of the journey :

"*From S. Quirico to Siena.* We arrived at Siena at half-past four in the afternoon, and alighted at our own house, had supper, and many Sienese gentlemen came, and at half-past eleven we went to bed. In this city (of which the description shall be written separately) we remained 5 months and 6 days."

Pippo's diary ceases here, to be taken up religiously when the family continues its very slow progress to Paris. His mother made the most of every excuse to linger by the way, hoping against hope for some unexpected intervention to liberate her husband and relieve her of the necessity of finally carrying out Napoleon's orders about the boys. The family was terribly embarrassed, financially, by the sequestration of its revenues, and to this, by Napoleon's personal order, was added the extreme annoyance of having all communications to, or from, the prisoner of Fenestrelle sent to Norvins and Danzer, the former Director of Police at Turin, the latter filling the same office in Rome. Later we shall see that even these restrictions were not considered sufficiently severe, and that the Patrizi correspondence had to be consigned to, and overhauled by, much more exalted personages.

But, as we know, the Marchesa Cunegonda had found at Siena a trustworthy person by whose good offices she was enabled to write almost every day to her husband, and to receive his letters, without their having been submitted to censorship. On February 3 she writes :

"MY DEAR GIO,

"I cannot understand why you do not receive the letters from Rome, and I know how much this must grieve you. As long as I am here" (in Siena) "it does not matter so much, since I can let you know all that happens at home—since, thank God, my letters reach you punctually. But, if I leave this before the communications are open, it will be a great hardship. To-morrow I will write to my mother-in-law and tell her how many letters you have written home, for in the last one to me she complained that she had received nothing from you since the 19th of January. I have caused inquiries to be made at the Police Office, but I fear they will prove useless. Really, if they keep them back there, it seems to me a cruelty which can give them no satisfaction, for surely you have not written anything that could cause alarm ; but it is true they find something to criticise in every word, and I heard that your letters to me from Civita Vecchia, which I missed for three posts, were kept back because they were found to be *boute feu*" (incendiary), "that was the expression they used ! "

The obstinate resistance of the Patrizis to the imperial demands were by this time made the more conspicuous to the Government by the submission of their many relations. All the other children ordered to go to France were either already there or were to start at Easter, including the sons of Cunegonda's sisters, Princess Altieri and the Marchesa Massimo. On February 7 she gave her husband some interesting details on the subject.

"Clementino Altieri will only be enrolled among the (imperial) pages after Easter. Every Sunday he is to have leave, like all the rest, to dine with his relations and stay with them all day. This does not seem to me such a very great thing. They tell me the Prince is rather anxious about Augusto, but they have not explained why. Marianna" (Princess Altieri) "went to dine with the Empress Joséphine, who made a great deal of her. On New Year's Day Marianna was in court dress for four hours on end, making visits to all the kings and queens possible, while it was snowing most fearfully. Christina" (Marchesa Massimo), "who is always joking, says that she can see from Rome the envy by which I am devoured, and of course she is right. You will understand that?"

There was great hope at Siena that the Marchese Giovanni's imprisonment would be commuted to mere exile from Rome, in which case he could have rejoined his family at Siena. In Cunegonda's letter of February 7 is enclosed one from Saverio to his father.

"Dearest Papa mine,—

"It would be a fine thing if, one of these days, while we are all here, you would give us a surprise. I warn you beforehand that you had better put on an iron collar, so as not to be thróttled by my hugging you. If I could see you, even at the cost of pulling your carriage all the way from your residence to ours, I would do it gladly, even all by myself. Papa mine, I pray you to believe me
"Your devoted, loving son,
"Saverio."

In addressing their parents, either by writing or speaking, the Patrizi boys, like all well-brought-up children at the present day, used the third person, the courteous "Lei," for which we have no synonymous form in English. Even the Marchese and his wife always employ the formal "You" to each other in their correspondence, "Thou," the *tutoiement* so familiar to us now, being considered in those days too common for the use of refined persons, even those most closely related. In the south of Italy "You" is the general form of respectful address, even to very exalted personages.

The stay in Siena proved the least painful stage of Marchesa Cunegonda's sorrowful journey. The children most tactfully managed to catch a very light form of measles, which gave her a good excuse to prolong the halt and nurse herself, instead of continuing to travel in the depth of winter. Her

SIENA. PIAZZA AND TOWN HALL.
Photo Moscioni, Rome.

A "FORTUNATE CONTRETEMPS" 165

pleasure at this fortunate *contretemps* causes her to reproach herself contritely for her selfishness later; but meanwhile valuable time had been gained. The prisoner at Fenestrelle was delighted at the news—anything was good which delayed the consigning of the boys to the abhorred French school. But the matter was viewed in a very different light by Giovanni's father and mother, who believed that he would be set at liberty as soon as the boys had arrived at La Flèche.

On February 12 Cunegonda writes to her husband: "I have sent the medical certificate to Paris in order that my delay may not be imputed to me as an added crime. My sister" (Altieri) "must have received it by this time. I have had a letter from her this morning saying that she has heard of the boys' illness, that she is sorry not to see me so soon as she had hoped, but that I must let the boys have every care. She added that, a few days earlier, the Minister of Police, the Duc de Rovigo, had inquired of her whether I had arrived, and she told him that I had stopped in Siena, as I was ill, a thing which she had certainly foreseen, knowing how bad the journey would be for me. She did not know then of the boys' illness, but she will tell him (the Minister of Police) at the first opportunity. Your mother, although she wants the children to recover completely, is frenzied to have me get to Paris, hoping that then I shall obtain your immediate liberation, and this is what was told to my sister when she interceded for you; but I, who know you, am more than sure that you are not in any such hurry to come out—on these terms" (of giving up the children).

The Archbishop of Siena, Cardinal Zondadari, who had shown so much friendship for Giovanni, manifested the most delicate and kind attentions to Cunegonda. He came to see her constantly, and was able, through her, to communicate with Cardinal Pacca, Giovanni's fellow prisoner at Fenestrelle, who was always designated in this clandestine correspondence as "La Pecorella," the "Lamb." The noble ladies of Siena vied with each other in showing courtesy towards the Marchesa Patrizi, and so overwhelmed her with visits that she had to make quite a struggle to have for herself the morning hours which she devoted to exercises of piety and to continuing the education of her children, teaching them some subjects herself and superintending the instructions of the masters she engaged for them, being especially anxious that they should progress in their Italian and in their French. It may sound strange that the Marchesa should have been anxious for her children to be instructed in the language of their own country; but her pre-occupation is explained when we remember that almost all regular instruction was given in Latin, and that, in consequence, the complicated elegancies of "high" Italian often remained a closed book to those who knew it merely as the ordinary medium of communication with their fellow men.

Siena was a gay, self-contained little city in those days, and many were the hospitalities offered to the Marchesa Patrizi; but she would accept no invitations till just before her departure, fearing that the authorities would, if she were known to be amusing herself, no longer allow the delay on the count of her health, which indeed made it more prudent for her to rest as much as possible before resuming the journey to Paris. There was then in Siena a stepbrother of her father-in-law, the 'Bailli' (acting Grand Master) of Malta, Ruspoli, a charming old gentleman whose quaint ways often afforded much amusement to his relations.

The Order of the Knights of Malta had been practically suppressed in 1798 when Napoleon, on his way to Egypt, took possession of the island and forced the Grand Master, Ferdinand von Hompesch, to resign. Paul I of Russia, although not a Catholic, was then recognised by the Pope and the members of the Order as Grand Master, but on his death in 1801 his successor, Alexander I, refused the honour, and the Order was administered for over seventy years by a vicegerent in Rome. There was a clause in the Treaty of Amiens (1802) stipulating that the island of Malta was to be ceded to its rightful owners; but the further outbreak of war prevented the restitution, and the Order was homeless till, in 1827, Leo XII invited it to take refuge in the Pontifical Dominion, an act of hospitality which Gregory XVI completed by authorising its definite installation in Rome in 1831. One of the first acts of Leo XIII was to restore the ancient dignity of the illustrious Order, and, after being in abeyance for seventy-four years, the title of Grand Master was revived on March 28, 1879. There is a curious provision in the Statutes that Knights of Bohemian extraction must have sixteen quarterings, but for those of all other nations only four are required.

The noble Order was suffering eclipse when the Marchesa Patrizi made her long halt in Siena, and 'Uncle Ruspoli,' who, since the Napoleonic invasion, had acquired the habit of spending a great part of each winter in the cosy Tuscan city, was a most cheerful companion in the house. Like every one else, he had fallen deeply in love with Cunegonda when she entered the family as a bride, and though he did not, like her father-in-law, exalt her charm in verse, he was to the end one of her most devoted adherents. He was a man who lived by rule even to his own inconvenience, for, regardless of what the weather might be doing, he always put on his heavy winter clothes on a fixed day, as also his nankeen breeches, at the cost of many a shiver, at a particular moment of the Spring; his ideal of comfort was stability, and poor Cunegonda, driven about the world in a tide of uncertainties, appeared to him deserving of the deepest commiseration.

A poor woman in Siena, whose aunt had been employed at the Palazzo Patrizi a hundred years earlier, told the writer of the Memoirs a quaint anecdote about the good 'Bailli.' Among the habits which he had formed, and which his methodical mind caused him to regard as solemn duties, was that of paying every day a visit to the Sanctuary of the Madonna of Provenzano, and of giving alms to at least one poor mendicant on the road. One day, in the heart of the winter, the snow was falling very heavily, and there was not a living creature in sight. Sighing deeply, but never dreaming of omitting his daily pilgrimage, the 'Bailli' came out, went down to the Provenzano Church, made his visit to his beloved little Madonna, and turned homewards, hoping with all his heart that he would meet one of his many protégés before he reached the Palazzo Patrizi. But fate was against him—even the beggars would not stir out of doors, and he found himself at home without having been able to bestow his alms! Well, since the beggars would not come to him, he must go and look for them—a Knight of Malta could not break his word. So, in face of the raging snowstorm, he trudged on to the Duomo, and just as a wild gust carried away his hat he perceived an old woman tottering towards him with outstretched hand.

"May God reward you for your alms!" she said, as he dropped the silver piece in her palm.

"May God reward *you*," cried the Bailli, "for having asked it of me! If you had not, Heaven knows how far I might have had to go!" And he plunged away, racing after his hat, which had fortunately taken the right road home.

CHAPTER VIII

ON February 24 Cunegonda Patrizi wrote an unusually long letter to her husband, having received two of his together on the preceding day.

". . . You describe your Carnival dissipations—a dinner party on *Jeudi Gras*—I am sure it must have been very cheerful; a good conscience and the company of gallant gentlemen could have no other result. My carnival was even less brilliant than yours, for I should have been unconscious of the season but for hearing others speak of it, and but for the annoyance of being waked up at night by the sound of the revellers' carriages. To-day I was obliged to interrupt the Lenten Fast, finding that I had not the strength to accomplish it, and now I have been forbidden to make the attempt at all."

It may be well to explain here that the Lenten Fast in Italy was exceedingly rigorous in those days, most of the faithful taking neither bite nor sup till three in the afternoon. The custom now is confined chiefly to the stricter of the religious communities, the Holy See having, in indulgence to the exigencies of modern life, enacted that there shall only be four or five such fasts in the whole year. But abstinence is still very strictly observed all through southern Italy. In many districts meat, milk, eggs, and lard are banished from the tables of the peasants from Ash Wednesday till Easter Sunday.

Cunegonda continues :

"Now I come to your letter of the 13th. There is no truth in what you say about standing idle with your hands in your pockets and not bearing with me the burden of the trial, and I will prove it to you, for what is the heaviest part of this cross? It does not lie in mere travelling and external discomforts, but in the separation and dispersion of the family, in the purpose of this journey, in the exile from home, and so on ; and all this you suffer equally with me, besides your isolation and your ignorance of what may be happening, which presents things to your imagination as worse than they really are ; so you see that I am right in saying that your part of the cross is sufficiently heavy! I admit that mine is not light, but I deserve worse things, and I am sure of being effectually helped, so do not make yourself unhappy about me ; but also do not cease to pray fervently for me and to recommend me to the special prayers of those your friends and companions, including the 'Lamb,' who I hope will not refuse me this favour for your sake. . . .

"I was sure that you would have been pleased

to hear that the good Tommaso * was destined from the first to bring me on this journey. We can really give him the diploma of *vetturino* of Casa Patrizi, for he always appears in Rome when we are about to travel. This time he remained long in the city in the hope of that which finally happened, namely, that he might accompany, or rather, conduct me to Paris. I must confess that it used to make me a little angry to see him sitting in the anteroom, knowing that he was promising himself the pleasure of taking me—when I had not yet decided on going at all. I told him so afterwards, and he replied that, on the morning of our departure, if I had lingered but half an hour longer, he would have got down from his horse and renounced the job altogether, so dreadfully cruel did the separation appear to him, so moved was he not only by our tears but by the tears and lamentations of the crowds that gathered on the stairs, many of them not even members of the household.

"It is true that he charges a great deal, but he takes the entire care for the travelling off my mind. Before I left Rome, foreseeing that I should make a little stay here (although I had no idea it would have to be such a long one) I wanted to arrange with him that he should leave me here and go to Florence meanwhile to take

* This man was an owner and driver of posting-horses and carriages in Rome.

advantage of any short engagements he could procure; but he would not consent to this, so we agreed that, while I should stay in Siena, I was to pay for the feeding of the mules, but no wages either to him or the other man.

"But, from the very first day we arrived here, he began to complain that the allowance for the mules was insufficient, so I sent for him and told him to reconsider my first proposition, since he could earn nothing while waiting here, while the mules were a sheer loss. That I would pay him his journey back to Florence, where he must go and work for some one else, and that as soon as I should need him again I would write to Pollastri to send him back to me—to all of which he consented, and it is much better so for him and for me. . . .

"You were mistaken in your explanation of the term, *boute-feu*, applied to your letters from Civita Vecchia. They" (the police) "called them so because, as they declared, you roused me to resistance, animating me to imitate your conduct, to be courageous, and showing that you regarded yourself as a martyr; for all these reasons, they said, the letters were as incendiary as the notes you had written to the Prefect and others. . . .

"Marianna" (Altieri) "is leading in Paris a life very different from her Roman one. The Empress Joséphine, who remembers being at school in the convent with her, overwhelms her with attentions and kindnesses; she constantly has her with her at Malmaison, and tells her to come and dine whenever she feels inclined. The first time Marianna dined with her it was by formal invitation, and Marianna says that the luxury and elegance of the dinner surpassed all imagination, particularly in the matters of flowers and porcelains. Afterwards there was music, the musician Crescentini and Maestro Pez being among the guests. In fine, Marianna only got back to Paris after midnight; what do you say of it? But I do not envy her at all."

Without feeling envy it must have been a little depressing to the Marchesa to contrast her sister's cheerful lot with her own rather isolated and melancholy one at this time. The course things were taking in Rome was not calculated to raise her spirits. On March 2 she writes to her husband:

"You may have heard that the" (religious) "Companies and Confraternities have been ordered to submit to the authority of the Delegates, and are invited (!) to pay all their revenues into a public coffer, because in this manner they will be better administered and the cult of religion much increased. Such are the motives furnished for this change, and as yet no word has been spoken of pillage or of diminishing the number of religious ceremonies—indeed, they are to be increased . . . if you can manage to believe it!"

A day or two later Cunegonda gives tidings of

some of the other children kidnapped for the famous
" Golden Levy."

" Clemente Altieri is to become a page after Easter.
Augusto is not yet sure of remaining with his
parents. Pippo Lante, also named a page, has
obtained permission to stay in Rome till he is fifteen
and a half, the age designated for entering that company. As he is scarcely twelve, he has time before
him! Alessandro Spada decided on military rather
than civil service. Guido is already in a regiment
of hussars, and Luigi is a page."

The next letter concerns the attempts of the
authorities to gather the foremost men of Siena into
its Government as a province of France. They met
with some difficulties, and it may have been that
Giovanni Patrizi, when he read his wife's communication, was inclined to congratulate himself on his
enforced absence; but it seems more likely, con-
sidering his fighting spirit, that he regretted losing
such an opportunity of causing trouble to the
detested usurpers.

"*March* 9, 1812.

". . . In Rome the nomination of electors,
senators, and dignitaries goes on. The retirement
of Doria and the 'Connétable' has been accepted,
but I fear they will not escape from having to take
the oath. Three lists have been sent to Paris: one
of those who refuse" (office) " flatly and without
giving any reasons; one of those who have valid
reasons for their refusal; and the third of those who

UNCOVETED HONOURS

have accepted. It is believed that the Duke Braschi will be chosen by the Emperor (for supreme office) out of the three proposed to him by the Senate ; the other two are Chigi and Giustiniani. Six deputies have been elected to thank His Majesty for the honour done to Rome ; but I cannot tell you in what the honour consists, unless it is that of having given it this new court of electors "—here follow six well-known names.

"*March* 16.

" Your father is apprehensive of being obliged to take the oath, as that condition has been laid on all those who refused to be electors ; among the rest is C. Viscardi, who gave as excuse that he was merely a 'fils de famille'" (without personal status, since his father was living), " that his father was already an official of the Government, and, finally, that he himself had been ill in bed for three months. He was told that his arguments were all perfectly sound ones, but that he could quite well take the oath—in bed!

" . . . The other day I had as a guest at dinner the Abbé Nicolai of the Penitenzeria, who was exiled from Rome to Florence after seven months' imprisonment in Castel Sant' Angelo. . . . Please thank in my name the 'Lamb' for having said his Mass for me on my feast-day. I very much appreciate his kind remembrance, and tell him that I return it as well as I can, by recommending him to God. . . . Parisani writes me that Cristina was paying a visit to Montbreton" (the Director of Police) "and that in speaking of you he remarked how well you write, adding that at the beginning he read all your letters, but that now he no longer does so. But this I do not much believe."

In fact, the Marchese's correspondence was being very strictly censored at this time, and even the harmless little letters of the boys were sequestrated as dangerous communications. Saverio, the eldest, describes to his father with much amusement the suspicions thus excited.

"I wrote a little while ago to Costantino" (the younger brother left in Rome) "a letter in Tuscan, with many words which are only understood here; but it was evidently mistaken for a dangerous snare, and my letter was sequestrated in the post. Oh, let them only get it interpreted and they will discover great conspiracies! Oh, what idiots they are!"

Naturally the correspondence of Patrizi and his wife could not long escape the watchfulness of the police. In the State Archives in Paris there is a great file of intercepted letters, police reports, secret communications, and imperial orders which testify most eloquently to the hatred, amounting to personal rancour, which Napoleon at this time nourished towards the Patrizi family. It had become an obsession with him, surprising even his own subordinates into something very like protests. From the political point of view Giovanni and his father were the most harmless of adversaries ; they did nothing to dissuade others from obeying the Emperor's behests, kept scrupulously apart from intrigues subversive of his authority, and only opposed him when he trespassed on their indisputable private rights regarding the education of the children, and in refusing to enter the public services to which his gallicising policy had, so to speak, condemned the Roman nobility. One would have expected the Conqueror of Europe to pass over their recalcitrance in scornful silence—the Statesman to have avoided the mistake of distinguishing them as martyrs to a lost and noble cause ; but they had committed the, to him, unpardonable crime of proving themselves unconquerable. This quiet, old-fashioned family had refused to be bribed or cajoled or terrified into even superficial submission to his will ; they had yielded to force, and force alone, and this was an intolerable humiliation to him, and one that evidently bit very deep into his proud spirit. There remained nothing for him to do but revenge himself, and he was by just so much wanting in real greatness as to be unable to do so with the laugh and the joke which would have consigned their rebellion to obscurity. His amazing brain found time, amid a thousand preoccupations of world-wide importance, to invent small spites in order to make them feel his power. He actually gave orders that their correspondence was to pass through his own hands. Every letter written by or addressed to Giovanni Patrizi, the prisoner of Fenestrelle, was to be sent to him so long as he should be in France, and, in case of his absence from the country, was to be *personally* examined by the Prime Minister ; so that, sad to say, the larger part of those letters, still hoarded in the State Archives in Paris, never reached their destination at all.

Cunegonda's joy, therefore, at finding a safe means of communication with her husband from Siena was very short-lived. One can imagine how the imperial wrath flamed out when it was discovered, as before stated, that the too soft-hearted M. Gazan of Fenestrelle was making himself and his old friend at Siena intermediaries for the correspondence of Giovanni Patrizi with his wife. The information was conveyed to the Ministry in a long and excited letter from Desmarets, the Agent of Police, to the Duc de Rovigo in Paris, and the various enclosures forwarded gave but too evident proof of poor M. Gazan's indiscreet indulgence. What became of M. Gazan the documents at our disposal do not say, but his name never appears again. M. David, the Commandant, seems to have been reprimanded for negligence, but he retained his position nevertheless.

It was unfortunately Giovanni himself who most involuntarily betrayed his benefactor. A letter from him to the Banker Rolli, in Turin, was intercepted there by the police, and was found to contain very questionable matter in the shape of two letters enclosed, one written by Count Baccili, a fellow prisoner at Fenestrelle, to the Bishop of Vienne (France), and another, from Giovanni, addressed to a certain Signora Camilla Cecchini in Siena. This last, being opened, disclosed another letter inside addressed to the Marchesa Patrizi, and the contents were at once translated into French and forwarded to Paris. Poor Giovanni writes to warn his wife against an indiscretion which, by his own inadvertence, was now to prove all but fatal to their communication with one another:

"In your letter of January 27 there was a great oversight which has caused me some anxiety. In this letter, which you sent through the post, you spoke of those which you had received through M. Louis Custode and M. Gazan. That might have compromised M. Gazan and the Commandant of the Fort. As your letter had passed through the hands of the police in Turin, I received it opened, as my letters always are when they are addressed directly to myself. Fortunately, it is said that the police there" (in Turin) "are not over strict. . . ."

Both husband and wife were kept carefully in ignorance of the fact that their secret was discovered, and they continued to write to each other without reserve, much to the satisfaction, no doubt, of the authorities, who were thus kept posted not only on all their private affairs, but on their plans and hopes for their immediate future.

The kind rigours of the winter, which had permitted Cunegonda to have some months of rest and comparative peace among her friends at Siena, had passed away, and the lovely Tuscan spring that called the almond-trees into blossom and the larks into song, sounded for her the hour when she must resume her sad journey to France. There was no further valid excuse for delay, and on April 3 she wrote, as she fondly believed for Giovanni's eyes alone, the following letter:

". . . I cannot tell you the precise day of my departure, for I have not decided on it yet; it depends on the letter from Florence" (presumably concerning the Vetturino Tommaso) "which I expect on Sunday. Naturally I shall be moving from here towards the 15th.

"On Sunday I am invited to dinner at Casa Chigi, to see afterwards the grand procession of which I told you in my last. The Marchesa had invited me as soon as I arrived in Siena, and both she and the Cardinal have done so repeatedly since then, but I always refused on the grounds of my health, and also because, as I was here in a kind of incognito, I did not wish to appear in the great world; but now that I am on the point of leaving I will not refuse" (the Marchesa Chigi), "and I foresee that I shall also have to accept an invitation from the Cardinal.

"The Prefect left for Grosseto the day before yesterday, to receive the Grand Duchess" (of Tuscany, Elisa Baciocchi, Napoleon's sister), "who was expected here in a few days, but she has changed her mind and is, instead, returning to Lucca and Piombino by the same road; it is said that this is in order to avoid finding herself in Tuscany for the execution of the terrible decree of conscription, of which you will certainly have read in the 'Gazette.' In Rome this Decree produced the greatest consternation, drafting away seven hundred out of eight hundred young men in the First Department alone.

"In order to make sure that I shall have news of you on my way, you might begin by sending me a letter to Milan, addressed to Sigra. Marianna Baccani" (this was Cunegonda's maid), "Poste Restante; I cannot tell you about other cities. I shall certainly find something from you at Turin, but meanwhile send me yet a line here addressed to Rosini. . . ."

The Marchesa's departure, however, was yet further delayed by the non-appearance of the Vetturino, the trusty Tommaso. He had undertaken to convey some travellers to Vienna, and Cunegonda entirely refused to let any one else conduct her over this part of her journey; so she waited on in Siena, expecting his return from day to day. On April 13 she finds time to discourse about the little boy left at home with his grandparents.

"You are quite right in saying that Costantino is very fortunate in having a grandmother who is so careful and so loving, and I confess that if

I had not been able to leave him in such safe hands I could never have consented to the separation at all. But my conviction that your mother and father will not alter in any way the system already adopted, sets my mind at rest, although I am so far from my child. You will have received by this time Costantino's French letter on the subject of which he reproached me, in another which he wrote, because I had not gratified your desire to peruse that *chef d'œuvre*! I replied to him that you had asked me to copy out the most beautiful parts of it for your benefit, but that I was embarrassed as to the choice, and, in order not to defraud you of his finest efforts, I had resolved to send it on to you entire.

". . . . I am sorry you should have taken so much to heart what I said about my headache. . . . you know that is my inseparable companion, and really the present circumstances are not exactly remedies for the trouble, but God gives me strength not to be cast down by it, and I only speak of it when it becomes more acute. . . . The order of sequestration has not been rescinded in Rome, but we have good hopes" (that it will be) "and there is an order exempting the tenants at Bracciano from paying the quarter's rent.

"SIENA, *April* 15*th*, 1812.

". . . . The four sons of Oligiati have been ordered to leave" (for France), "and as their father cannot afford the expense of the journey the Government will pay for it. Pippo Lante, who had been assured that he might stay with his mother till he should be fifteen, and then was to enter as a page, has now been ordered to La Flèche to remain there until he reaches the required age. These are the last news from Rome. The Senator Orville has arrived in Rome to take up his senatorship, which brings him in ninety thousand francs a year paid out of the revenues of the Roman States; but the office confers on him no authority whatever. He is staying at the French Embassy, and will remain for three or four months. . . ."

In another letter Cunegonda says: " I have read to Pippo the extract about his birthday; may God fulfil your and my desires for the child, desires which only point, so far as this world goes, to see my sons true Christians; the two eldest already begin to give us great comfort, being most excellently inclined; and I trust the third will not disappoint our hopes. It seems to me that I, on my part, am neglecting no means of having him turn out as we desire; may the Lord cause my care to bear good fruit!

". . . My sister Altieri wrote to my mother-in-law that the Minister had told her very distinctly that there is no hope of having the order of sequestration removed until the boys shall have reached Paris. Behold how many good things I am to obtain in that place! First, your liberation; second, the removal of the sequestration; third, that which most interests us" (that the children might remain with their mother); "fourth, the restoration of my father's property" (confiscated at the time of the Revolution); "and so forth and so on. The flattering hopes held out to me of obtaining all these things are really marvellous! It appears that I shall have but to open my mouth and ask—and all will be granted! Were that so we might indeed talk about miracles!

"Siena, *May 1st*, 1812.

"King Murat came through here quite suddenly on Tuesday. I think I told you that he was expected some days ago. At least he dashed through, at full gallop, in a little carriage with eight horses. Everybody is talking—and each gives his own views of the incident. The deputies from Rome chosen to go and thank the Emperor (I have no idea what for) have been ordered to leave in twenty-four hours, as His Majesty will receive them at St. Cloud on the 7th. I do not know whether they will get there in time.

"The Mayor" (of Rome) "and his Councillors have resigned because Montbreton" (the actual Prefect) "mixed himself up in business which was purely their concern. He refused to accept their resignations, and it was hoped things could be arranged amicably in a private conference."

THE ARCHBISHOP ZONDADARI 187

Saverio adds a postscript to his mother's letter :

"Dearest Papa mine, We began to-day with Mamma the month of Mary, and I will also begin a Novena which says at the beginning, 'A prayer for obtaining any kind of grace,' and I want to see if it says the Holy Truth. . . ."

On May 6, Cunegonda, still detained in Siena by the non-arrival of Tommaso, writes to her husband: "I went yesterday to pay a visit to the Cardinal" (Zondadari, the Archbishop whom Giovanni had seen for a moment when he was on the point of leaving Siena) "at Murlo, fourteen miles from here. The expedition was most successful, and His Eminence, to whom it came as a complete surprise, was delighted. Casa Chigi was also there, all but the Commendatore. The boys enjoyed the outing immensely. . . . I wished to pay this visit to the Cardinal to show him my gratitude for all the kindness he has extended to me during my stay here. . . .

"To-morrow there will defile into Rome the twelve thousand men from Naples who are to be passed on into the Grand Army. This makes the politicians think that, as was reported, Naples is to become a part of the Empire, and that Murat will not return there."

"*May* 18*th.*

"I was arranging to leave on Tuesday the 12th so as to reach Florence on the 13th, and I think of doing it all in one journey. . . . I was finally induced to start by a message which the Marchese Chigi conveyed to me from the Prefect" (of Siena), "who said that he feared, if I lingered longer, he might get some stringent orders from Paris, and might even be instructed to take the boys away from me. You see that prudence required that I should take note of this warning, and in fact, a few days after receiving it, I went to pay him my first visit, which also had to serve as farewell. He is a good old man, incapable of injuring any one, and he does kindnesses whenever and however he can—as was proved by the affair of the sequestration"—(it seems that the Prefect had made an attempt to have the Patrizi property in Siena exempted from that order)—" although he has every right to be rather annoyed with me, as until now I have never given him a sign of life ! "

Saverio adds:

"Dearest Papa mine,—

". . . Too clearly I see that we must leave this amiable town, but God's will be done. Who knows ? We have not gone yet ; perhaps the mules will break their legs, or something else happen. Well, whatever happens will be for our good. . . . So be it, so be it, verily so be it."

Cunegonda, on the 11th, explains that she is still detained. Tommaso has not turned up, and the mules, which apparently were out at grass in the neighbouring country, have not been sent in as she expected, so a few days more must pass before she can get off. The poor lady had managed to get the whooping-cough, and the children had caught it from her. "But now," she says, "we have all recovered, so do not be anxious about us; the journey will not hurt us. Indeed, I am a little afraid we shall feel the heat, for it has been very oppressive for the last few days, and in the mountains near Bologna we shall get the full force of the sun. Patience! First I was afraid of the cold, now of the heat; and when I left Rome that was the last thing from which I expected to suffer in this journey. Who knows? 'The hand of God is not shortened'; and I did not put that in Latin, for fear you would make fun of me.

". . . To-morrow I must write to Rome to let them know of this last delay, and I am sorry to have to do so, as they are anxious to know that I have started, fearing always some new hostility; but to you I give the news with pleasure, knowing that you will be glad, although you are the person most interested."

"SIENA, *May* 20.

"We have decided to leave, certainly, on the 27th. . . . Great numbers of troops are passing here. Of the twelve thousand ordered from Naples, twelve hundred came through the day before yesterday, and the same number is expected to-day. They come every other day; but I am told that, instead of fresh men, it is the same column that has already passed, which we shall see to-day going the other way, a galloper having been sent to tell them to turn round and get back to Naples. I cannot even imagine the reasons for all this, but it is accepted as certain. To-day we shall find out the truth."

"*May* 25.

" Our departure is still fixed for the day after to-morrow, but I must write you a few lines.

" . . . The passage of the troops still continues . . . only the first detachment was ordered back to Naples. The rest continue to come, about two thousand every two days, and the men parade in the Piazza, making really a very fine spectacle. But at night it is dreadful. There is no possibility of sleep; they begin beating the drums at one or half-past to call the soldiers together again in the Piazza, and they do not get away until five. Imagine how pleasant for us! Yesterday there were many negroes among them, and they look hideous in uniform. This business is to go on until the 5th of June."

The long-delayed and dreaded departure from Siena took place according to schedule, Saverio's prayers and his hopes of a happy accident remaining unfulfilled for the moment. On June 1 Cunegonda writes to her husband, in deep depression, from Bologna :

" . . . At last, to my intense regret, I must change

the heading of my letters. You can imagine how I grieved at leaving Siena, where for five months I enjoyed a tranquillity that must be discounted now. Before I left I received your letter of the 11th" (of April), "and I was amazed to find that I had told you I felt more full of strength and courage than usual. It must have been true at the moment, but the scene changed afterwards, and I cannot possibly describe to you the trouble, the sorrow, the apprehensions, and so forth, by which I am surrounded now. I have suffered in these days all that it is possible to suffer physically and morally; the burden of this journey makes itself felt more and more. . . .

"You tell me to write in French if that is easier for me, but I assure you that I write quite as easily in Italian. Perhaps I make absurd mistakes, but you will be indulgent about them."

After this protest, Cunegonda suddenly begins a sentence in French, the language of her childhood—and always of her heart—pulls herself up and goes on in sober Italian to describe the first stage of her journey, a long one, for the party left Siena at a quarter to seven in the morning and did not reach Florence till ten that night.

"There," she says, "we stayed over Thursday, the Feast of Corpus Domini . . . and I had a visit from the Prince and Princess of Palestrina and their sons, as well as Don Orazio Borghese.

"On arriving in Florence we went to the

'Pelicano,' which I think was the inn you spoke of to me; but it was quite full, so I went to the 'Four Nations,' where I was very well satisfied, and where even the hotel-keepers showed the interest they felt for us, assuring me, with tears in their eyes, that they would certainly not take advantage of my circumstances; and indeed they charged me much less than they are accustomed to do.

". . . The next morning we started off again, halted at 'Le Maschere,' and slept at beautiful Covigliano. . . . On Saturday at nightfall we reached this place. Immediately Benedetto and Clementino Spada came to see me, having come expressly from twelve miles away in the country, where Clementino is in *villeggiatura* with his wife; I shall see the villa when I pass."

Bologna was full of friends and relations who vied with each other in showing their affection and sympathy for the travellers in this time of trouble. Clementino Spada insisted on having the whole party stay at his house in the town, and poor Cunegonda was already so worn out that she decided to rest there for a few days before going farther. The physical repose, however, seems to have in no way lightened the heavy weight that lay at her heart; on June 11 she writes:

"What I have become, Giovanni mine! I can truly say that I am a reed shaken in the wind, for every moment some new fear takes possession of me; the only thing that consoles and reassures

THE FATIGUE OF TRAVEL

me a little is that when I am most troubled is the time when I turn with most faith to prayer.

". . . Yesterday the ex-Court of Spain * arrived here and was to go on to-day. They have to move in instalments, as they require sixty-nine horses, and could never find them if the whole company travelled together!"

The next little note is written somewhere between Modena and Saliceta, on June 17. The heat was becoming overwhelming.

"I cannot describe to you," Cunegonda says, "what I am suffering from heat and the fatigue of the journey. . . . I have to stop constantly to rest. I propose to do so in Milan, and I am sure you will approve. It is no exaggeration to say that I have not strength to do anything else. Oh, if I knew how to accept all this, how much of my purgatory could I be sparing myself!"

* Charles IV of Spain travelling to Rome with his Court. He remained there for some time.

CHAPTER IX

MILAN was reached on June 20, and the next day the Marchesa wrote to her husband:

"I left Modena, or rather Saliceta, on Thursday. The Marchisios, husband and wife" (friends with whom she had stayed near Modena), "did everything they could to show their cordial affection. On Friday we dined at Piacenza and slept at Lodi, and yesterday morning at half-past ten we arrived here. I am lodging at the Hotel Imperial, an excellent inn in a quiet situation, where I found both the Bailli Ruspoli and Cardinal Albani. . . . Monsignor Odescalchi and Count Francesco Scotti came to see me and send you many greetings.

"I forgot to tell you in my last letter that at Bologna I had to part with Tommaso and take to the post. His demands became so outrageous that I could not consent to them. I am quite satisfied with the new arrangement, as the roads as far as Turin are splendid; at Turin I must consider again what I had better do.

". . . I should be telling you an untruth if I were to say that my health is good, and you would perhaps not believe it; may the Lord help me to

CASTLE OF BARD.
On the road from Turin to Courmayeur.
Photo Alinari, Rome.

bear the fatigues and mental sufferings I sustain, and I hope He will accept them in place of that which we fear, a hope that inspires me to bear them willingly. . . . I cannot say when I shall leave Milan. . . . Unless I rest now, there will be nothing to send to Paris except my bones!"

"*June* 25th, 1812.

"I am pleased to hear that you are occupying yourself in studying Spanish. I held up your example to Pippo, showing him how happy are those who love to be occupied, and how bad idleness is for the soul and the body. Why do you doubt that I shall obtain the happiness of seeing you again? I, on my part, promise it to myself; and of how many things we shall have to tell one another! You say that you wish me to be cheerful. . . . This I cannot promise; one thing alone can restore cheerfulness to me, and you know what that is; I shall rejoice to see you in good health, and for that I am thanking God now—that, to so many sorrows, is not added the one of knowing you to be suffering physically. I hope you will experience the same about the boys; the quiet life and the good air of Siena caused them to flourish again (after their slight illness) in a way that amazed me. . . . Like you, the benedictions I ask for our children are all celestial ones, for I cannot bring myself to ask for them the goods of this world."

The Marchesa was at this time ardently nourishing the hope that she would be permitted to visit her husband in prison on her way north from Turin, a hope which he, sadly wise, dared not entertain. On June 28 Cunegonda apprises him of the coming of some new comrades in misfortune to Fenestrelle.

"I hear that the brigade in your hermitage is very soon to be increased. This morning I was given the names of the Abbés Guidi and Caprani, both of the Roman College; and there may be others coming to you. I had been told the two Canons Fratini were condemned to Corsica, but there are already so many prisoners in that island . . . that Corsica can maintain no more."

At last Cunegonda accomplished the journey to Turin, where she hoped to obtain permission for her visit to Giovanni. On July 6 she writes:

"I got here on Thursday evening, and am stopping at this inn of 'The Red Bull.' The journey from Milan was quite a fortunate one, thank God; the heat was not oppressive, and here it is almost cold. . . . You exhort me to be courageous, and I will try to obey you, knowing what great need I have of courage even to keep up physically, for I have periods of such exhaustion, not only of spirit, but of body, that, were they to last any time, I should succumb completely, and those are not moments when moral reflections are of any assistance. There is nothing to do but wait till the paroxysm has passed; but I do not wish you to be troubled about this. God, who has helped me so far, will certainly continue to help me; only ask Him to give me all the faith I ought to have in His goodness."

"Here I shall be obliged to go out more than I did in Milan, for we have an apartment so small and restricted that I cannot turn round in my room, which is also the family sitting-room, dining-room, study, and so forth. Luckily for me, the weather is not warm. We often say that we should be profoundly grateful if you would engage an apartment in your cloister for me and my whole party."

As soon as she reached Turin Cunegonda began to make every effort to obtain permission for herself and the boys to visit Giovanni at Fenestrelle. On July 8, by the hands of the Marchese d'Azeglio, she sent her husband a long letter describing her many futile errands and expeditions, for, as she said, "They send me from Herod to Pilate" (still the Italian synonym for our phrase 'From pillar to post'). The Commandant of Fenestrelle, who happened to be in Turin at the moment, received her courteously, listened with gratification to the warm thanks she offered him for his many kindnesses to the beloved prisoner, but told her that it was not in his power to grant her permission to visit her husband in the fort. The Director-General of Police, Danzer, only went so far as to advise her to apply to Don Camillo Borghese, the Governor of Turin; and she tells Giovanni that she has tried this last resort, and is awaiting the answer with feverish impatience.

Here is her letter to Don Camillo—and how bitterly it must have gone against her proud heart to have to write it!—

"Monseigneur,
"After being separated for more than seven months from my husband, and finding myself now so near him, I have taken all the steps which appeared necessary to obtain the ardently desired permission to see and embrace him for a moment before continuing my journey to Paris; but, contrary to my expectation, I have encountered many obstacles, and am told that without the express permission of Your Imperial Highness" (to such rank had a Borghese attained by becoming the Emperor's brother-in-law!) "it is impossible that my request should be granted.

"I therefore venture to address Your Highness directly to implore you not to refuse me the favour that, after such a long separation, I and my children may have the joy of seeing and embracing a tenderly loved husband and father. Your Imperial Highness's good heart and humane feeling will, I am sure, induce you to give the favourable reply which we await and desire with

the most eager impatience. I am, Monseigneur, with the most profound respect,
"Etc., etc.,
"CUNEGONDA OF SAXONY PATRIZI."

His Imperial Highness, Don Camillo Borghese, had not the least idea of offending his all-powerful brother-in-law by acceding to the poor wife's request. To favour a Patrizi would have been to incur Napoleon's certain displeasure, and Cunegonda's heart-broken entreaty received this curt answer :

"MADAME,
"I will not lose a moment in answering the letter which you took the trouble to write me to-day ; I should do so with much more pleasure if I could grant what you ask. I advise you to get to Paris as quickly as you can and there ask permission from the Minister of Police to visit your husband on your return journey. I do not imagine that you will then have any difficulty.
"Pray accept the assurance of my esteem and high consideration.
"CAMILLO."

This letter was a double-edged sword to Cunegonda's hopes ; not only was she forbidden to see her husband, but it showed that the enforced sacrifice of the children would not, as she had hitherto believed, procure their father's liberation. She broke down completely under the disappointment, and had to stay several days in Turin before she could find strength to resume her journey.

Meanwhile, at Fenestrelle, her husband was the victim of similarly deluded hopes. "On the 9th of July," he writes in his journal, "by some extraordinary and incomprehensible combinations, my hopes"—of seeing his family—"suddenly became almost certainties. I was shut up in my room towards four in the afternoon when there came a knocking at the door. I opened it to find some of my companions in captivity, one of whom declared to me, on the assertions of two others, that my wife was just about to arrive at the fort. Those others told me that, with the aid of a small opera-glass, they had discerned on the road leading hither a tall, well-dressed woman with two boys, accompanied by other persons, one of whom looked like a servant, as he kept some paces behind; the party were on foot, and kept constantly turning to look at the fort. My friends reminded me that the road was new, and still unfinished, which would explain why the strangers had had to leave their carriage and approach on foot.

"All these details made the thing appear so probable that they blinded me for the moment to its greater improbability. I flew down to the lower bastions to look closer at the road which skirts the Mosino fort, and on which I was told the travellers must very shortly appear. I saw indeed some persons moving on the road, but at that distance could not make out whether they were men or women, big or small, and all the time heart was beating wildly, I thinking they might be those tenderly loved beings! . . . Alas, they were only gendarmes, as some who had seen them more clearly than I explained to me. . . . Oh! the terrible disappointment! I stayed there, gazing out for a little while ; then, when no one appeared, I realised that the kindness of my friends, and their desire that I should have this consolation, had completely misled them.

"I did not, however, lose all hope of that dear visit ; on the contrary, I expected it hourly until the arrival here, on the 10th, of the good Marchese Taparelli d' Azeglio of Turin, who had come here to visit two friends of his and fellow-prisoners of mine, Mancini and Berrera, Canons of the Cathedral of Florence. Then all my hopes were dashed, for the said Marchese, while bringing me the last news as well as the letters of my most beloved wife, of my dearest children, and of that incomparable friend, Giustiniani, told me that, in spite of every effort, of every possible means employed both with the police of Turin and the Governor (Borghese), my wife had been unable to procure the desired permission.

"I cannot deny that this was a blow which I felt very deeply, but I adored the dispensations of our good God, who had refused me the consolation in order to spare me the pain of the parting which must have followed it, and which would indeed have been greater than the consolation itself.

"The never sufficiently to be praised Marchese

d'Azeglio, a man estimable in every way, but most singularly so for his intrepid religious spirit, shortened his visit here and renounced the pleasure of being with his friends in order to hasten back to Turin and give my wife all the news about me, and the letters I entrusted him with, before her departure, which finally took place on the 15th of July."

On the 9th, after receiving Camillo Borghese's refusal of her request, Cunegonda had written : " I am only forty-five miles from you, and I must go on without seeing you ! I never expected this ! Goodbye, my dear Giovanni—until now every step brought me nearer to you ; henceforth each one will take me further away. Lord, give me strength, courage, constancy, and patience ! "

On the 19th she wrote from Chambéry :

" I was hoping to find a letter from you here ; but, so far, it has not come. You will have heard of my departure ; what I felt at coming away without seeing you God only knows. All through Wednesday I kept gazing at the mountains until we reached Susa, hoping to distinguish the spot you inhabit, although I was told that one could not see it from the road. But I seemed to remember that, when I came to Italy, some one had pointed it out to me from a distance. At Susa I learnt that I was only five miles away from you ! Oh, how gladly would I have gone over them—but to what purpose ? The best thing is to be resigned, and to hope that God has only deprived me of this one

SUSA. THE ANCIENT GATEWAY.
Photo Alinari, Rome.

consolation in order to give me many others all together. The journey from Turin here was, thank God, very fortunate. The first day, Wednesday, we slept at Susa; on Thursday we travelled over the Mont Cenis, in such cold that, as soon as we reached the Grand Cross which stands at the summit of the Pass, I had a great fire made, as we were all frozen. After dinner I went on foot to the Hospice of the Cistercians, and there the good Fathers wanted me to stay the night, which I should have been glad to do, for the apartment they offered me was so elegant that one could find nothing better in Paris. I saw the room where the Holy Father lately spent three or four days, and where they feared he would expire; but, thank God, his health improved during the hurried journey, and the surgeon of the monks, who accompanied him as far as Fontainebleau, has already returned, having left him quite well. When I had seen all, and heard all, I had a cup of coffee and took the road to Lans-le-Bourg, where I slept that night. On Friday we got to St. Jean de Maurienne, and yesterday, after a long and tiring day, we reached this place, where I shall rest and wait for the answer from my sister" (Princess Altieri, in Paris) "to the petition which I have asked her to get strongly supported for me—with what result we shall see. I imagine it will have the same fate as all my former ones."

Here we must insert an extract from little Filippo's

faithful journal of his travels, which, as the compiler of the Memoirs remarks, is not without interest for his descendants, who to-day cross the Alps in automobiles, and to-morrow may be flying over them in aeroplanes!

" From Susa to Lans-le-Bourg :

" This morning, July 16, we left Susa at about six o'clock, and as soon as we were out of Susa began the ascent of Mont Cenis, one of the highest mountains in the Alps. Three years ago people passed over it in winter on sledges, and in summer on horseback or in sedan-chairs, on account of the very bad and very steep road there was ; but now one can go most comfortably in the carriage over the new road just finished, which is really beautiful and broad. . . . On this mountain there are twenty-six little houses where people live to help travellers in case of necessity ; these houses are at small distances from one another. In one place on this mountain, as rocks often fall on the road, they pierced a tunnel through the rocks, so that one passes very well. . . . The road is not very steep. At half-past four we reached the Great Cross, an inn on the top of Mont Cenis, and so named because, when in the winter the road is all covered with snow, there is danger that people will fall over the precipice, and so there are crosses to let them know the way, even when it is all under the snow ; and the biggest of these crosses is at this inn, and it is the first, and the others follow all the way down to Ramace.

"A little while after leaving the inn one begins to go down the mountain, and there is an inn called the 'Ramace'"—a zig-zag path—"because when people came by the old track on sledges it was here that the mule which had pulled the stranger from the Novalese so far, was left, and then they did the rest of the way with the sledge sliding down over the ice."

One sees from Pippo's careful account how it all must have impressed the Roman children, to whom ice and snow had been so far mere geographical fairy tales!

The Marchesa remained at Chambéry until August 5, waiting in vain for letters from Paris, and much incensed at the outrageous delays imposed on those which her husband sent from Fenestrelle. On July 24 she had written:

"I received your two letters dated the 10th and 15th, and this morning the one of the 17th; the two first were folded one within the other" (this was before the days of envelopes), "and the inside one was addressed to me in Turin, the other to Chambéry, which made it quite clear that they had been opened and read. I cannot understand how, after seven months, these gentlemen of the police can still find amusement in this useless reading of our letters, of which they have not yet tired! They ought to know them fairly by heart by this time, for almost the same things are said in them all. You see that even yours of the 17th has been long kept back, for it seems impossible that it should have taken seven days to reach here from Fenestrelle. . . . I see you have had all the accounts of our journey to Chambéry, where be sure I am leading a life more solitary than yours over there. I do not know a single soul. In the morning, at six, I go to church with the Cavaliere "—Don Lorenzo—"then we return, and have breakfast at half-past eight. At nine the boys sit down to their lessons, and at eleven we go out to Mass, and after that we take a walk. . . . Dinner is at two, and after that the Cavaliere has his nap. At five the boys study again; and after six we all say the Rosary together, and then comes another walk. For the most part I let the Cavaliere take the boys, and I stay quietly at home. They come back after eight, supper is at nine, and by half-past ten we are all in bed. The life is much the same as we have led ever since we left Rome. Good-bye, my Giovanni. Courage!"

CHAPTER X

The Marchese Patrizi was badly versed in the ways of duplicity and intrigue. While his wife was still hoping to obtain his immediate liberation, a letter which he had written to her in May, openly mentioning the names of friends who facilitated the correspondence, had found its way into the Emperor's hands, and had roused him to such wrath that he resolved to make Giovanni's punishment more severe than ever. It had been forwarded to Paris in a French translation with this information on the margin : " This letter, written in Italian, was enclosed in one addressed to M. Le Comte François Scotti at Milan, which was itself put into the post at Pignerolle."

" The Marquis Jean Patrizi to Madame his wife in Milan.
"Fenestrelle, *May* 21, 1812.

" After having sent you a very long letter yesterday by the ordinary way . . . I now address this one by the surer means which you requested, by the good Count Scotti.

" My object this time is to make some observations about the renewed supplications which you propose, while in Milan, to make through your sister." (The translator here explains, for the Emperor's benefit, that these referred to the Marchesa Patrizi's hope that her husband would be set at liberty in order to accompany her and the children for the remainder of the journey to Paris.) "In the first place, I wish that such requests should be made solely in your name, for I would fear that, if mine were appended to them, it might be supposed that I am tired of my present position; the God Who commands us to be humble forbids us to degrade ourselves, and a base action now would injure the cause for which I have thought it my duty to affront any and every vicissitude. Therefore, if you are really resolved to take this step, let it be absolutely in your own name; you could even tell your sister that you are only induced to do so in order to have the pleasure of my companionship on the journey, and not because you imagine *I wish to come out of prison* to travel on my own account. You can tell her this in all good faith, for to tell the truth I do not in the least wish to see Paris, and would never have thought of proposing such a thing, except for the sake of sharing with you the many tribulations which you must doubtless encounter. Make your sister clearly understand that I do not propose to buy this favour by any yielding whatever (on the point of the removal of the children), and suggest, if that question is put to her, to reply that you have not authorised her to accept any conditions, but merely to present the request. The conditions in question might be that you were to say precisely on what day you would be in Paris, that you would present the children (at La Flèche), and other things of the kind which must not be promised, for all sorts of good reasons. I foresee, in any case, that nothing will be obtained, given the absence of the Emperor, and if you are also convinced of its uselessness do not take the step at all. Do not think that because I write you all this now, I regret having suggested the idea. . . . I was only wishing to do what would be most agreeable to you. Consult with your good friend, whom I greet affectionately, for I am ready to do whatever you and he think right, even as a child submits to his father and mother.

"As the result of something that has happened in this place our walks" (about the fort) "have been much restricted for the last few days, and are now confined entirely to the courtyard. Nothing remains but to forbid us to go out of doors at all. But I must say that our good Commandant does not do all this from unkindness or caprice; and I think he takes it more to heart than we do, for, personally, I am utterly indifferent."

The letter is taken up again the next day:

"I have had a letter from my father, which caused me the greatest pleasure in every way.

They say here that the Roman priests who are at Pignerolle are going to be summoned once more to take the oath, and they are threatened, if they refuse, with confiscation of all their goods and exile beyond the confines of the Empire. I fear this measure will be extended to those in other places.

"The 'Lamb'" (a note on the margin explains to the French authorities that this is the name by which Cardinal Pacca was always designated in the correspondence of the various prisoners) "and all the others here send you many greetings."

On a scrap enclosed and marked 'Post Scriptum,' Giovanni writes:

"I forgot to tell you not to mention this letter when writing. . . . To let me know you have received it merely say, 'Count Francesco Scotti salutes you.'"

On the margin is another note of the translator-censor. "In writing to M. Scotti (enclosing the above) M. Patrizi says, 'Please do not acknowledge the receipt of this, as it has not passed by the ordinary channels, and I should be sorry to have it known that I have written to you. I am telling my wife how to let me know that she has received it.'"

Various letters of Giovanni and Cunegonda had already found their way into the Emperor's hands, and had irritated him so furiously that he gave orders to the Duc de Rovigo that a means must be found immediately and once for all to put a stop to their clandestine correspondence.

Giovanni's phrase, "The God who bids us be humble forbids us to degrade ourselves," had struck his unacknowledged readers with something like panic. A prisoner who nourished such sentiments was evidently a dangerous person, not to be subdued by ordinary methods. Only some very strict enactment could reduce such a one to silence.

The facilities were all at hand. There arises from the Mediterranean, just in front of Marseilles, a sharp crag crowned with a fortress—the Château d'If, famous in history and romance, defending the port and providing a dungeon from which evasion is well-nigh impossible — who, indeed, has not gasped over the miraculous escape of Monte Cristo? This was the fortress in which the dangerous criminal, Patrizi, was now to be immured. Here is the order from the Duc de Rovigo, written evidently with some irritation, for his removal from Fenestrelle. The prisoner's title is not mentioned. He has become plain 'Mr.'

"*July*, 1812.

"To the Director-General of Police of the Transalpine Departments.

"I have decided, sir, that the Sieur Patrizi shall be removed from the castle of Fenestrelle where he is now detained; the object of this step is to put a stop to the correspondence which the prisoner has never ceased to keep up and which my orders to that effect have been insufficient to prevent.

"I send you herewith the order of the Commandant to hold this prisoner at your disposal. I beg that you will take the necessary measures for his safe conveyance to Marseilles. On his arrival at that city he is to be delivered to the Commissary-General of Police, to whom I have given instructions as to the ultimate destination of the Sieur Patrizi.

"You will render me an account of the result of your care for the execution of this order.

"I am, sir,

"Etc., etc."

The final instructions were these:

"PARIS, *July* 18, 1812.

"The Duc de Rovigo to the Commissioner of the Château d'If:

"I notify you, sir, that the Commissary-General of Police at Marseilles is charged to bring to the fort which you command the Sieur Jean Patrizi; you are to receive him and register him on the books of the prison according to the order of imprisonment which will be remitted to you. It will be necessary for you to superintend very carefully the correspondence of this prisoner; you must send to me all the letters which he writes, and all those which come addressed to him."

The same notification was posted the same day to the Commissary-General of Police in Marseilles. It ends with instructions to inform the Duke at once of the arrival of the prisoner and of his transfer to the Château d'If.

The sharp reprimand contained in Rovigo's letter to the Director-General of the Transalpine Departments called forth an indignant protest from that functionary :

"Monseigneur," he writes from Turin on July 24, "in conformity with the orders Your Excellency condescended to lay upon me . . . I have made arrangements to have the Sieur Patrizi removed from the Castle of Fenestrelle, where he is at present detained. He will be conveyed to Turin with an escort, and I will see that the same care be taken to bring him to Marseilles and place him at the disposal of the Commissary-General of that city, who, as Your Excellency informs me, has received your instructions as to his ultimate destination.

"Your Excellency tells me that this step is taken to put a stop to the correspondence maintained by this prisoner. May I be permitted, Monseigneur, to submit to you a few remarks on this subject? Until now, prisoners not sentenced to solitary confinement have had permission to write letters; this was the custom before Fenestrelle came under my superintendence, and I always rendered account of it and of the precautions which I took to prevent its entailing any abuses.

"I charged the Commandant of the fort to have brought to him, and to read, himself, all the letters written or received by the prisoners who were not sentenced to isolation and only to permit the passage of those which treated of purely personal matters, and to send to me, on the other hand, all communications which touched on politics or contained matter requiring consideration.

"As for the prisoners of State under sentence of secrecy (complete isolation) the commandant was instructed to send me all the letters they wrote or received, for my personal examination.

"For some time past I had included the Sieur Patrizi in this special order, although he was not under sentence of secrecy, because Your Excellency had instructed me to exercise particular watch over him.

"Mme Patrizi, his wife, passed through Turin on her way to Paris a few days ago, and asked my permission to pay her husband a visit at Fenestrelle. . . . I refused unconditionally. She then addressed herself to H.I.H. the Prince Governor-General, who, having done me the honour to consult me, also refused her request; she then continued her journey to Paris.

"Nevertheless, in spite of all the precautions I take, it is possible that some letters escape all our watchfulness; this is due to the locality of this state prison. It was one of the most pressing reasons why, last year, I begged you to permit all the prisoners to be lodged in Fort Mosin. In truth, the building where they are now housed cannot be closed to the military agents who have to visit their stores—a state of things which makes it necessary for many persons from outside to enter the prison. It is impossible to make sure that some one of them, tempted by bribes, does not make himself the carrier of secret letters. On the other hand, when all the repairs at Fort Mosin are completed and the prisoners can be kept there all together, they will have no chance of communicating with any one except the turnkey and the guard, which will render the surveillance far more exact, this fort being entirely under the control of the Minister-General of Police and used exclusively as a State prison.

"I am, Monseigneur,
"Etc., etc.,
"L. Danzer.
"Director-General of Police of the Transalpine Departments."

The benevolent authorities were now only worried by one possibility, which they were anxious to avoid at all costs, the fortuitous meeting of husband and wife on the road to France. It seemed that they might be dangerously near one another, so the Marchese's itinerary was modified to meet the situation. M. Danzer appears to have taken to his bed after the passage-at-arms with his irascible superior in Paris, but a subordinate writes to the Duke for him :

"Your Excellency's orders regarding the Sieur Patrizi have been executed; yesterday morning he arrived under a sure escort at Turin, where he is closely guarded by a gendarme who permits him neither to speak or write to any one.

"To-morrow morning he leaves for Marseilles in a carriage for which he is to pay, accompanied by the Quartermaster of Gendarmes, to whom I have imparted Your Excellency's instructions. . . . The road which I have directed for the prisoner to take is the one by Nice and the Col di Tenda. I could not permit him to pass by Lyon, because it seems that Mme Patrizi, who is travelling by slow stages to Paris with her children, is at Lyon at this moment."

So far the official view of the Patrizi case. How these ominous changes affected Giovanni himself we shall read in his Journal. The blow which, to all appearance, amounted to doom, fell upon him quite suddenly, and Cunegonda, awaiting in eager suspense at Chambéry for the hoped-for permission for her husband to accompany her to Paris, was, perhaps fortunately for herself, kept in ignorance, for some time longer, of the impassable barrier now raised between her and the man she loved so wholeheartedly.

"On the afternoon of the 26th of July," the Marchese says in his Memoirs, "I was taking my usual walk in the courtyard when I met my confessor, the Canonico de Berrera, who asked me at what hour he could come the next morning to speak to me in my room. This inquiry surprised me, and I began to have gloomy premonitions, increased by the fact that I had already noticed that my friend Baccili had been looking disturbed, and had let drop some disconnected and mysterious phrases about the many troubles to be encountered in this world—phrases which I had at first not regarded as having particular reference to myself.

"But from that afternoon till the following morning I was in an agony of anxiety, apprehending some great misfortune and unable to divine whether it threatened myself or those my very dearest ones. With the morning came the Canonico de Berrera at the hour I had named, and, after those preambles which religion dictates when a painful announcement is about to be made, informed me that I was about to be removed from Fenestrelle and carried into France. The news had been conveyed in profound secrecy by our friend Rolla, in Turin, to Count Baccili, and the next courier would bring to the Commandant the order for my transfer.

"I was turned to stone. Then I could not restrain my tears. I asked if it were known whither I was to be sent, and the Canonico replied that no one appeared to know. Then I bowed my head to the divine ordinances, and waited quietly for these new blows of a cruel Government.

"On the evening of the 28th, after the arrival of the courier, I was summoned to the presence of the Commandant, who communicated to me an order just received from the police at Turin; instructing him to have me sent as rapidly as possible, and under the guard of a gendarme, to that place, where I was to be put at the disposition of the Director, and this by order of the Duc de Rovigo, Minister of Police of the French Empire. I pretended to be surprised at the announcement, of which I could foresee all the unpleasant consequences, and I felt renewed regret at having to leave this prison, to which, after seven months' residence, I had become so reconciled, for a new one, where it was not at all likely that I could adapt myself so well.

"I wrote to Turin by the same courier, who went back the next morning, for my travelling carriage, which I had sent there some months earlier to have it properly taken care of, and this arrived at Fenestrelle, with friend Rolla inside, on the morning of August 1st. That same day, towards four o'clock, having mingled my tears with those of the good friends and compatriots whom I was leaving behind, I left Fenestrelle *en route* for my new destination, accompanied by Rolla and a quartermaster of gendarmes.

"At Pinerolo I supped, and, after some rest, resumed the journey, arriving at Turin about seven in the morning. There I went to the inn of 'The Red Bull,' where my good wife had stayed when she passed through, and I was given the very room which she had occupied with my dear sons."

The Marchese was visited on his arrival in Turin by a certain Avvocato Ferrero, who was acting as substitute for the still indisposed Director of Police, M. Danzer. From this gentleman Giovanni learnt that he was to go to Marseilles, and obtained permission to remain in Turin until August 4 in order to arrange for his money matters and various business. His route to Marseilles was laid down for him, by Cuneo, the Col di Tenda, and Nice. He says that he wanted to find a body-servant, but, not liking the looks of those sent to him, he resolved to do without. The gendarme who had brought him from Fenestrelle seemed a good fellow, and on the Marchese's request was designated as his escort on the journey. And then "friend Rolla," the Turinese banker, cast about for an introduction to a banker in Marseilles who could be relied upon to do whatever lay in his power to accommodate the prisoner of State. It seems that Rolla had no connection himself with any house in Marseilles, so he applied to a colleague in Turin, a certain M. Gabbi, who, knowingly or unknowingly, gave over the unfortunate Marchese into the hands of a double-dyed traitor, a certain Signor Carminati, a banker in Marseilles, who, under the most glowing protestations of friendship, was secretly an agent of the police and betrayed punctually to them every confidence with which the too trusting prisoner honoured him during his stay at the Château d'If. So perfectly did he conceal his transactions with the authorities that Patrizi never discovered his treachery, and it was only when the compiler of the Memoirs obtained access to the police archives in Paris that it was brought to light, in a series of letters of which the first, written on August 18, 1812, explains the gist. It is addressed by the Commissioner-General of Police in Marseilles to the Duc de Rovigo in Paris, and is marked " Bureau of the Secret Police. *For the Minister only.*

" The Sieur Joseph Carminati, a Genoese merchant established in Marseilles, has handed to me the enclosed literal translation of a letter of credit and letter of introduction which his firm has received from the Quartermaster of Gendarmes who escorted the Sieur Jean Patrizi, prisoner of State, from Turin to Marseilles. The Sieur Carminati wishes to know if he may fulfil the commissions which the Sieur Patrizi may entrust to him, and if he may furnish him with money to the extent covered by the letter of credit. . . . The Sieur Patrizi sent a message to ask M. Carminati to inform his family of his arrival in Marseilles. He (Carminati) will send me all the letters which M. Patrizi may write, and I will hasten to send them on to Your Excellency.

" The Sieur Carminati has an excellent reputa-

ARRIVAL AT MARSEILLES

tion; his intention is to watch M. Patrizi carefully and inform us of everything he does. Madame Jolielen, the wife of the Comr.-General of Police in Genoa, always stays with Mr. Carminati when she comes to Marseilles; she is in his house at this moment.

"Pernon."

Such was the man whom Giovanni Patrizi trusted with his most secret affairs during his long imprisonment in the Château d'If, and whom he regarded as such a faithful friend and benefactor that when Napoleon fell and the captives were set at liberty he chose to go and lodge in his house, refusing to stay with Cardinal Consalvi, who had come all the way from Lyon to hail and take possession of him!

On August 4 Giovanni, always calm in the presence of the decrees of Heaven, and counting on still being able to communicate with his family, set out on his journey to Marseilles with a quiet mind. He reached that place on the 11th, at eight in the evening, and with his watchful escort descended at the Hotel du Suisse in the main street. The next morning he was permitted to call, as he says, on the " highly commended Signor Carminati, who received me with every politeness and offered me all possible courteous services. Towards midday I was presented to the Commissioner of Police, who caused me to be accompanied back to the hotel by two of his own men. There I took a few moments to put my things together, and, having commissioned my gendarme to go and ask Signor Carminati to be so kind as to have my travelling carriage bestowed in safety, I walked with the Police Agents down to the port and took boat for the Château d'If, the State Prison which stands on a small island about a league out at sea. . . .

"Arrived at the fort, I was presented to the Commandant, and in his presence the jailer made a most minute inspection of everything contained in my baggage, after which this functionary conducted me to the prison. On entering this, the jailer made a rigorous search of my person, and took possession of my pocket-book to show it to the Commandant. I cannot deny that this search was excessively painful to me, never having undergone such treatment before. I was then taken to the room assigned to me, which I was to share with another prisoner, a very old Frenchman. The room was truly horrible—a typical prison indeed! The only piece of furniture shown me was a wretched bed supplied by the Government. Oh how regretfully I thought of my nice room at Fenestrelle! When night came I heard the bolts drawn across the door; the same was done to all the other prisoners, but it was irritating to my self-respect.

"The next day I took steps to obtain what was

MARSEILLES. THE CHATEAU D'IF.
Photo Giletta, Nice.

A FRESH PRISON

requisite to make my situation less uncomfortable, and the most necessary things were provided by Signor Carminati, to whom I addressed the request. After a few days of imprisonment I asked the Commandant for my pocket-book, and this was instantly returned to me, minus some letters from my relations which the Commandant thought it his duty to keep. But after a few days more these were also returned, as, I was told, there was nothing suspicious in them."

It was several weeks before Giovanni Patrizi's wife, and his family in Rome, were apprised of his removal to the Château d' If. He relates in his Memoirs that he had no news of his father and mother for eighty-three days, and Cunegonda, writing on September 10 a letter which took six weeks to reach him, said that she had had no word of or from him since August 3. The correspondence of the Patrizi family was already piled high on the writing-table of the Duc de Rovigo!

CHAPTER XI

CUNEGONDA arrived in Paris on August 21, 1812, having stopped for a day at Pont-sur-Seine, her father's once-beautiful château, and her own birthplace. The boys were intensely interested in their mother's first home, and Filippo, the irrepressible writer of the family, describes the visit, in his journal, and, like a good little boy, puts down all the information that his elders imparted on the subject.

"This morning, the 19th of August, we left Troyes, and at about . . ." (he forgets to state the hour) "arrived at Pont-sur-Seine, the property of Prince Xavier of Saxony, my mother's father, and now unjustly held by the French Government. Julius Cæsar speaks, in his 'Commentaries,' of this place, which was then called Pons ad Sequenam, and where one can still see traces of an ancient life. About two miles outside the town is a great palace, where the above-mentioned Prince lived with his family. This palace has two beautiful façades, one that looks on the posting-road and one that looks on the garden; the façade on the posting-road has statues and two big pavilions (wings) which project far forward, forming a courtyard open in the front ; and these two pavilions are united by a great arch with a terrace on top of it ; the side that looks towards the gardens has no pavilions ; to enter the palace from that side you must cross a bridge over a great trench made to keep the stags and the deer in. In the palace are 300 rooms, not including those for the servants. Behind the palace are many gardens and a beautiful wood, where there is an open-air theatre. In these gardens are three great fish-ponds, and the Seine flows at the foot. Near the palace, on the side towards the road, there are two houses opposite one another and surrounded with a wall which makes an enclosed court ; in the middle there is a stone basin for water. These were built by the afore-mentioned Prince Xavier to keep all his hunting-dogs of every kind, he being very fond of hunting.

"Of the town of Pont-sur-Seine I can say nothing, because I did not see it. We went to lodge in the house of the Curé, Monsieur Pesme, a man most estimable for his good qualities, of which esteem is also worthy his brother, the Curé of Sévigny. By these two excellent personages we were extremely kindly treated, and we stayed till the 20th."

The compiler of the Memoirs tells us that there are two copies of Pippo's journal in the "archivio" of Casa Patrizi, but that one of them has been evidently much revised and corrected by well-meaning elders. That here given is from the little man's own point of view, pure and simple, and strikes one as a remarkably lucid and intelligent production for a child who was not yet nine years' old.

Upon her arrival in Paris, the Marchesa Patrizi was informed that henceforth all her letters to her husband were to be written in French, for the convenience of the police. She heard rumours that he had been transferred to a new prison, but for a long time remained in ignorance of his real address.

"I did not know how or where to send you news of us," she writes at last, "and I was going to risk writing to the Commandant of Château d'If and the Commandant of Hyères to ask if you were in either of those prisons; but, thank God, your letters received yesterday have relieved my suspense, and, what is more, tell me that you are well. They are of the 24th and 28th of August, and you say this last is the sixth you have written to me, so four are missing. I wish I could give wings to mine to-day to make it reach you more rapidly, for you must be anxious about us. I will hasten to say that all went happily during the second part of our journey; our dear children are well; they kiss your hands, and only do not add a few lines to this letter because they cannot write in French. Our excellent friend" (Don Lorenzo Giustiniani) "for the same reason commissions me to give you a thousand and yet a thousand affectionate greetings from him. I will not talk about my own health, because it is always bad. My address here is Rue Jacob, Hôtel d'Hambourg, 18, Faub. Saint Germain. My lodging is clean but very small, our finances permitting nothing more expensive. My life is solitary. . . . I rarely go out, as the least walk fatigues me. I am glad you are getting some sea-baths; they will do you good. I fancy you have made up for all the cold you endured at Fenestrelle, for it must have been very warm on those lonely rocks" (of the Château d'If). "I will write to Rome about you, in case they have had no news of you there. Good-bye, my very dear Giovanni. Keep well, and think of me as I think without ceasing of you.

"GONDINA."

On September 16 a hurried note says:

"I am longing to know that you have received my first letter" (from Paris) "and also news from Rome. I was in a fever of impatience to write to you; but, not knowing where you were, or whether it were permitted that I should write to you, I searched about in vain for means to let you have news of us. I wrote to-day by the Government messenger to your mother, that she might the sooner have yours, for which she was in mortal anxiety. . . . Have you found any one to wait upon you? Oh, how many things there are that I want to know!"

Then comes the account of poor Marchesa Patrizi's efforts to see the Duc de Rovigo. On the 27th she says:

"Last Friday I went to see the Minister of Police. This makes the fifth time I have been to his door, and this time at last I was admitted. Before I could speak he told me that I was to ask nothing for you, since you yourself had forbidden me to do so in your letters, a fact which it would be useless for me to deny; I replied that I felt free to ask, in spite of that, and that I did ask for your liberation, and I continued to urge the point very insistently. He gave me no definite answer, but I do not abandon the hope of obtaining what I desire, and I assure you that my own wish united with yours and that of your mother as well as of our mutual friend keeps me in a state of intense impatience to obtain the favour. I spoke also (to the Duke) of the sequestrations, and he promised me that if he found the order emanated from himself he would have it rescinded at once; if, however, it had come from the Emperor we should have to wait for the latter's return; I hope it did come from the Duke, and that so it will soon be removed. There, my very dear one, is all that I have been able to do so far! Keep up your courage and let us be confident that at last God will grant us all that we desire. . . ."

The worst cruelty of Giovanni Patrizi's imprisonment was the absolute ignorance in which he was intentionally kept about his wife and family. It was maddening to Cunegonda to discover that her long, faithful letters never reached their proper destination. She was, in spite of all her exalted training, a very human woman, and sometimes her feelings got the better of her prudence.

"Oh! how I wish you could send me word that my letters reach you," she cries, on the 8th of October, from Paris, "I am more and more surprised that you have as yet received not one of them. Every time I get one of yours I dream that it will be an answer to mine—but nothing of the kind! It is always the same thing for both of us!"

And a day or two later: "This will be short, for when I have told you that we are all well there will be nothing more to say. Here is the eighth letter I have written you—it is terrible to think that for two months and a half you have been in complete ignorance of what had become of us! . . . I feel it is useless to write you letters doomed to be lost, but as I hear now that mine are all in the hands of the Commandant of the Château d'If, I am sending this one to him direct, begging him, as a favour, to let you have the others, or, if that is impossible, at least to tell you our news, which, thank God, is good. . . ."

Ten days later, on the 21st of October, she writes: "Your last letter, my very dear Giovanni, of the 7th, was a very sad one, but I am glad you wrote it, since it eased you. I beg you not to think of the pain which the relation of your suffering may cause me, but to write as fully as you feel disposed; I am only too glad if, by doing so, you can gain a few moments of consolation. . . .

"I wrote you that I was working for your liberation and the removal of the sequestrations. I continue to make these attempts, and though as yet I see no results, I do not lose courage. . . ."

November 1, 1812.

"It is almost a year since we were separated and it seems very long ! . . . I am sure my letters (if they ever reach you !) must seem very dull, for to me they seem all alike, and there is nothing new to tell you . . . everything revolves round our mutual sorrow and our much-broken-up correspondence. . . ."

On November 15 Cunegonda gives her husband some quaint details of the restricted housekeeping made necessary by the low state of her funds. She had tried to give up her one cup of chocolate a day " for the sake of economy," but to her regret had to commit the extravagance of returning to it. She chronicles with much disapproval the fashionable hours in vogue in Paris—dinner at five o'clock, sometimes actually as late as six ! She, however, resists all temptations to be drawn into this vortex of dissipation, and says that the family keeps severely to the primitive Roman regime !

On the 12th comes a little cry from her heart : "If only I could set you free by taking your place ! . . . You ask me for more details about the children. . . . I scarcely know what to tell you . . . everything goes on precisely as it has done wherever we have stopped on the way. I make them continue their studies as far as possible, and not a moment of the day is ever wasted. Xavier grows very rapidly; I think he must already be taller than you, but he ought to grow stouter—he is as thin as a lath, but quite well, which is the essential. Pippo stays where he was, is pretty fat, and as cross as ever at growing no taller!"

"*Nov.* 16, 1812.

"Though I have not had any letters from you, my very dear Giovanni, I will write two lines just to give you news of us—thank God, good, in spite of the rain, the fog, the mud, and the cold, for we have all this at once. You can have no idea what the streets of Paris are at this season; one walks on a mattress of mud, so I stay indoors as much as I can. . . . The children take long walks with the Cavaliere, and that does them much good. When they cannot go out they play at battledore and shuttlecock to get a little exercise, although it is true our rooms are so small that we can scarcely move. Xavier's room is so tiny that the bed fills it completely, and the bed itself is too short for him; and if the window is open one cannot get into the room at all! Luckily he is only there at night. . . . My own room is more a passage than a bedroom . . . but the lodging is cheap, and the proprietors of the hotel very good people and most obliging. Monsignor Marini and his nephew are also staying in this house, and we see them often."

The Marchesa's long stay in Paris—for she showed no disposition to move until her petition for her husband's liberation should be granted—began to irritate the Duc de Rovigo, and called forth an order to conduct her sons at once to the Prytanée de la Flèche. This command, though not unexpected, troubled her greatly. On November 22 she wrote: "After remaining for many days in ignorance as to the result of my two petitions, and hearing nothing from the Minister regarding the origin of the order of sequestration—tormented greatly, too, by not having obtained your liberation—I again importuned the Minister on both those subjects, and, by way of reply, was ordered to present myself to the Prefect of Police, by whom I was informed that, according to the Minister's orders, it was impossible to consider either of my petitions until my children should have been received into the College at La Flèche. I was overcome with sorrow at this news, and could only answer by imploring again and again that *you should be given back to me!*

"Having afterwards received your letter in which you advised me to refer our sad affairs to our relative, Prince Corsini, whom you supposed to be in Paris at present, I found and spoke to his brother, Don Neri . . . but unhappily he had been charged by the Minister of Police to repeat these threats, which melancholy commission he carried out on Monday. On Wednesday I received orders from the Prefect of Police to go to him again on Thursday morning; but, having learnt from Don Neri just what the Prefect would say, and being completely worn out both physically and morally, I sent word that I was not well enough to go, that I understood what it was that he wished to say to me, and that I would send my answer the next day. . . . This I did . . . the answer being a letter to you, telling you all that had occurred, and asking to know your wishes before taking any decision on such an important subject. This letter I enclosed with a note to the Prefect, in which I begged him to give it to the Minister, with the prayer that he would have it conveyed to you quickly and safely, and let me have your answer to it in the same manner. An hour afterwards the Prefect returned me the letter, saying that I was at liberty to send it direct to the Minister if I liked, but that he himself was charged with the execution of the Emperor's command in regard to my children, and, seeing my resistance, he warned me that he would be obliged to take the necessary measures to carry them out. So yesterday, while we were at dinner, a Commissioner of Police came to tell me that the Prefect had named a person to take my children to La Flèche within twenty-four hours. I asked if I too might name some one to go with them; he said, certainly,

I could go myself if I wished. Meanwhile this Police Agent has established himself in the house to keep the children under his own eyes, and to travel with us. This being Sunday, I asked for a delay till Tuesday; the banks are closed to-day, and it is impossible to get any money. I do not know yet if the delay will be granted, but I hope so, and I will tell you before I close this letter. I have been assured and assured again that in fifteen days you will be set at liberty. I hope it, and in my extreme sorrow that will be a very great consolation to which I look forward eagerly.

" P.S.—I have obtained the respite till Tuesday. Be quite happy about my health—God sustains me."

Here little Filippo takes up his chronicle.

" On the 24th day of November 1812. Tuesday.

" As a number of things happened to us (!) we were made to leave Paris for La Flèche accompanied by a certain M. Martin, Commissioner of Police. So we started with six horses (though we were paying for seven), being six people in the carriage, my mother, the Chevalier Giustiniani, my brother, a maid, and M. Martin and Giuseppe our servant; but he went outside. Leaving there at about ten in the morning, we passed out of the barrier of Chaillot, following the Seine on our left, and one sees on the right a big town. The road is flat but stony, which caused the lock of a trunk on the back to be broken, and so we lost something.

"After passing the Seine we reached Sèvres, a post and a quarter from Paris. This post is a city, and there is a beautiful avenue. Here a coachman of a diligence brought back to us some of the things which, as I said above, we had lost.

"After Sèvres there is nothing much. One post further we arrived at Versailles, a city of 3,000 souls, where the Kings of France used to live, and there is a beautiful palace on a great Square, all ornamented with colonnades.

"Here there is now the School for Pages (*Pageria*) of the Emperor Napoleon I. Here we changed horses and hurried on. Just outside the city there is a big frozen fish-pond. On the rest of the road nothing worth noticing. At half-past one we reached Coignière, a small place and an ugly one; we stopped at the only inn, the "White Horse," of which I cannot judge, having seen only one poor old room on the ground-floor where we had dinner. But I was told that there are some decent rooms. The owners of this inn are very moderate, having only asked us 12 francs and 10 sous for an excellent dinner. . . .

"After a post and three-quarters we got to Rambouillet. We went to the Hôtel St. Martin, which is very clean but also very dear.

"Second day.

"After a discussion with the innkeeper, who insisted on charging 32 francs, we came downstairs at half-past eight to go away; but, the postilions having broken the coach-ladder (to climb to the top), we had to wait to get it mended; but that could not be done, so it had to be taken off. On leaving Rambouillet we took the road to Chartres . . . it passes by many small frozen lakes and ponds, and also many little villages consisting of a few huts . . . thatched with straw. . . . We reached Chartres at half-past twelve and went to the Hotel of the 'Grand Monarque.' It is very clean but very expensive, and is outside the city, which has about fifteen thousand inhabitants and a beautiful Cathedral of Gothic architecture. At a quarter past five we got to Courville, an inconsiderable town, where we passed the night.

"Third day.

". . . At the posting-station of Nogent-le-Rotrou one of the postilions fell with his horse and the wheel passed over his thigh, but, thank God, did not injure him. . . . While we were at dinner at La Nerté-Bernard they put two wedges in the centre hole of the big wheel because it was broken and the axle was wearing through it. We reached Conéré at a quarter-past six, and stopped at the good and moderate hotel of St. Jean, which is outside the town, and forty years ago was all burnt; but it has been rebuilt.

"Fourth day.

"Feeling very much satisfied with the inn-keeper of the hotel, we left Conéré about 9 o'clock; but there was such a thick fog on the road that I could not see if there was anything to note about it. . . . At Mans we had to wait half an hour to get a wheel mended. . . . At last, to our great sorrow, we approached our sad destination. . . . Arrived at the town of La Flèche, we got down at the least bad of the inns, the 'Golden Lion,' kept by Mme. Boisseau, a good honest woman."

In the last note in Pippo's diary is added, later: "Here we stayed till December 3, on which day took place our hard separation from our Lady Mother."

So it was done at last. All Cunegonda's innocent plots to gain time, all her valiant rebellions, her agonised prayers, had been in vain. The boys were taken from her and shut up in the detested school, and she, poor faithful soul, bravely turned her eyes towards her husband's liberation, which both he and she then believed would be granted as the price of the enforced sacrifice. What the weary journey from Paris to La Flèche, through the frozen country, meant to her no one ever heard her say. She never even referred to her feelings during those last few troubled days that she had her children with her—dear and precious days in spite of all fatigue and discomforts of the long rough journey. Her first letter from La Flèche to her husband is all cheerfulness and good sense, intended to comfort him for the sorrow that lay so heavily on them both. This letter describes the surroundings in which, taking every possible chance of seeing the children, she was to remain for nearly two years!

On November 29 she writes:

"I arrived here on Friday evening . . . and I would have wished to write to you at once, but yesterday I was, as you may imagine, so tired that I had neither the courage nor strength to do so. Our journey was prosperous, but very cold; everything was frozen. The Commissioner of Police put in charge of our children behaved very properly, but you will understand how it annoyed us to have him in the carriage; he goes back to-morrow.

"I have already seen the Sub-Prefect of the town; he is the brother of the Prefect of Paris, and exceedingly gentle and polite. He came to see me last evening; and this morning General Duteil, the Director of the Prytanée, paid me a visit. Every one seems to speak well of him. We are still at the hotel, which is anything but good, but the General has already found me a small furnished house, which I will go and look at to-morrow. We are all quite well, thank God, and indeed it is by a special grace from Him that I have been able to bear up under so many sorrows, following one upon another and ever increasing. I am actively working for your liberation, and hope to obtain it soon now.

"What happiness it will be for me, my dear,

THE BOYS ENTER COLLEGE

when I can see you again ! What a quantity of things we shall have to say to each other after over a year of separation—and a year so crowded too, with events !

"This place is ugly and small, but I care little. The life I lead does not foster the desire to live in a great city ! Our good, excellent friend makes himself ever more helpful to me ; he salutes you, and the children kiss your hand. They see with heavy hearts the approaching moment of our separation ! "

The next letter, dated December 8, informed Giovanni that his sons had entered the college. Cunegonda writes bravely as usual.

"Our boys entered the college on Thursday. I have facilities for seeing them during their hour of recreation. They are well, but each day makes me more unhappy at being separated from them, and I need to make constant acts of resignation. . . . Good-bye—I must go and warm myself, for I am as frozen as the wells of La Flèche."

On the 13th of the month she says : "Each letter I write to you now I promise myself that it is the last I shall have to address to the Château d'If, and that from one day to another now I shall receive the joyful news of your liberation. Heavens ! how long the time seems till it shall come ! Every time I hear a posting-carriage go by I fancy that you have come, without reflecting that it would be all but impossible for you to get here so quickly.

"Since my last letter to you I have received three of yours, dated the 18th, 22nd, and 23rd of November. In that of the 22nd you proved a true prophet; for, without knowing at all what was happening, you wrote that you had a presentiment that I was more than usually troubled just then, and it was precisely then (as you will have seen if my letter of that time has ever reached you) that they had obliged us to leave Paris so suddenly. It surprised me, as it did our friend" (Don Lorenzo), "that you should have had this intuition about me.

"I come now to your letter of the 24th. You divined rightly in thinking that our talk reverted constantly to the sad anniversary of the day after . . . it made our journey yet more mournful, as we remembered it. . . . At last you have had letters from Rome! I can imagine what a comfort they must have been. But they were very much retarded, even as mine of the 13th of October, of which you now speak; but it is better than nothing, at any rate. I got a" (Roman) "letter of the 25th of November yesterday. That is a little more recent than yours. I think I forgot to tell you that your father made a little expedition to Siena; he was four days at Quirico with the Chigis and one day at Siena. The 'Bailli'" (Ruspoli) "declares that the object of the journey was to make an inventory of the old pictures and arm-chairs which are still in the apartment your father rented to him, so that at his death there should be no disputes with the Sovereign Order of Malta, if it ever be revived.

". . . You ask after my health; but how is it possible to feel well in such circumstances? It is a miracle that I am alive. I will not give you details about the children. We can talk about them when you get here. I will only say that, but for colds, they are well, and they ask for your blessing. It is bitterly cold. If one leaves the fire for a moment one is frozen, and my fingers just now are like ice."

If ever a heart knew the torment of hope deferred, it was that of Cunegonda during these months at La Flèche. She had regarded her husband's liberation as certain from the moment when the children had been brought, practically under arrest, to the college, and she even shows some little impatience when Giovanni's faith in the happy event does not keep pace with hers. He writes to ask her to have some portraits taken of herself and the boys, that he might have the consolation of looking at the beloved faces in his solitude. On December 16 she replies, apparently for the second time, to his request:

"I told you that I hoped it would be only a short time before you would see the originals, and as this hope is now greatly strengthened it seems useless to have the portraits made here, and in any case it would be very difficult, if not altogether impossible. However, if my anticipations should unhappily not be realised, I will try to procure what you desire. I will give Xavier your messages for his fête-day. You wrote this " (last) " letter on the eve of the anniversary of our cruel separation. How many tears and sorrows do these children cost us? Xavier understands it all; Pippo is still very heedless for his age, and this makes me troubled for him and keeps me in continual sharp anxiety on his account, apart from the pain of being separated from him. I cannot get accustomed to this loneliness, especially after having the boys with me from morning till night for a whole year. May the will of God be done."

The correspondence between husband and wife was at this time all but paralysed by the severity of the police and the all too ready zeal of the Commandant of the Château d'If to carry out and even surpass the Minister's instructions. On Christmas Day, 1812, Cunegonda writes in great depression:

"I have let a few more days than usual go by without writing to you, my dear Giovanni. I confess that I am getting weary of writing uselessly, for I reflect that if this letter reaches you at all it will be over a month hence, and that is discouraging. After all, the only interesting subject on which we can speak to one another is that of our own and our friends' health—and if I tell you that we are all well

PETTY PERSECUTION

to-day, you will only know it towards February—and it takes away all one's wish to write.

"Never mind, let us persevere, in the hope that 'they' will get tired of always reading the same thing and will at last permit our letters to go through directly. It will be a year to-morrow since I left Rome—my dear Rome!"

A day or two later she remarks sarcastically: "It is really delightful to hear, on the 28th of December, that you have received my September letters! That becomes really interesting!" Then, softening, she says, as her New Year's greeting: "God grant that this coming year be happier than the one we have just passed through—at least, it could scarcely be worse!"

Indeed, the correspondence which could so greatly have lightened this time of trial for Giovanni and his wife had now become a source of constant worry and irritation. Although restricting themselves to the constant repetition of one or two uncompromising facts, which had to pass the judgment of the argus-eyed police, nothing was allowed to be forwarded to either of them without many weeks of delay, and, so long as the Empire lasted, it seemed to give actual pleasure to the authorities to make their situation as painful as possible. Giovanni's letters were allowed to pile up on the table of the Commandant of the fort, day after day—sometimes he waited till there were seven lying there before he sent them on to Paris—a negligence, indeed, for which he was at various times reproved by the Duc de Rovigo, who wished to be kept *au courant* of the Patrizi sentiments and concerns. These packets of correspondence lay about in the police office for an infinite time before being sent on to Rome or La Flèche, if they were judged innocuous; but if they aroused the slightest suspicion they were, as we have seen, forwarded to the Emperor for his personal perusal. The result was that very often a perfect mass of Patrizi correspondence lay jumbled up on the Minister's table. Those of Giovanni to his wife would (when somebody undertook to clear the papers up) all be forwarded together with those to his parents in Rome. Thence they were returned to the Château d'If, to start once more on their travels to Paris, and again reach the Duc de Rovigo. No wonder that months and months intervened between the writing and the reception of the missives!

CHAPTER XII

THE Marchesa found much consolation in the kind and amenable attitude of the Director of the College at La Flèche, General Duteil. This good man always sent the boys home for their holidays, and took advantage of any little indisposition of theirs which could furnish an excuse, without infringing the rules of the college, to let them be with their mother for a time.

Once, however, the good General becomes almost panic-stricken on hearing of a threatened visit of inspection, and writes in great haste to Cunegonda:

"MADAME,

"Having been informed by M. le General Bellevue that he is coming here immediately to make his inspection, it is indispensable that Messieurs your sons should at once return to the school. I know that the youngest is ill. You will keep him until he has recovered, but I must rely for this on your own delicate feeling, for you will understand that the sudden arrival of the Inspector would put me in an awkward position. It cannot be doubted that other parents, whose requests to have their children at home I have refused, would instantly inform him that I have permitted you to have yours. I will do everything in my power to facilitate your interviews with your sons. Pray believe, Madame, how much I desire to be agreeable to you. . . .

Your very humble and very obedient servant,

"Gen. Duteil."

On January 1, 1813, Cunegonda received from Rome the welcome news that the order of sequestration had been removed from all the Patrizi property except the estates in Tuscany, and these too were freed a few weeks later. Encouraged by this alleviation, Giovanni's mother urged him to write directly to the Duc de Rovigo, petitioning that his sentence of imprisonment might be commuted to one of exile, at La Flèche. This was unconditionally refused. Napoleon, who boasted of having introduced into Rome a judicial system which precluded the smallest possibility of partiality or injustice, was inflicting on a Roman citizen a severe imprisonment, without trial, without defined limit, an imprisonment which might well have proved life-long had not he who imposed it himself reached the extreme limit set for him by Divine Providence, and beyond which he was nevermore to exercise his own will.

But for those who loved Giovanni hope suddenly rose high. News had come of a reconciliation between the Pope and the Emperor.

THE "NEW CONCORDAT"

On the 31st of January Cunegonda writes:

"In your letter of the 10th, my dear Giovanni" (the letter must have echoed the sentiments of the authorities, to have been permitted to travel so fast!) "you beg me to speak no more of my hopes for your speedy liberation. At any other time I would have obeyed you, but to-day these hopes are too well confirmed to keep me from communicating them. The happy news of a new Concordat between our Holy Father and the Emperor seems to promise the accomplishment of our desires; so hope, my very dear one, hope! I trust that the hope I now bring you will not prove unfavourable to your health, for indeed it rests on solid foundations; you will agree with me on that point—and I begin to breathe again. Be sure that I shall neglect nothing to obtain this grace—it is too close to my heart. My sister writes that the Cardinals who were imprisoned at Vincennes have already been set free, as well as Monsignor de Gregorio and the Père Fontane, and that orders have been sent to Fenestrelle to bring Cardinal Pacca to Paris. That is all I know, for the moment."

The "New Concordat!" The words mark the saddest of all the sad pages of the life of Pius VII, and, one cannot but think, the darkest in the record of Napoleon. The Emperor, as every one knows, was threatening the Church with a Schism of the West which would have been more far-reaching in its direful consequences than any that had gone before. The ambassadors whom he selected to lay his terms before the Holy Father allowed themselves to be terrified into submission by the violence of his threats, not perceiving that this very violence betrayed an intense anxiety to come to an understanding. He felt not only that the moment had arrived when it would be to his advantage to put an end to the damaging spectacle presented to the world by the imprisonment of an aged and saintly Pontiff and all the most respected and influential members of his ecclesiastical Court; but, still more forcibly, that he could never overcome the stubborn opposition of the Roman people until he should be, in appearance, at least, reconciled with the Pope. He wished for peace; and, expecting the terms to be discussed and to some extent modified, he laid them down with a completeness and arrogance which one fancies he was far from expecting to see satisfied. He chose his ambassadors well. The four Cardinals, Doria, Ruffo, Dugnani, and de Bayane were men of timid dispositions, and were convinced that the Emperor meant what he said, and they exaggerated the import of his threats in repeating them to Pius VII, so that Napoleon himself must have been secretly surprised at the result.

On January 25, at Fontainebleau, the Pope, worn out, ill, vanquished more by the entreaties of his friends than the fear of his enemy, yielded so far as to allow his signature to be extorted—no other word suits the case—for the plan of a Concordat, which, it was clearly stated, could not come into force until approved and ratified by the whole of the Sacred College. Until that ratification should have taken place, all the parties to the proposition were bound over to maintain complete secrecy in regard to it. By the terms of this fatal document the Pope renounced his temporal power and obliged himself to reside in France or wherever the Emperor might wish to send him.

Napoleon, delighted with his victory, immediately set at liberty the Cardinals and Bishops detained in his various prisons. Then, reflecting that their representations might induce Pius VII to change his mind—and sure, moreover, that the approval of the Sacred College of Cardinals, on which the legality of the agreement was to depend, could never be obtained—he made one of those *coups de main* for which the Bonapartes are famous; he flung his promises of secrecy to the winds and published the text of the Concordat entire, stating that it was already agreed to unconditionally by the Holy See. The Chancellor Cambacérès read it aloud to the Legislative Body, the newspapers published it in full, salvos of artillery informed the people that peace was concluded, and Napoleon ordered Te Deums to be sung in all the churches to celebrate the happy event. Wise people said little; many, on reading the published text, believed it to be a forgery; others were convinced that the Pope's consent had been extorted by force, and thus rendered entirely illegal. All waited, eagerly or anxiously, according to their dispositions, for what would happen next.

Meanwhile the unfortunate Pontiff, torn with remorse at having even conditionally acceded to the Emperor's outrageous demands, fell into a state of such despairing melancholy that for several days he could not nerve himself to celebrate Mass. He accused himself of betraying his trust, forsaking his sheep, delivering the Patrimony of Peter into the hands of the spoiler. The Cardinals Pacca and Consalvi, who flew to his side the moment they came out of prison, had to use a gentle violence to draw him once more to the Altar which he said he had betrayed. The sustaining presence of these two faithful friends roused him at last from his despair. It was not enough to repent; he must undo the harm he had so unwillingly done. He must retract publicly. To this end he began to compose a manifesto, every word of which he submitted to the Cardinals and Bishops who were near at hand. But all this while he was under strict military surveillance, and it was exceedingly difficult to treat of such an important matter under the watchful eyes of the chief jailer, Colonel Lagorse, who had the strictest orders from the Emperor to prevent the Pope from touching in any way on public affairs in his interviews with the prelates until Napoleon himself should grant permission for him to do so. The strictest prohibition of all regarded Cardinal Di Pietro, of whose influence the Emperor stood in such fear that his first words after obtaining the Pope's signature to the Concordat were, "Now that Cardinal Di Pietro is coming, I suppose you will instantly go and confess to him!"

But the holy Cardinals and Bishops were too astute for the fierce Colonel. They were not in the least afraid of Napoleon, and the preparation of the manifesto went on quietly and carefully, as Cardinal Pacca relates in his Memoirs:

"In the morning, after the Pope had returned from Mass, Cardinals Di Pietro and Consalvi entered his apartment and passed him the sheet which he had written the day before. He then continued to work for a little. At half-past four I went to see him, and sometimes he added a few lines to what he had already done in the morning. Then I, slipping the notes and his manuscript under my robe, took the papers to the house where Cardinal Pignatelli was lodging, and from which they were returned to the Palace (to Di Pietro or Consalvi) by a sure hand the next morning."

All these precautions were necessary to prevent Lagorse from discovering that the Pope was preparing some document of importance and also to have none of the papers left in the Palace, where he might make some secret raid of inspection during the night. Also it was necessary that the Holy Father's advisers should be able to consult together and make suggestions or amendments on what he had written, and the fact that Cardinal Pignatelli was confined to his lodgings by illness gave him and the other prelates, who were allowed to visit him freely, the opportunity they required for reflection and discussion. "This went on for several days," Cardinal Pacca tells us, and when at last the letter was finished every point of importance was clearly set forth in it. To justify his action the Pope invoked the example of one of his predecessors, Pascal II, who in rather similar circumstances retracted a concession made to the Emperor Henry V, declaring it null and void because extorted by violence. Pius VII, however, desiring to be conciliatory, declared himself ready to accede to any terms which his conscience, aided by the Council of Cardinals, would permit.

The Emperor flew into one of his epic rages when the letter reached him. He communicated the contents at once to the Privy Council, abused the Pope, whom he called an "obstinate priest," and declared that he would have the heads of some of the prelates at Fontainebleau. There were not wanting among the imperial advisers some who pressed him to follow the example of Henry VIII of England and at once declare the independence of the Church in France; but the cold sense which rarely deserted Napoleon made him brusquely reject the impolitic proposition. Instead it was agreed that the initial violence should be supported by a particularly black piece of treachery. The Pope's retractation was to be quietly suppressed, and the terms of the already published Concordat further published, rigorously upheld, and, as soon as possible, carried out. It all seemed perfectly simple. But Napoleon did not deny himself the pleasure of punishing those who were responsible for his annoyance. In the dead of night on April 5, Colonel Lagorse entered the apartment of Cardinal Di Pietro, roused him from his sleep, and handed him over to a delegate of the police, who at once carried him off as a prisoner to Auxerre. And from that moment Pius VII and the Cardinals who remained in Paris became more than ever conscious that they were prisoners too. New and stricter regulations were ruthlessly enforced. Lagorse had orders to prevent all private intercourse with the Holy Father or among the prelates themselves. It was a persecution of every moment, and more than once the unfortunate Pontiff was forced to regret the comparative peace of his incarceration at Savona.

Thus matters dragged on through 1813, the Pope a helpless prisoner kept in complete ignorance of what was taking place around him in Paris, or—a far more painful privation—in his beloved Rome. Had he known the condition of things in France he might have drawn consolation from the heavy clouds which were gathering over his enemy's head.

Napoleon was losing his prestige; Europe, no longer hypnotised by his marvellous force and audacity, was preparing to dismember his empire; he was no longer constantly victorious, and the tremendous sacrifices demanded of the French, particularly the last levy, which had swept in recruits of barely fifteen years of age, had aroused universal indignation. Napoleon was no longer sure of himself. It was the beginning of the end.

The pretended Concordat, disastrous as it appeared on general grounds, was, very naturally, hailed with joy by some who saw in it the termination of their own sufferings. Cunegonda Patrizi, like a loving wife, could only think of one aspect of it. To her simple and honest mind it meant the liberation of Giovanni. She was sure now that any request made by the Pope would be instantly granted, and on February 7, just after the publication of the document, she wrote to her husband:

"If you have read the Gazette you will have seen . . . that there is an article in the Concordat which appears to touch you and many other persons, and in view of this I and all others who have read it believe that you will very shortly be set at liberty. You said that you thought I must have got tired of expecting you by every post, and had probably by this time ceased to think of your coming at all. But I assure you that it is quite the contrary. Only yesterday I believed it still, and Marianna" (the maid), "who was crossing the square when the *calèche* arrived, was much agitated because she made sure that you were in it. So you see I am not the only one to have faith in your coming; every time the Chevalier hears the crack of a whip he thinks it is you!"

Fired with hope and confidence, the Marchesa wrote to her old friend Cardinal Pacca:

"Since I was not able to have the good fortune of personally congratulating Your Eminence, may I be permitted to do so most warmly in these few lines, which must also express all the gratitude I feel for the repeated remembrances with which Your Eminence has honoured me in my husband's letters. At the same time I will venture to remind Your Eminence of that companion of your imprisonment, who has now languished for six months, immured in the Château d'If, my many efforts for his deliverance having all been made in vain. This is the time when Your Eminence can show greater kindness than ever to that unhappy man by persuading our Holy Father to ask for his liberation, and let him add that of our sons, the only children who were brought here and consigned" (to the College) "*by the direct hand of the Government.*"

This was a proof of Patrizi's loyalty to his Sovereign, which certainly contrasted favourably with the supine acquiescence of other Roman parents of his own class. Cunegonda continues:

"No one is better acquainted with all the facts of the case than Your Eminence, and from Don Marino, who will have the honour of presenting this letter to you, you will learn of all that has happened to me recently. So I look to Your Eminence for consolation after all these misfortunes, and I have the firm trust that you will not only grant the favour I ask, but plead for it so zealously that I shall soon experience the happy result, and thus have still new motives for the gratitude, affection, and respect which I have for so long professed for Your Eminence, and which I now renew.

"Remaining Your Eminence's humble, devoted, and obedient servant,

"CUNEGONDA OF SAXONY PATRIZI."

Cardinal Pacca's reply, of which the reasons are clear to us, must have puzzled and discouraged the poor Marchesa, ignorant of the circumstances attending the publication of the new Concordat. After the usual friendly greetings he says:

"I would at once have executed the commission you entrusted to me had I considered the present circumstances propitious; but, unfortunately, they are not that yet. Rest assured, however, that I will take advantage of the earliest favourable moment. I will not talk to you of my recent fellow prisoner, for fear of saddening you; I will only say that I love him as tenderly as a brother.

"Let us pray continually to God that He will reunite us where we have lived in the past, and yet more that He will deign to do so in that life where there is no sorrow or trial or bitterness. . . ."

On the same day Cunegonda was writing to her husband:

"*February* 13, 1813.

"I will do as you wish and wait till the end of this month before taking any new steps to obtain your liberation. It is too true that the fifteen days at the end of which the promise had been held out to me have been unduly prolonged; God grant we may be nearing the end now; as for me, I hope it more and more, and you can imagine how I desire it; on Friday it will be fifteen months since we were separated. How much we have suffered in that time!"

She draws, or pretends to draw, hope even from Cardinal Pacca's letter. "Barthelmie, the Lamb, writes to me showing the greatest interest in you, saying that he loves you as if you were his brother. I did not doubt it, indeed; but his expressions were very consoling."

As the Government were sedulously circulating the terms of the Concordat, which implied amnesty for political prisoners, the Marchesa very soon attacked the Cardinal again on the subject of her husband, making her excuse for writing her wish to thank His Eminence for his kind letter.

Her graciously worded acknowledgments only thinly veil the real purpose, her feverish anxiety to have him plead Giovanni's cause. Her surprise and mystification were great when a tiny note, undated, unaddressed, and written in a disguised hand, was secretly conveyed to her. It seemed as if the Cardinal were once more undergoing the rigours and espionage of imprisonment. Its contents show that he thought her plea would have a better chance coming directly from herself.

"Do not hesitate to address to the Government a petition demanding the full and complete liberty of your husband, and suggest to him that he do the same. . . .
"The Lamb."

The advice seems rash, and nothing that can be found in the papers of the persons concerned appears to justify it at that moment; but the Cardinal may have had some kind of verbal encouragement from one in authority which led him to give it. In any case, we know the attempt was doomed to failure. Cunegonda's multiplied applications and petitions could not have been launched at a worse moment. The Emperor and his underlings were too thoroughly out of temper with the Holy Father to set at large one of his most ardently devoted subjects just then. But Cunegonda was incorrigible. No disillusion discouraged her for long, and her enthusiastic trustfulness came, very naturally, to add pang after pang to the sorrows of the lonely prisoner in the Château d'If.

We get a pathetic glimpse of him from time to time. He had been shut up in his room for three whole months when he received permission to go out and walk about the fortifications.

"A small consolation!" he exclaims in his journal. The monotony of his existence must have been fearfully wearing, for he says later that this incident was the only new thing that happened during nine months of his imprisonment. He tried to shorten the unending days by study and some literary work, one item being the translation into Italian verse—and a very fair one—of Racine's tragedy *Bajazet*. There are also some original dramatic pieces; but one feels in all this the lassitude of a brave mind that occupies itself merely not to give way to despair. It was, after all, only his deep religious faith that supported him through this dreary period and enabled him, deprived of all outward exercises of piety—for the celebration of Mass was forbidden in the fort—to still resign himself wholly to the Divine Will.

Had his correspondence with his wife been less cruelly trammelled he would have drawn great consolation from her loving, hopeful letters. But the barbarous restrictions placed on the interchange caused those letters to reach him only two, three, sometimes even seven, months after they were written, and it is small wonder that Giovanni came to feel that he scarcely belonged any more to the land of the living. This depression shows through his fortitude in the letters he writes to his wife. He is longing to speak to her, but he fears to impose the weight of his own melancholy on her gallant spirit ; and, too, the knowledge that every word will be read by hostile eyes before it is allowed to reach the person addressed is anything but an inspiring factor in correspondence.

With himself in his Journal and Memoirs he can be quite frank, and one gets a very graphic idea of his circumstances. Certain regulations were bitterly humiliating to the noble and the gentleman, however the Christian in him might strive to regard them.

"On the 23rd of May," he writes (1813), "there came to the fort the Count Thibeaudeau, Prefect of the Department of Bouches-du-Rhône, with the two Privy Councillors Appelins and Fort. These last had been sent from Paris to make the annual visit to the state prisons, a visit which was omitted last year. I was called, like the rest of my colleagues here, into their presence, and had to answer their questions as to my name, age, my country, my status, etc., etc. They asked if I was married, if I had children, whether these were boys or girls, and what was the age of the eldest. They ended by asking me where my sons were, and I, having answered all of the other questions, replied that two of them were at La Flèche, having been seized and placed there. Then I was asked if I had been arrested in Rome, and if I had been in prison at Fenestrelle, and the Privy Councillors said that if I had complaints to make or petitions to present they would see that these should reach the Emperor.

"I replied that many applications had been made for me in vain by other persons, and I asked that, if I was not to be set at liberty, I might be allowed to return to my former prison at Fenestrelle, where I had the advantage of being with my compatriots; and I added that, since I was in any case a prisoner, the authorities could just as well keep me in one place as the other."

Some more perfectly futile questions followed, and Patrizi returned to his cell, congratulating himself, one imagines, on having kept his temper through the interrogatory. But that day, at sunset, he and the other prisoners had at least the diversion of real excitement, for an English vessel, coming very close in, opened fire on the fort with a fierce cannonade, and the fort instantly touched up its mouldering guns and answered the compliment. The exchange of shots continued for about an hour in quite a lively fashion. The result of this affair was the capture of a mercantile vessel by the English in the port of Marseilles; but it was almost immediately set free, being furnished with papers which proved that it was not proper booty of war.

"On the 22nd of May the representatives of the

Imperial Procurator-General came to the fort to verify the list of the prisoners. They asked me my name and nothing more."

The year 1813 was to be a sadder one yet for Giovanni, and marked by an irreparable loss. His father's health had long been failing, and the recent trials and anxieties had greatly enfeebled him. So early as May of the year before, the grief of Giovanni's imprisonment had brought on an illness which threatened to be mortal, and under this impression he had written what he thought might possibly be his last letter to the dearly loved son, who was never absent from his thoughts.

"ROME, *May* 12, 1812.

"MY MOST DEAR SON,

"Aboccultis meis libera me Dne, et ab alienis parce servo tuo." *

"Here is a fine beginning for the letter of a father to a son, particularly when he has not written to him for so long, except in postscripts to your mother's letters!

"But I believe you will find it right and just, for the reasons which I will now expose to you.

"I believe that every man, and more especially the father of a family, when the passing of the years brings him near the last great step, should try to repair the scandal he may have given, and should

---

* "Deliver me from my secret faults, O Lord, and forgive Thy servant his errors!"

MARCHESE FRANCESCO NARO PATRIZI.
The Father of Giovanni.

ask God for grace to be able to do so. This grace I have asked and still ask constantly.

"I am old, you are far away from me, I do not know how long that absence will last, and consequently I do not know whether you will be at my bedside in my last illness as I should wish; so it is right that now, when for a few days, through the mercy of God, I am suffering less from my infirmities and the oppression of my spirit, I should anticipate the fulfilment of this duty to you, and I propose to do so in this present letter.

" By the grace of God, I think I have given no direct scandal to you or to others; ' nil mihi conscius sum, sed in hoc non justificatus sum '*; but indirectly, who can say how much? With my whole heart I ask pardon for it of the Divine Majesty, and I beseech that no one may have to suffer misery through my fault; God grant it.

". . . To speak of other things . . . your Costantino is as good as possible, and provides all our amusement at the dinner-table, and he is my best solace when he comes into my room after his hours of study and spiritual occupation. He opens every book he finds, so it seems as if he would grow up into a great literary man. Joking apart, he is a good child, and I as well as you must thank God for the good characters of your children. May He confirm that which He has worked in us!"

* "My conscience does not reproach me, but not for that am I justified."

Towards the end of the year the Marchese's condition grew rapidly worse. On December 2, shortly before his death, he dictated what he knew would be his last letter to his son (in order to conform to the prison regulations at Château d'If it was written in French):

"My very dear Son,
"May the Father of Mercies and the God of all consolation be ever blessed and praised! You suffer, in this present life, but you are acquiring at the same time great merit for the life to come. If you have not quite the patience of Job, at least you have enough to ensure the salvation of your soul, for the good God permits us to be tempted to prove our virtue, but never beyond the limit of our strength. The deprivation of the Angels' Bread, which so deeply afflicts you, can be and certainly is a source of merit, and the ardour with which you so eagerly desire it and the spiritual Communion, which you can renew as often as you like, will take the place of actual participation in the Sacrament. The penitent Mary of Egypt, during the twenty-three or twenty-five years which she passed in the desert, only received Holy Communion at the time of her death—yet she is a saint, and even very famous in the Church. Courage, then, dear son; endure all that the good God asks of you, and keep ever before your eyes the great maxim that we suffer here for

only a short time, while that" (happiness) "which awaits us is, God helping, eternal.

"As for examples, your good mother has given you excellent ones to follow; but, alas! we will not speak of mine. I fear to have had the misfortune to have given you none that you should imitate. I wrote you this on the 12th of May, 1812, and I pray in the bitterness of my heart that the good God will forgive me all and accept the sacrifice of my heart united to the infinite merits of the blood of Jesus Christ. Add your fervent prayers to mine. . . .

"You have chosen an excellent author—Thomas à Kempis! What a beautiful book, and how helpful it will be to you in your solitude! If it arouses in you the desire to approach the Holy Table, and this unsatisfied desire disquiets you, you must not value it the less for that, for it will be to you the occasion of gaining new merit. . . . Your mother blesses you and embraces you; Costantine kisses your hands and asks for your blessing. Your aunt and your sisters send most loving greeting. . . . The Secretary does the same. I embrace thee with all my heart and bless thee, for I am thy loving Father,

"FRANCESCO."

The last words are written in his own hand; the rest was apparently dictated to Don Joseph de Ligne, the children's tutor.

Giovanni received this letter, written on December 2, some days after his father's death, which took place in January 1814. The prisoner could not even have the comfort of writing to his wife in this great sorrow, for he feared that she might still not have received news of their loss, and felt that it would cause her less of a shock to learn it from her mother-in-law than to be told of it by himself. But in truth the sad announcement had arrived at La Flèche sooner than it had at Marseilles; and Cunegonda was also afraid to write of it, wishing that her dear prisoner might remain in ignorance of his bereavement as long as possible. At last, in a letter written on March 13, she gave voice, though still restrainedly, to her feelings:

"You dare not write openly to me about your father's death, because you fear I may not yet have been informed of it. What new kind of torture is this, to be kept two or three months in ignorance of something which touches us both so closely! One has to fall back on saying, 'God wills it so,' otherwise our human weakness could not bear it; but He gives His aid in the measure in which it is needed. So let us have ever-increasing confidence in His infinite and all-powerful goodness. . . . Continue, my well-beloved Giovanni, to seek your only consolation in raising your thoughts to Heaven. . . . As long as I know that you have recourse to this, I shall fear nothing for you!"

Cunegonda's words were notably verified at this

moment, for the loving Providence of God, on whose assistance she counted for her husband in his grief, sent him that for which he had been longing so earnestly, an opportunity of approaching the Sacraments. Two good priests, one French and one Italian, were unexpectedly transferred from the prison of Compiano to that of the Château d'If, and obtained from the Minister of Police the permission to celebrate Mass. The first occasion on which they did so was Easter Day (April 10), and Giovanni Patrizi was able to assist at the Holy Sacrifice and receive Holy Communion, after being deprived of that inestimable benefit for two years and two days.

CHAPTER XIII

WE must retrace our steps a little in order to follow the thread of Cunegonda's life at La Flèche during her husband's second year in prison. Now and then some friend or relative came to visit her, or the parents of some of her sons' companions at the school passed a few days in the dull little country town. In May her brother-in-law, Prince Altieri, brought a breath from her own world, which must have been refreshing to the lonely lady. Her faithful companion, the "incomparable friend," Don Lorenzo Giustiniani, was apparently as silent as he was devoted, and her letters give us glimpses of the appalling monotony of their existence when the boys were shut up in the college. She always shows her relief when some real incident has occurred with which she can enliven her husband in his distant solitude. Without possessing a particle of malice, Cunegonda was a keen observer of human nature, and her curt yet graphic descriptions of people bring the subjects of them very vividly before our eyes.

Of Altieri she writes: "He arrived here the other night with his son Auguste, all his representations and petitions to have the child dispensed from coming to this school, on account of his delicate health, having been made in vain. I found the Prince looking much aged, and Auguste is thinner than before—if that was possible! I hope my sister" (Princess Altieri) "will come and establish herself here too. . . . I never told you that her eldest son was sent back to her by the Emperor's order, at the beginning of this year, on account of his health."

The Marchesa learnt from Prince Altieri that her eldest sister, the Duchesse d'Esclignac, whom she had not seen for twenty-three years, had come to Paris, and was arranging to pay her a visit at La Flèche. They had parted in haste at the outbreak of the Revolution—what memories they would call up together, what confidences they would be able to exchange! "With Altieri," Cunegonda writes, "came Count Baglioni (an Umbrian nobleman) to visit all the boys who were brought here from Perugia, and of whom a large number are his own nephews. He passed the greater part of his time while here in sleeping; in the day, in the evening, he falls asleep with a facility which I have never seen in any one else. If he has not spoken for a minute or so you may be almost sure he is asleep, and since Altieri (as you know) never wants to sleep, they form an amusing contrast."

Then the Marchesa hears from the Patrizi Steward in Siena that the Bailli Ruspoli has left that place suddenly, in the night, without telling any one where he was going, but saying mysteriously that he had a long journey before him! Towards the end of May the good old gentleman appeared in Paris, and announced his intention of travelling sixty miles farther to visit his beloved niece and her children at La Flèche. But to his and her disappointment some very urgent question relating to the Order of Malta demanded his instant presence elsewhere, and he had to leave France without carrying out his intention. At the end of June three of the five daughters of Prince Xavier of Saxony were at last reunited for a short time, and great was Cunegonda's joy when she and Lise (the Duchesse d'Esclignac) and Marianna Altieri could " talk out," as women love to do, all big and little things that lay nearest their hearts. The two weeks they passed together were the least sad part of Cunegonda's exile.

On July 4, 1813, she writes to Giovanni:

"My sisters are here since last Thursday. I found Lise much altered, but still very sweet and gay. We take long walks together; that is the only diversion I can offer her here; but, as she does not care about worldly amusements, she does not seem bored. She has brought Ernest, the youngest of her boys, who is three months older than our Xavier; he is big and strong for his age, but nothing like Xavier, who is already much taller and stronger than he. Ernest arrived here pretending that he was

Lise's courier, and told us that she would come in a quarter of an hour, and that I was to go and wait for her at her house. As I did not know the boy, I believed him at first; but after a little it struck me that the pretended courier might be my nephew, and I asked him where my sister had left her son Ernest? He smiled and said she was bringing him with her, and then I understood. Lise is longing to make your acquaintance, and I am sorry she is to stay here such a short time."

Always the hope that Giovanni would come! The load of disappointment and weariness settled very heavily on Cunegonda after her sisters had left her; but, as she tells Giovanni, she had become so accustomed to trouble that it would have seemed to her quite unnatural to have any lasting pleasure or consolation now.

From August onwards the correspondence becomes sadder and sadder. Patrizi was tortured by having his wife's letters kept back month after month, and during those cruel silences he was left to imagine the thousand misfortunes which might already have fallen on those he loved. He wrote few letters himself now—it seemed almost useless—but from those which Cunegonda never ceased to address to him it is easy to reconstruct the history of this, the most mournful period of their long separation. In truth, after making sure that he was to be immediately set at liberty, it finally became clear to both husband and wife that an imperious and inexorable will had been imposed, and that all entreaties, all attempts to change it, were doomed to be hopeless. Giovanni fell into such profound mental prostration that he at last told his wife that it would be better for them to give up writing to each other altogether, since the letters were either never delivered at all, or else came so long after they were written that they only added to the agonies of the suspense; and also that he found it intolerable only to treat of matters which could pass the censorship of the police when aching to speak of things infinitely closer to both their hearts.

La Flèche was anything but a salubrious residence, lying, as it did, close to great marshes, which spread the miasma of malaria over all the district, and in September poor little Filippo was laid low with Tertian fever. The Marchesa writes that this was regarded as an ordinary indisposition at La Flèche, and expresses her surprise at the happy-go-lucky methods prevailing for the treatment of it.

"They do not even think of giving Pippo quinine!" she exclaims. "Yesterday they administered an emetic . . . to-morrow he is to have an infusion of bitters, and the fever will disappear little by little! Here they think only unhealthy old persons can catch a 'pernicious' fever, so they very rarely give any quinine to children."

It seemed almost as if the French doctors might be right, for a few days later the Marchesa writes that the trouble seems to be passing. She had, however, insisted on some small doses of quinine.

"I hope Pippo's fever is over," she writes, "for it was due yesterday and did not come. He had only had three-eighths" (of a grain) "of quinine, and that smelt of nothing but mould! It shows the difference of climate, for in Italy they would have made him take at least a grain."

She has but little to relate to Giovanni at this time, and tries to make up for the exclusion of her former all-absorbing hopes of his liberation by writing of any small change or incident that takes place. In looking at the long, beautifully written letters (for Gondina was one of those people who put the touch of exquisite care on everything they do) one feels that the "miraculous hands" must often have ached with weariness—that only the valiant woman's heart gave her courage to write at all! She tells of little indispositions of the children, of making acquaintance at La Flèche with the Duchess of Bracciano (Bracciano was held by the Odescalchi at that time) whom she describes as "a very good sort of woman, who asked after you with much interest"; she tells of Romans who came from time to time to see their boys at the school, of births and marriages among their friends, now and then of some strange dream she has had. She scarcely knows what to write; life is very grey and sad, and now and then, in spite of all her courage, she nearly breaks down. Only nearly, for her faith always triumphs over the momentary weakness in the end. Once she writes:

"What a comfort it would be to you to weep on the heart of some one who could understand and sympathise with your sorrows! I can do that sometimes; but more often my tears flow in solitude, and I find great easing so, because, although apparently alone, I offer the tears I shed in the Presence of the only true Consoler."

The autumn vacations brought a little more brightness into her life and that of the two boys. She had had a letter from Giovanni in which he told her he had dreamt he was a Cardinal.

"Your letter of the 20th made us all laugh at the curious dream you describe; I was quite pleased to find myself, in spite of your new rank, recognised as alive, since you say I am to address you as 'Eminence'! We, too, often amuse ourselves by recounting our dreams. At least, it makes us laugh—and then it is so hard to find anything to talk about, especially when I am here alone with the Chevalier. Just now I am so happy as to have my children with me, and, as you know, the silliest little thing is enough to interest them and set them chattering!" In the same letter she speaks of the portraits that Giovanni had asked for, many months earlier. "You reproach me with my credulity which prevented me from having them taken and sent to you, as you wished. I have reproached myself many times since then!"

In October Giovanni obtained the Commandant's permission to have a little dinner in honour of his mother's name-day.

"I was very pleased," Cunegonda writes, "to learn that you had celebrated your mother's birthday with some of your companions in misfortune, and I am not surprised when you tell me that your tears fell when her health was drunk!"

The little relaxation at the prison was followed by—perhaps, caused—new strictness to be exercised towards the Marchese and his companions. Orders came to forbid the prisoners to take any more walks round the bastions, and the deprivation of even this slight solace was very keenly felt. Giovanni began to feel more acutely than ever the sad isolation of his lot, and spoke in his letters to his wife of the constant longing for home and family which tormented him, and which she felt too, although all her thoughts seem to have been for him.

"I know too well," she writes, "that our union has not been a source of happiness for you, although in your goodness you say that it has." (Here she seems to be referring to Napoleon's marked hostility to her own family, which she believed had been the real cause of many of her husband's misfortunes.) "God give me grace to make it true in the future! ... You had a moment of consolation in seeing the handwriting of our children, and they, on their part, were enchanted yesterday when they received your reply. I can assure you that I have been, and am, very satisfied about them in every way, and I hope, when you see them, that you will be as pleased with them as I am. I am sure your prayers have done much for them. Xavier is already taller than I am—I just reach to his ear; Pippo, too, has grown, but not much. Yes, most certainly I insist upon your regarding me as a Roman! I am, because I have my home there; but much more because I love it dearly . . . for many years I have had the good fortune to be able to regard it as truly my own country. God grant that we may see it very soon!"

The year 1814 opened sadly enough for Cunegonda. In January she writes: "Humanly speaking, I am happier in the night than in the day, for scarcely a night passes that I do not find myself transported to Rome. . . . What a sad kind of pleasure it is to have to be impatient for night to come—to bring consolation in a dream!"

She is pleasantly surprised to find that there is a circulating library at La Flèche, and that " for forty sous a month " she can have " as many books " as she likes! Immediately she plunges into reading. "It is my only distraction," she says, and at once begins to speak of Chateaubriand. " I have never read the 'Génie du Christianisme'; but I hear it favourably spoken of, and sometimes unfavourably. The author was Secretary of Embassy at Rome in the time of Count Fesch—not under the Consulate.

I have just finished another book by the same writer, 'Itinéraire de Paris à Jérusalem!' I found it extremely interesting, not so much for the matter itself as for the manner in which it is written. They gave me after that 'Les Martyrs'; but, finding that it was merely a romance, I did not read it."

Cunegonda, it will be remembered, had been described at the time of her marriage as 'very cultured,' and the years that followed had not been intellectually idle; capable of appreciating the best, she had not fallen into the modern error of reading for the 'style' alone, that vain excuse offered by so many persons now for poring over abominations presented in precious vessels. Apart from her unceasing striving after perfection, she felt, at this period of her life, when she was left alone to face terrible difficulties and still heavier responsibilities, the necessity of strengthening herself for the conflict by feeding her mind and heart with serious reading, and she voluntarily puts aside everything which might in her forlorn condition, ever so slightly even, savour of worldly vanities.

The sweetness and humility of her character are very charmingly revealed in a letter a little later than the last. She says, "For about a month we have had here three or four hundred Spanish prisoners who have been in France for three years. They are excellent fellows, and everybody likes them because they are so gentle and quiet. They work to earn a little money, and this morning one of them brought me some straw baskets made with great delicacy and taste. I like to talk Italian to them, as they understand it better than French. The other day one of them was sawing wood and bringing it into the house for me. He told me he had been in the army for thirty years, and had served under Carlo Tercero" (Charles III of Spain). "I did not tell him that the king was my uncle, because that seemed to me proud; but I am sure the man would have been pleased if I had, for he seemed to speak of him with affection."

How did this letter strike the Duc de Rovigo when it passed through his hands, coming from her who was called by the police " that arrogant Saxon Princess "?

During this long, quiet period at La Flèche the 'incomparable friend,' Don Lorenzo Giustiniani, a man who had the rare talent of devoting himself to the Marchesa, her children, her interests, without claiming a moment of her time, without ever getting in her way, always effacing himself but always there, a silent, faithful, lynx-eyed guardian, had thought it incumbent upon him also to improve his mind and increase his mental resources by prayer and study—Cunegonda often speaks of him in her letters to Giovanni, and says that he is "always serene, and utterly undisturbed by the discomforts of a small establishment and a climate so different from the Roman one." Before leaving home he had begun to write a résumé of Ecclesiastical History, and at this he continued to work regularly during the whole two years of absence, for five or six hours every day.

The love of work is catching. When the boys came to their mother for the holidays they invented various occupations for themselves. Filippo sends his father a map which he had drawn, and Patrizi, pleased with its execution, writes to his wife that he would like to have the boy take drawing lessons. Cunegonda replies, " If you knew this enchanting spot you would never have written that I would do better to let Pippo copy some original from the ' Beaux Arts '; it would be difficult—I fancy impossible—to find such a thing here! Besides, the copying of the maps was only done in his hours of recreation; it amused him so much, and I was better pleased that he should do that than nothing at all. My house is so tiny that the boys cannot even run about; sometimes they go for a few minutes into the garden, but that, I think, is hardly as large as the courtyard of our house in Rome."

Once before, she had spoken frankly of the dullness and ugliness of La Flèche, where, as she puts it, " everything seems to be wanting." But, she adds patiently, " Perhaps my opinion of it should not be taken too seriously. I see it only through tears. I suffer here too much in every way to be an impartial judge."

Before the end of 1813 she tells Giovanni of the vicissitudes of various friends who are serving—

much against their will, doubtless—in the imperial army. "Don Pompeo Gabrielli and Don Giulio Lante have been taken prisoners; the former is wounded in the thigh. Don Mommo Odescalchi was at Hamburg on October 1; Don Camillo Ruspoli is a prisoner of the Austrians at Prague."

Among the great names the humble one of Marianna, the maid, is never omitted. She sends "handkissings to the master," but she cannot get on at all with her French. Her vocabulary is limited to "Oui, Madame," "Venez ici," "Monsu' Cavalier," and "Madame est sortie!" and she is dying of longing to be in her own country, where she can make people understand her!" "Monsu' Cavalier" (Giustiniani), who had suffered at first from the same disabilities as poor Marianna—(how strangely it strikes one now that a man of his position should never have taken the trouble to learn French!)—has overcome the language with a mighty effort, chiefly, it would seem, in order to be able to write to his friend at the Château d'If, where such letters as were passed at all had to be written in French. By December 1813 he acquits himself with much credit.

"My very dear friend," he writes, "Madame, your wife, reproaches me very justly for never having written you a few lines in this language, which is so foreign to us, even after your children had already succeeded in doing so. I blushed with shame, I admitted my fault, for which, indeed, I intended to atone last week. . . . But what shall I say to you in the conditions in which both you and we are at present? Simply that I love you dearly, that you are always present in my heart, which remembers you even without my consent; that is to say, when I am asleep. And then I wish to recommend to you my poor sister, for whose health, now exceedingly enfeebled, I tremble continually. I beg you, my friend, to offer fervent prayers to the good God that He will dispose all things for the best for her, and, when you pray, remember her brother, who is also more yours in Jesus Christ than simply your very affectionate friend,

"LORENZO GIUSTINIANI."

As we have seen, this year of 1814, which was, indeed, to end all their troubles, began sadly enough for the Patrizis, in Rome, at La Flèche, and at the prison rock of the Château d'If. Towards the middle of February some excitement was caused in the latter place by the sudden appearance, one afternoon, of a barge displaying the imperial flag, and evidently conveying some high official. The personage proved to be M. de Vandouvre, the Commissioner-General of Police at Marseilles, with a number of persons in his suite, some of them wearing the tricolor sash of office. The party went to the Commandant's apartment and immediately from thence to the prison, where M. de Vandouvre entered the room of one Rochelle, where he remained shut up a long time, putting the prisoner through a very severe examination and sequestrating a great quantity of his papers. On emerging with these in his hands, he ordered that M. Rochelle should be kept in the most rigorous solitary confinement. Patrizi, recording the incident in his diary, says: "While this was going on the Chevalier Lehara and I, who had been having our meals together since the 7th of January, ordered our dinner to be brought in. One of our guards who waited upon us, having brought the first dishes, remained in the room—a strange thing, which he had never done before. When we asked him to go and fetch the rest of our dinner he replied that he could not. We insisted on further explanations, and then he told us, with much confusion (for he was really a very honest fellow), that he had received orders not to leave the room. This answer surprised us, and caused our appetite to disappear on the instant. The matter seemed so ominous that we plied him with questions, and at last he told us that he had been commanded not to lose sight of M. Lehara, adding, however, that the order did not regard myself, and that I was at liberty to go in and out of my room as I pleased.

"I must confess that, in spite of my anxiety for my friend, this news consoled me a good deal. Had the case been different I should have had to be anxious both for him and myself! I at once profited by the liberty granted me, to leave my friend's room, where we had been dining, and go down to my own, which was reached by a small wooden staircase, that of M. Lehara having been built into the lower room like a closed 'loge' at a theatre. As soon as I was in my own apartment I hastened to sort out some papers which I thought might prove dangerous and threw them into the stove. The dinner now being terminated, the Commissioner and his suite . . . entered the room of M. Lehara. I left at once." (The Marchese has evidently returned upstairs to his friend.) "There were loud words between the Commissioner and M. Lehara; a strict perquisition of his effects was made, and he was condemned to solitary confinement." (This meant no communication with any person except his jailers.)

"Two days later the Commissioner returned with his satellites and carried out the same measures with regard to Major Rousillon, also examining five other prisoners, who had been implicated in the celebrated affair of Moreau, Pichegru and Georges Cadoudal in 1804.*

"At his first visit the Commissioner-General had left new and rigorous orders. The prisoners were not to be allowed to come down from the prison building to the 'place,' or square of the fort; they were not to receive any newspapers, and no person whatever was to enter the prison itself except the turnkey and his two assistants, which order appeared to exclude even the Commandant. No

* See Appendix, "A Diplomatist's Wife in Many Lands," Vol. II.

explanation was given, and we could not divine the motive of all this severity, or of the measures taken against the three men who had been placed in isolation. On the 21st and 22nd of February thirty prisoners were transferred from Compiano in Italy to the Château d'If, because of the approach of the Allies; and on this occasion the three men who had just been condemned to isolation were once more put on the same footing as all the rest, which made us think that there was nothing in particular against them, and that the whole thing was merely an attempt on the part of the already tottering Government to inspire terror at that critical moment.

"For, in spite of the prohibition of all newspapers, there came through to our ears the comforting news of the war, which showed that Napoleon's affairs were already going lame" (*andavono zoppe*). "The very guards set to keep us . . . made a merit of telling us all that was going on, and it was the turnkey himself who gave me the news of the taking of Paris by the Allies.

"Therefore we lived in the sweet hope that our troubles would soon be ended, our shackles struck off. On the 14th of April another prisoner confided to me that an ecclesiastic had come from Marseilles, and, having gone to visit Olive, the good, honest man who supplied our food, he had announced to him the abdication of Bonaparte and the proclamation of Louis XVIII, and told him further that the island of Elba had been assigned to the discredited Emperor, with a good sum of money. I made haste to tell all my colleagues these most comforting news, and it can easily be imagined what our emotions were. The adorable Providence of God thus gently prepared our hearts for a joy which, had it come too suddenly, would have been too great to be borne."

At La Flèche they were still in ignorance of the march of events, and Cunegonda, all unconscious that her sorrows would be ended in a few days, seems at last to have given way to the lassitude of despair. So late as March 27 she writes :

"I received this week, my dear Giovanni, your two letters of the 18th and 25th of February. The first was sealed and bore the Marseilles postmark, so that I had a moment's hope that some change had been made in your circumstances, and I opened it hurriedly. I understood my mistake when I saw that everlasting date of the Château d'If. My God! how it hurts me to see it, and how it must hurt you to write it!"

Fifteen days later Cunegonda addressed a letter to Giovanni, not to the Château d'If, but to Marseilles . . . and the letter began, "Alleluia! Alleluia!"

In Giovanni's diary, kept for nearly two years, the record of his weary imprisonment at the Château d'If closes with the simple word "Liberty."

CHAPTER XIV

"On that same evening, the 14th," Giovanni Patrizi writes in his Memoirs, "our guard, when they came as usual to lock us up, asked us if we had seen the illuminations made in Marseilles to celebrate the 'Peace' of which the news had just arrived. I laughed at this word 'Peace,' employed to mark the downfall of the Tyrant. Luckily the one tiny window of our room looked towards Marseilles. I flew to open it, and saw the glow of the *feux de joie* blazing in the great city.

"The sight sent us nearly mad with joy, and, as soon as the guards had locked us in and gone away, we began to give vent to our delight, embracing one another, dancing up and down, indulging in every wild demonstration that the unfortunate are capable of when they see that their troubles are over. I instantly brought out my whole provision of tallow candles, some twenty in all, and, in the absence of candlesticks, stuck them in bottles and lighted them to celebrate the coming deliverance. My four colleagues did the same, so that our dark cell looked like a brilliantly lit ballroom. Nor did we forget to turn gratefully to our Heavenly

Benefactor, singing in low voices the Te Deum, and closing with the prayer designated for it, as well as with those for the Supreme Pontiff and the King of France.

"Very little did we sleep that night, in which we had the certain hope that all would now be changed for us. The longed-for dawn came at last, and very early we heard the beating of the drums, which announced the arrival of an official launch. We climbed to the terrace to see what was going on, and perceived that, the moment the persons in the boat disembarked, the garrison of the fortress crowded round them to read a paper they had brought. The next moment we heard some one exclaim, 'The eagle is not upon it!'—for the newspapers till now had all been marked with that emblem. The paper was brought into the prison. It was stamped with the three lilies, and contained the act of the Senate of Paris, which, Bonaparte being deposed, had proclaimed allegiance to Louis XVIII. After this good news our French priest made ready to say Mass; but, just as he was about to begin vesting himself, he was requested to wait awhile, as another official boat was approaching the fort.

"I quickly returned to the terrace above, and, oh! what was my joy to see that they were flying the white flag! To greet and honour it, I pulled out my pocket-handkerchief; a companion helped me to hold it out wide, so that it waved above the towers of the fort—so that to a Roman fell the honour of once more raising the royal standard upon those walls from which it had been torn twenty-five years before in the insane frenzy of mistaken liberty!

"The common rejoicing was increased when there disembarked from the boat several officers decorated with white cockades, and we heard them raise the great French cry, 'Vive le Roi!' Most heartily did we all echo that cry; and then we were immediately informed that we were all free, but they begged us to wait where we were till the following day. The Commandant now approached our jubilant group, looking very confused and dismayed, and I think he was going to complain about our shouts; but some newspapers closed his mouth, and one of the prisoners ordered him to shout 'Vive le Roi!' which he promptly did. Indeed, we were out of minds with joy, and were showing it in a thousand crazy ways, when we were suddenly told to get ready to leave the fort, as we were to be taken away in a very short time.

"I cannot say what the others did at this announcement, but I ran to my room and began to pack my properties in a great hurry. I had completed my task some hours, and yet there appeared no prospect of departure from that miserable island.

"It was almost night when another officer arrived, sent from Marseilles by the Commandant there, who we hoped would prove to be our angel of deliverance ; but he, after saying a thousand amiable things, and embracing us all one after the other, quenched our hopes of liberty for that day, and made it seem doubtful whether they would even be realised on the next. This intimation put us in rather a bad temper, and we decided to send back by the officer a letter to the Commandant at Marseilles . . . begging him to hasten the fulfilment of our desires. . . . The officer took the letter back with him, and, as he left, cried again, 'Vive le Roi!' We echoed the cry, but with less enthusiasm than we had shown in the morning.

"The night being come, certain that we must pass it, and perhaps others yet, at the fort, we fell into conversation, the subject of which can easily be imagined. I had pulled my bed to pieces, and now began to think that I had better go and make it again if I wanted to rest at all comfortably. It was now one hour of the night, by Italian reckoning" (an hour and a half after sunset), "when we were told that a boat had come from Marseilles to remove fourteen prisoners who were to be set at liberty that night. Not imagining that I would be included in the fortunate number, I was not at all electrified by the news; but I was really much surprised at the attitude assumed by two Italian fellow-prisoners, who began to grumble violently at the indiscretion of coming to set them free at such an hour, and declared that they would not move, even if their names were on the list. I protested against this extravagant resolution, saying that at whatever time I might receive permission to go, I should instantly avail myself of it. Exactly at that moment I received word that I was among the chosen number, and my compatriots had their wish, for there was no message for them.

"Beside myself with relief, believing it could be but a happy dream, I asked myself, and my companions too, if I were really awake! I picked up my cloak, resolving to return for my baggage the next day, came out of the prison, and got into the boat with thirteen of my colleagues (among them was the Curé, Don Giuseppe Venere), regretting indeed to have left in that dolorous dwelling twelve of our companions. These last had to remain there for some days yet; we learnt that the Commandant of Marseilles had set us free on his own responsibility, in order to appease the populace, which clamoured loudly for the liberation of the prisoners detained in the Château d'If. The Commandant thought that, if he sent for some of us, the people would be pacified, as indeed they were, being quite ignorant of how many the fort contained. Before quite emptying the prison the Commandant wished to have orders from Court, and these he received about a week after our liberation.

"After a crossing which did not occupy more than half an hour, the wind being favourable, we entered the port of Marseilles, which presented a really beautiful spectacle; every habitation in the city was illuminated, and the place was one vast brilliant amphitheatre. On every side one heard cries of joy, flags were waving, bands playing. When we reached the quay where we were to disembark we stepped on shore into an immense concourse of people who, having heard of our sufferings, welcomed us with noisy enthusiasm and with demonstrations of the most lively cordiality. I could not escape being kissed by one good woman who threw her arms round my neck, but whose white hair reassured me that there was no diabolical suggestion in an act so irregular for any one, and particularly for an Italian! Accompanied by all this crowd, which faithfully clung to us, we were conducted to pay our respects to the Commandant, but we had not the good fortune to see him, as he had already gone to bed.

"And now the group of ex-prisoners broke up to go and seek for lodgings. I turned my steps to the house of Signor Carminati, the Italian banker, to whom I had been directed on my unhappy arrival in Marseilles, and from whom I had received an infinity of kindnesses during my imprisonment. During the earlier months of it, when we did not imagine it would last so long, he had begged me, when I should come out, to be sure to go and stay in his house. I now found that he was absent, having been obliged to travel to another part of Italy; but his wife and family received me with the greatest cordiality."

It is to be hoped that Signor Carminati's family was in ignorance of the incredible treachery of his conduct towards his trusting fellow countryman. The Marchese himself lived and died without becoming aware of it, but the revelations contained in the archives of the Secret Police, and only discovered in recent years, appear to supply a motive for the Italian banker's presence being so " urgently required elsewhere " when Patrizi came out of prison !

Giovanni continues : "The next morning, in spite of the heavy rain, I returned to the fort to fetch my effects, and was touched with pity at the sight of my late companions who had remained there and were still uncertain as to the happy moment which should deliver them from their troubles. There were some whose condition really aroused compassion, for their fortitude failed them altogether in this new and wearing trial. Twelve remained there for a week longer, and the other two for a couple of days more after that before obtaining their freedom.

"How great was my own consolation, two or three days after I was set at liberty, on receiving a letter from my beloved wife, in which she informed me that La Flèche had also been freed from the yoke of the tyrant, that her sons had already returned to her side, and that, in spite of the perils to which they had been exposed, they had, by the Divine Mercy, remained faithful to their principles ! May God's Holy Name be blessed ! "

It may strike the modern reader as something of an exaggeration to talk of the ' principles ' of boys of the age of Xavier and Filippo, but the home education of those days did not hesitate to teach even the very young that they were primarily responsible for their own souls, that in a world full of the enemies of religion they were expected to play their own modest part as faithful Christians and good soldiers of the Church. It was Cunegonda's good fortune to be at hand at La Flèche to remind them of all these things whenever they could be with her ; and her merit that she had sacrificed home and comforts, and her health too, in order to stay near her boys. But one must remember that she only saw them for short intervals now and again, and that for the greater part of the time they were entirely in the hands of instructors who would do everything possible to make them imbibe the Voltairian theories which they held themselves—men who would never miss an opportunity of trying to weaken their pupils' respect and loyalty to the Church. It says something for the characters of the Patrizi boys, as well as for their early upbringing, that all these contrary influences cast no taint or shadow on their young minds, and that they returned to their home as pure and simple and devout as they had been when they left it.

Giovanni had planned to go to Lyon to meet his wife, but he changed his route on hearing from her that she intended to make a little stay in Paris to try and recover the property of her father, Prince Xavier of Saxony, who had departed this life some eight years earlier. The Marchese's widowed mother was eagerly awaiting him in Rome, and he was in haste to console her for his own long absence and her great loss. An old and dear friend of them both, Cardinal Consalvi, urged her claims too, very warmly. The Marchese writes : "Great indeed was my joy when, after another day or two in Marseilles, I had the satisfaction of once more embracing the Eminentissimo Consalvi, my valued friend, who was also returning to Italy and had come fifty miles out of his way to see me in passing. At the moment of our reunion I could not refrain from recalling to him the memory of my dear father, and our tears fell together, mine for a parent, his for a friend. Having then spoken to him of my design of going to Lyon to wait there for my wife to rejoin me, he showed me such excellent reasons for at once proceeding to Rome that I decided to follow his advice and do so. . . . I engaged a posting carriage to carry me from Marseilles to Nice, taking as my

A MASONIC FESTIVAL

travelling companion Don Giuseppe Venere, the Curé of Civitella Cesi, who had been my colleague at the Château d'If; and I fixed our departure for April 27, it being well understood that the carriage was to take no other passengers."

The Marchese's own luxurious travelling carriage, confided the year before to the lauded Signor Carminati, seems to have been sent back to Nice for some reason. The Memoirs do not enlighten us on this point, but they contain here the description of a curious sight that the writer beheld during his halt in Marseilles.

"Returning to the house alone one evening, after assisting at a musical gathering, I heard from far away the sounds of drums and other military instruments, which seemed to be accompanying a funeral. Then I saw the light of many torches, flaring in the wind, coming towards me, and curiosity made me halt to see what it was all about. The procession was headed by a banner inscribed *The French Lodge of St. Louis*, which, being interpreted, meant 'The Masonic Lodge hypocritically called of St. Louis.' I perceived that this was a Masonic festival, and I confess that I shuddered at the thought; but I determined to see what was taking place. After the standard-bearer came a considerable number of persons carrying torches, some of pitch, some, if I am not mistaken, of wax. They were followed by a bier carried by four men, and covered by what looked like a black pall; on the bier was fixed a bust, evidently the portrait of one of the royal family of France, and I imagined that the show was intended to do honour to the unfortunate Louis XVI. I said as much to another spectator at my side, but he replied that the bust represented Louis XVIII, and that the Freemasons were carrying it in triumph about the city!

"The procession went on, and halted at the house of the Mayor, and, under the windows, one of these unhappy men addressed a complimentary oration to the Magistrate. I was told that the company had already visited the theatre, with equal pomp. . . . Afterwards, that abhorred pack retreated to its lair, and I came home, indignant at what I had seen, and forming melancholy auguries of the fortunes of a monarchy which, at the moment of its restoration, permitted the public celebrations of an impious and revolutionary sect!

"On the afternoon of April 27 I left Marseilles, with my travelling companion, Don Giuseppe Venere, and before arriving at Aix we overtook Cardinal Gabrielli, who was returning by that road. I was glad, truly, to salute the most worthy prelate, who also greeted me with very great cordiality. . . . We reached Fréjus" (on the 29th) "and were told that the errant usurper Bonaparte had embarked from the little port eight hours earlier to be conveyed to the Island of Elba. That same evening we reached Cannes, where we passed the night. Leaving Cannes on the 30th, we crossed the Var, and said the Te Deum with all our hearts when we found ourselves once more in our beautiful and beloved Italy. At midday we drove into Nice, and I at once made inquiries for my own travelling carriage ; but heard, to my great disappointment, that it had been put on board a vessel bound for Marseilles. It was suggested to me that I should wait for its return, which could be effected by writing at once to that place, but I would not submit to such a waste of time. I decided to stay one day in Nice to procure a coach as far as Turin, and from thence I would post it back to Rome.

"That evening I received visits from the Cardinals Brancadaro and Gabrielli, who had come to Nice in the hope of meeting the Holy Father ; but they could get no news of him ; nobody knew in the least where he might be."

On May 3 the Marchese and the Curé reached Tenda, where elaborate arrangements had to be made for crossing the pass.

"The Vetturino," Giovanni writes, "arranged for us to have horses to ride, and also to carry our possessions over the Col di Tenda. The coach was left here, and another was to be found for us at Limone, a small town on the other side. So, on the morning of the 4th, we mounted and ascended to the top of the pass quite easily ; but there we had to alight and go forward on foot, as it was impossible to ride down. So I started on the descent with a man on either side to hold me up, for the ice caused me to slip at every step. But, further, the path was so narrow that three could not walk abreast, and I foresaw that the journey would be long and tedious. I was bewailing this to the two peasants who were helping me, and they at once proposed that we should take a short cut, and I most gladly assented; but when they showed it to me I was utterly dismayed, for it was simply the steep slope of that towering mountain thickly covered with snow! As I did not want to pass immediately from the Col di Tenda to a better world, I hesitated a little . . . but my guides, who were practical men, assuring me that there was no danger, I allowed myself to be persuaded, and, almost carried by them, started to slide down that break-neck slope, of which I could not even see the termination. From time to time we halted to take breath; often we were above our knees in the snow, but I accomplished thus in half an hour the descent which would have occupied two if I had kept to the beaten track.

"My companion had not followed my example . . . and made his journey over the path followed by the packhorses, with various tumbles on the way. I arrived alone at the village of Limone, and had to go to bed while my breeches were being dried, for they were soaked through with the snow.

"That evening we reached Cuneo, which was crowded with French troops returning to France. At Cuneo I again had the good luck to find Cardinal Brancadaro in the same hotel, and the next morning he went publicly, though still in a layman's habit, to the Church of a Confraternity where my travelling companion Don G. Venere said Mass with the accompaniment of the organ."

The journey continued without much incident except the frequent falling in with other joyfully returning exiles, till the travellers approached Modena, when, the Marchese says, "We were accosted by two ecclesiastics who begged us to come and stay at a certain palace of the town, which, by the kindness of several pious persons, had been converted into a hospice where all returning exiles were entertained free of charge by the charity of that Benevolent Society. A fine example, which does great honour to the good Modenese! We thanked the ecclesiastics very gratefully for their kind offer, but excused ourselves from accepting it, as we were in a great hurry to continue our journey.

"On entering the city I went to visit my friend, Count Marchisio. . . . In his house I found Cardinal Pignatelli, who was staying there, in a very pitiable condition, the result of repeated and violent fits of apoplexy which he had suffered in France. This most worthy prelate, the moment he saw me, burst into uncontrollable weeping, the usual consequence of that distemper, and embraced me with much tenderness, at which I was greatly touched.

"Meanwhile the Curé had betaken himself to the hospice for the returning exiles, where he was regaled with chocolate. There I went to fetch him, and we got into the carriage and resumed our journey, arriving towards evening at Bologna, where we stopped at the Hotel del Pellegrino. In Bologna I saw my cousin, Donna Prudenza Spada, the wife of Marchese Valerio Boschi, and also Count Baccili and the priest Don Girolamo Ricci, both old fellow prisoners with me at Fenestrelle.

". . . On the 12th we reached Siena, where I went to my own house. I had intended to leave on the 13th, but, some repairs to the travelling carriage being required, I remained for two days.

"During this time I enjoyed the company of my delightful uncle, the Bailli Ruspoli, who was now permanently established in Siena, in my house; and I received innumerable kind attentions from his Grace the Archbishop Zondadari, as well as from many others of the good Sienese gentlemen. The archbishop invited me to dinner, and among the guests was Cardinal Ruffo, who was staying with him. While there we received the comforting news that the Pontifical Government had been restored in Rome on the 11th.

"On the 15th we left Siena and arrived that night at San Lorenzo Nuovo. Passing through Acquapendente, we saw the illuminations and celebrations in honour of the restoration of the Pontifical Government.

"Leaving San Lorenzo Nuovo on the 16th,

we reached Viterbo about noon. . . . In this town I parted from my companion, the Curé Venere, and went on towards Rome with a young Roman, who in Turin had begged me to take him on the box as my servant, so that he could get back to his own country. We left Viterbo at about two in the afternoon—two hours after midnight I at last entered Rome!

"How can I describe my joy in approaching, in entering, the gates of my beloved country (*patria*)! With what ecstasy I sang the Te Deum as I passed through the Porta del Popolo!

"But yet greater was my joy on entering the house from which the most cruel of tyrants had barbarously kept me torn away for more than two years! Only one cloud was now cast over my happiness by the reflection that I would not find there my most beloved father, passed already, as I hope, to an infinitely happier dwelling.

"Many of the servants, as well as the good tutor, came down the stairs to meet me. Near the door of the Sala, preparing to follow them, was my darling Costantino, with my dear sister Maria, and in the doorway of the second anteroom stood my beloved mother, leaning on her stick, for she had not quite recovered from the bad fall she had had in September. . . . Oh the tenderness of those embraces and kisses when I pressed to my heart those dear objects of filial, paternal, and brotherly affection! How the tears flowed when

I threw my arms round my good mother, both of us remembering him whom we had lost five months before!

"That same night, even, and in the days that followed I received continual visits from relations, old friends, and numbers of other persons, who flocked to congratulate me on my return. . . ."

Giovanni Patrizi's troubles were over, the reward of his constancy and courage was meted out to him at last. Of all the nobles, not only of Rome but of Italy, he was the only one who had resisted unflinchingly the odious enactments of the "Golden Levy," the only one, as the French historian, who abuses and decries him, is forced to admit, who never cringed or yielded for a moment to the overwhelming forces opposed to him. He himself was taken by force; his boys were the only ones who had to be conducted by force to Napoleon's school, and he would have met death smiling had death meant the safety of his children's souls. The sons of such a father were very precious in the eyes of God. All three justified their paternity. Xavier, the eldest, entered the Society of Jesus a year before Giovanni's death, became immensely distinguished for the holiness of his life and for his vast learning, especially in exegesis and Oriental languages, of which subjects he held the chairs at the Sapienza College for many years. Constantino entered the ecclesiastical state, became a prelate, "Maestro di Camera" to Pius IX, finally cardinal, and—strange turn of Fortune's wheel !—was deputed to represent the Pontiff as godfather at the baptism of the Prince Imperial, the son of Napoleon III. As to Giovanni's third son, the irrepressible " Pippo," he grew up, married, first, Giovanna dei Conti Somunaglia, and, after her death Giulia Chigi, widow of the Marchese Lavaggi. He had several children, and his direct descendants to-day number just one hundred. The shadow of the Patrizis has not been allowed to grow less.

CHAPTER XV

On April 10, in that particular year of 1814, the sun had risen again for the exiled wife and children at La Flèche. Cunegonda's words seem to fall over each other in the letter which begins " Alleluia ! Alleluia ! " " La joie fait peur ! " The intensity of the relief was almost more than she could bear.

" At last we are free," she writes ; " our sorrows are over. Be patient if this letter is disjointed, for, what with joy and talk and packing-up, I have lost my head. I leave on Wednesday, the 13th, for Paris, to find out if you have been set free, and, if not, to have you brought out at once. I will stay there as short a time as possible, and hope to get through with my business in a very few days. I leave orders here for any letters that may come to be sent on to Paris. . . . If the King is already in Paris, or if he is just coming there, I will wait to see him about my own and my sister's interests in our father's property. The moment that affair is set going I will leave for my dear Rome. Write to me at Paris, Hôtel Hambourg, 18 Rue Jacob, and tell me if you are starting at once for Rome, as I imagine you will be. . . . My dear Giovanni, after nearly twenty-nine months of separation, we are on the eve of being reunited, miraculously reunited. The Chevalier is crazy with joy—as we all are. . . ."

Xavier adds a postscript : " At last we can write to one another in our own language and without any mysteries."

Pippo, too, puts in his word : " At last the hour has come when all the bonds that kept us in France are broken ; we can go back to our dear Rome! Oh, what a beautiful Easter!"

Cunegonda could learn nothing definite about her husband when she reached Paris, and, writing to him again, on April 19, still addresses her letter to Marseilles. Her brother-in-law, the Duc d'Esclignac, had already on the 11th written a very pressing letter to some high functionary, although precisely which it is impossible to say, as the letter still preserved in the Paris archives bears no address.

"Monsieur le Baron,

"I wish to speak to you about the Marquis and Marquise Patrizi" (the latter) " my sister-in-law, exiled or imprisoned on account of their opinions, on the subject of which I had the honour of speaking to Your Excellency already six months ago.

"The letter of M. le Comte de Nesselrode leaving no doubt whatever as to the manner in which they, as well as their children, who were sent by force to la Flèche, are to be treated, I should have considered it superfluous to present my request but for the fact that the many occupations laid upon you by present circumstances made it my duty to remind you of the Patrizis, knowing well, Monsieur le Baron, how unwillingly you consented to the execution of the unjust and hard measures used towards this family; this knowledge assures me of the promptness with which you will give the required orders for their liberation.

"I am, etc., etc.,
"Le Duc d'Esclignac."

The return of the little family from La Flèche to Paris is described by Xavier when he conscientiously writes up his journal there.

"When we entered the city on the 14th of April, by the Barrière of Passy, situated on the Seine, I saw a double stockade that had been set up to impede the entry of the Allies, a purely nominal thing which might have delayed them three or four minutes at the most. The barricade was guarded by Russian troops and the National Guard. At the Champs de Mars there was a small Russian camp with a great many mortars. The same was on the field of the Invalides; but there was no artillery there or at the barricade either. The Emperors of Russia and Austria were in Paris, the King of Prussia, and Bernadotte the King of Sweden; but the last was treated as of no importance at all; so he is preparing to leave, with the excuse of attending to affairs in his Kingdom. The Comte d'Artois, called ' Monsieur ' because he is the own brother of Louis XVIII, arrived on the 11th inst., receiving tremendous acclamations from the populace, accompanied by 600 men of the National Guard, and he himself in the uniform of the said Guard; he, the moment he arrived, went to give thanks to God, at the Church of Notre Dame. He is now Lieutenant-General (viceroy) of the Kingdom till the King's arrival. The Emperor of Russia, Alexander, entered Paris with the King of Prussia, on the 31st of March; after a fight which lasted twelve hours, 20,000 Frenchmen were overcome by 200,000 of the Allies, and Paris was obliged to capitulate. He" (the Emperor of Russia) "having been asked by all the inhabitants to place a Bourbon on the throne, he promised to do so. On the 14th the schismatic" (Russian orthodox) "priests sang a Te Deum on the Place de la Concorde, otherwise Place de Louis XV, the Emperor of Russia, although a schismatic, acknowledging that his victory was all the work of God. The Emperor of Austria entered on the 15th" (of April). "Besides the troops of the said sovereigns there are also English. All the troops in Paris are 50,000; and there are 100,000 in the environs.

"On coming into Paris I saw the Dome of the Invalides with the gilding finished; only on the upper part, however. The so-called Palace of the King of Rome has been left six or seven palms high. It is pleasant to see the Eagles, etc., taken down . . . all that belonged to the past Government. Bonaparte is derided in many papers which are scattered about the city. He is at Fontainebleau, where he amuses himself with making decrees and distributing decorations, notwithstanding his abdication.

"Before the arrival of Monsieur, a provisional Government of three persons was formed.

"It is notable that the first decrees of the said Government were: first, the liberation of the Pope; second, the restoration of children to their parents. The Senate has made a constitution, which is in vigour now, although it seems that the King will not be able to accept it.

"On the 16th, returning from St. Germain des Prés, at the end of the Rue Bonaparte I found that the name had ceased to exist, and they say it is to be called the Rue de la Paix. On the 17th I heard for the first time the "Domine salvum fac Regem" sung in the above-mentioned church.

". . . At the Champs Elysées there was much baggage of the Allied Troops, and also of the Cossacks, famous robbers and destroyers, and therefore very unfavourably regarded (!) I passed before the hotel called L'Elysée Bourbon, where the Emperor of Russia is staying, and the Hôtel de Saxe, where the Emperor of Austria lodges: both are in the Rue Faubourg St. Honoré. There were other Palaces in the same street guarded by troops.

"On the 21st arrived the Duc de Berry, son of the Count d'Artois and nephew of the King. . . .

"I also went to the Place Vendôme, where there is the great bronze column from which the Emperor of Russia had removed the statue of Bonaparte to take it away to Russia, and put it on top of a pyramid made of all the cannon taken from the French. It is well to remember that the said column was made out of the bronze of cannon which Bonaparte took from the Austrians at the battle of Austerlitz."

There are gleams of philosophy in Xavier's journal!

On April 30 Cunegonda, with her boys and their faithful Cavalier, Don Lorenzo Giustiniani, started on their return to Italy. Their immediate objective was Lyon, where the Marchesa made sure she would find her husband waiting for her. He, as we have seen, imagined that the business would detain her much longer in Paris, and had returned back to his mother in Rome. It was a bitter disappointment to his wife when she arrived at Lyon, tremulous with joy at the thought of seeing him at last, to find that he had travelled by another route. She had flown from Paris at the first moment possible, in spite of feeling really ill with fever and her torment of headache, and, the disappointment coming after so much strain and agitation, quite overcame her fortitude. She tries to catch up with her dear traveller—hears that he is only three days ahead of her—and then, hearing that he is travelling night and day, resigns herself to accomplishing the rest of the journey in shorter stages.

But at last, at last, on May 22, at two o'clock in the afternoon, the husband and wife, the children and the parents, were reunited under their own roof—and how the old house must have rung with the greetings, the laughter, the sobs of happiness, the voices of the boys as they scampered about with the stay-at-home brother! The letters cease here. The conflicts were all over, the battles won; the after-history of Giovanni and his wife is the history of character, and for those who have accompanied them so far some details of it may not be without interest.

Two days after Cunegonda had reached home, Pius VII was brought back to Rome in triumph. That return awoke to new life the population which for six long years had remained obstinately deaf to French orders and French cajoleries; which, though passionately fond of amusements, had refused to be amused by the invader; though devout, had refused to enter the Basilica for his Te Deums; had, in dead silence, obeyed scrupulously the slightest indication of a wish on the part of its absent sovereign; for, as the French authorities themselves complained, "The Pope has, even now, more power in his little finger than we with the Empire at our back!"

Active resistance there had been none to speak of; the Romans, pure and simple, are not a factious people, but the dead wall of deaf-and-dumb obstinacy presented an obstacle impossible to overcome. Deluded, like Alaric, by his own passionate desire to possess the capital of Christendom, his dreams nursed by only too willing agents, Napoleon discovered, at last, that the capital of Christendom would have none of him, and that all his genius and power could not shake the strange, deep-seated loyalty of the people to their own ruler. Many and good reasons have been supplied for his failure; but even had he gone about the matter differently—even had he refused to listen to the scruples from which, in fact, he was never free, or to the lures of popularity which he promised himself to the end—and had he treated Rome as he did other conquered cities, he was doomed to fail. Rome has capitulated, since, to a greater force than Napoleon could bring to bear on it; a hundred years of human development in anti-Christian directions has produced generation after generation to whom it is all one who rules so long as their own existence can go comfortably forwards. Feeling is dead; the mob, more than ever in the world's history, crawls on its stomach. But a hundred years ago it was not so; there was something of the spiritual still in the composition of the man in the street, unsatisfactory as he might be in many ways.

It seems unlikely that the world will ever again witness such an outburst of emotion as that which greeted Pius VII when he entered the gate of Porta del Popolo on May 24, 1814.

He was dressed in full pontifical robes, and sat in the amazing old Spanish gala coach in which Charles IV of Spain had entered Rome as a refugee (and pensioner of Napoleon) two years earlier, a conveyance of which the Romans had never seen the like for massive gorgeousness. Before the Pope's cortège had reached the gate a crowd of young nobles flung themselves upon the carriage, took out the horses, and dragged it themselves to St. Peter's through streets where the crowds, weeping and shouting for joy, prostrated themselves at every step to receive the Sovereign's blessing. Windows, balconies, roofs, every point where standing room could be obtained swarmed with human beings; every window was hung with bright draperies; the air was a cloud of waving handkerchiefs and showers of flowers. For once St. Peter's was full to danger point. The French historian * says : " The flood of humanity, beating against the enormous walls of the Basilica, resembled a great sea, long held back by an invincible dyke, and now suddenly dashing through. The dyke had been built by the frail hands of this aged

* Madelin.

PIUS · VII.
From the Statue by Antonio Canova.
Engraved by Balestra, after a painting by Camucini.

man, who now broke it down ; Pius VII had said, 'Anathema on whomsoever shall take part in the work of the French.' 'Roma locuta est'—and the Romans, in their strange, silent way, which seemed so supine and inefficient to onlookers, had obeyed to the letter, and, by their dumb obedience, had paralysed all the efforts of the conqueror of Europe.

"Now they were dumb no longer; sorrow is silent, but joy loves to rend the skies. The day and those that followed were one long festival in the city. The Pope entering the Quirinal, and beholding all the sumptuous preparations (in true first-Empire taste) for its occupation by the 'King of Rome' and his imperial mother, merely remarked, with an amused smile, 'Ah, they were not expecting *us*! We can replace their gods and goddesses with saints, and every one will have had his way!'"

If he could laugh, others could, too, and Rome was itself again!

Among the first to throw themselves at their Sovereign's feet was Giovanni Patrizi. The Holy Father recognised him at once, and embraced him tenderly. In a private audience granted to the whole family a few days later the Pope expressed his desire to give the Marchese a public proof of his favour; but Patrizi deprecated all recognition, saying that he did not wish to hear the word "merit," and far less to receive rewards for having done what was purely his duty.

Nevertheless, in the ensuing September Pius VII named him Senator of Rome, the highest civic dignity, corresponding, though with far greater power and distinction, to the office of Prefect. In doing this the Pope departed from the invariable law hitherto observed which forbade that the Romans should be governed by one of their own fellow-citizens. But every one concurred in the justice of the nomination, for Patrizi was the only noble who had publicly and consistently proclaimed his allegiance to his rightful sovereign. He made his state entrance into the Capitol on January 1, 1815, and was the last Senator who did so with all the antique pomps of procession and cavalcade.

In the two years that elapsed before his death he devoted himself with his whole heart to the great duties of his position, sparing no efforts to maintain order, salubrity, and decorum in the beloved city committed to his care. But, side by side with this public life of pomp and place, he was leading in the privacy of his home a life of constant detachment, all-embracing charity, self-denial, and prayer. His long imprisonment, its sorrows and anxieties, as well as the many months during which he had been forbidden fresh air and exercise, all these things had seriously undermined his health and brought on the cardiac affection which ended his life almost before he had reached his prime. But to Giovanni Patrizi the solitude of his prison had brought a great flood of inner light; the reward of his simple, unquestioning loyalty to duty had been for this true Paladin the revelation of things unseen. While scrupulously fulfilling his great public responsibilities and continuing in his home to be the most loving son and husband and father, the eyes of his soul were fixed on the distant bourne, and he approached it gladly and readily, as a child turns to its home.

All the love and care by which he was surrounded could not delay the end. On January 1, 1817, he found that he could no longer rise from his bed. With all his dear ones kneeling around him he received the last Sacraments of the Church he had loved so faithfully. On the 8th he passed away, serene and conscious, breathing his Saviour's words, "Lord, into Thy hands I commend my spirit."

They buried him in the Patrizi chapel in Santa Maria Maggiore, beside his father. Cunegonda was laid there with them in 1828. The two older boys had already heard and obeyed the call to Perfection; and the youngest, as has been said, remained in the world to follow in his father's footsteps and raise up many sons to honour his name.

TRANSLATOR'S NOTE

In view of the fact that those incapable of estimating the man and his extraordinary qualities have seen fit to cast aspersions upon the high intelligence and clearsightedness of Giovanni Patrizi, the compiler of these Memoirs, the Marchesa Maddelena Patrizi has judged it as well to append to her work a just and conclusive appreciation of him from the "Memoirs of Cardinal Pacca." It will be remembered that Cardinal Pacca was for a long time the Marchese's fellow-prisoner. The terms in which he speaks of him leave no doubt as to the high consideration with which Patrizi was regarded by the most thoughtful and distinguished men of his day. We reproduce the extract word for word.

"The year 1811 closed with the arrival at Fenestrelle of a prisoner worthy of particular mention. This was the Marchese Giovanni Naro Patrizi; he arrived on the 28th of December, the day on which the Church celebrates the Slaughter of the Holy Innocents. He had earned his sentence by refusing to consign his sons to the French Government, which insisted on educating them in one of the French Colleges, a possibility which

Patrizi regarded as a far worse fate than death for them—the destruction of their innocence and religious faith. I had often seen him in Rome, but had never conversed with him. This young Cavalier had no taste for noisy entertainments and the gay society of fashionable people; he was constantly seen in the churches, and gave much edification by assisting, in the habit of the brotherhood, at the religious functions of the Confraternities of which he was a member. This was enough to cause him to be looked down upon, laughed at, and generally regarded as a man of limited intelligence, dull, and more fitted for the cloister than the world. The occupation of Rome by the French, and the change of government, demonstrated how mistaken was this opinion of his character.

"While other gentlemen of the first nobility, either through base cowardice, or the even lower motive of personal interest, made efforts to obtain employments and appointments from the usurping Government, and crawled to the feet of General Miollis and the other French Ministers, Patrizi preserved intact the rare and exalted sentiments of a true Roman noble. Of these he gave brilliant proof when it was intimated to various parents that the Emperor required them to give up their children to the authorities to be educated in the schools and colleges of France. Patrizi instantly understood, and was revolted at the perfidious motive of this pretended paternal solicitude, and, rather than consign his own sons to the new Moloch Idol, exposed himself to the indignation and fury of Napoleon, who had him arrested and kept prisoner, first at Città Vecchia, and then at Fenestrelle.

"As the extreme rigour which had been exercised towards me in the first years of my imprisonment was then somewhat relaxed, and some of the other prisoners were allowed to come to my room and keep me company, I had full opportunity for knowing Patrizi well and forming my judgment on him. I can therefore say emphatically that he appeared to me a man well gifted with culture and erudition, and, further, one possessed of such principles of piety and religion that he was the edification of his fellow-prisoners."

INDEX

A

Albani, Cardinal, 194
Albano, 14–15, 21
Alexander I of Russia, 167, 306–7, 309
Altieri, Auguste, 268–9
Altieri, Clementino, 163, 176, 185, 269
Altieri, Prince, 48, 54–5, 58, 138, 142, 268
Altieri, Princess, 138, 143, 163, 165, 174–5, 203, 209, 269, 270
Amiens, Treaty of, 167
Angèles, M., 121
Appelins, Councillor, 260–1
Appolloni, Filippo, 119
Arnim, General Sixtus von, 32
Artois, Count d'. *See* Charles X
Aspern, 20
Austerlitz, Battle of, 5
Azeglio, Marchese d', 197, 201–2

B

Baccani, Marianna, 183, 280
Bacchi, Canonico, 143
Baccili, Count Andrew, 134 *et sq.*, 180, 217, 300
Baglioni, Count, 269
Balbo, Cesare, 16, 19
Barberini, Prince, 58
Barberini, Princess Cornelia, 40
Bassi, Cavaliere, 126
Battaglia, Felice, 26
Bayane, Cardinal de, 248
"Beato Tarlato," 48 *et sq.*
Beauharnais, Eugène de, 15
Bellevue, M. le General, 245
Belli, 113, 120
Benedetti, 114

Bennini (Valet), 117
Berrera, Canon, 201, 217
Boisseau, Mme., 237
Bologna, 31, 125, 128, 130, 189, 192, 194, 300
— Palazzo Spada, 128
Bolognetti, Canon, 130
Bomba, Doctor, 156
Bonaparte, Jerome, 53
Bonaparte, Joseph (successively King of Naples and Spain), 6, 12, 53
Bonaparte, Lucien, 1
Bonneval, Monsignor de, 126
Borghese, Prince Camillo, 13, 198–9, 201–2, 214
Boschi, Marchese Valerio, 130, 300
Bracciano, Duchess of, 273
Brancadaro, Cardinal, 297 *et sq.*
Braschi, Duke, 177
Bruschi, Francesco, 126
Bucci (Steward), 101 *et sq.*, 106–7, 115

C

Cadoudal, Georges, 283
Calabrine, Vincenzo, 126
Callo, M., 112
Cambacérès, Chancellor, 249
Canova, 48
Capotti, Signor (Mayor of Civita Vecchia), 105, 115–16, 118–19
Caprani, Abbé, 196
Carminati, Signor, 219 *et sq.*, 291–2, 295
Catherine of Russia, Empress, 36
Ceccacci, 113
Cecchini, Signora Camilla, 181

Cenis, Mont, 203 *et sq.*
Chambéry, 202 *et sq.*, 216
Charlemagne, 5, 53
Charles III of Spain, 278
Charles IV of Spain, 193
Charles X of France, 307, 309
Chateaubriand, 276
Chiara Spinelli, Contessina. *See* Xavier
Chigi Giulia (afterwards 2nd wife of Filippo Patrizi), 303
Chigi, Marchesa, 177, 182, 187-8
Chiuchiulini, Signor Giacomo, 159
Civita Vecchia, 6, 95 *et sq.*, 128-9, 135 *et sq.*, 162, 174
—— Palazzo Montoro, 103, 105-6, 108, 126
Collia, Brigadier, 118, 120
Collicola, Signor Carlo, 93, 96-7
"Concordat," 2, 5, 24, 52, 247 *et sq.*
Consalvi, Cardinal, 46, 250-1, 294
"Consulta," 17 *et sq.*
Corsica, 196
Corsini, Don Neri, 232-3
Corsini, Prince Tommaso, 75, 232
Crescentini, 175
Custode, Luigi, 152, 181

D

Dall Pozzo, 17, 19
Danzer, M., 131, 161, 197, 213 *et sq.*, 219, 220
David, M. Bernard, 134, 152, 180
— Madame, 134
De Filippi, Captain, 91-2
De Rossi, Canon, 130
Descartes, René, 17
Desmarets (Agent of Police), 180
Di Pietro, Cardinal, 251, 253
Doria, Cardinal, 248
Dugnani, Cardinal, 248
Durand, 26
Duteil, General, 238, 245

E

Egidio, Fra, 13
Elba, Isle of, 285

Ema, Monastery of, 22
Esclignac, Duc d', 39, 305-6
— Duchesse d', 39, 269 *et sq.*
— Ernest d', 270-1

F

Feltre, Duc de, 67
Fenestrelle, 117-18, 122, 128, 132 *et sq.*, 140 *et sq.*, 150 *et sq.*, 196-7, 200, 205, 211 *et sq.*, 222, 227, 247, 261, 300, 319
Ferdinand IV (King of Naples), 54
Ferrero, Avvocato, 219
Florence, 8, 16 *et sq.*, 127, 177, 187, 191-2, 201
Fontainebleau, 248, 252, 308
Fontane, Père, 247
Fort, Chancellor, 260-1
Fouché, Duke of Otranto, Joseph, 23, 26-7
Francis, Emperor of Austria, 26, 306-7, 309
Fratini, Canon, 196
Frederick Augustus II (King of Poland), 35
Frederick Augustus III (King of Saxony), 35, 37, 39
Frederick William III (King of Prussia), 307

G

Gabbi, M., 219
Gabrielli, Cardinal, 55
— Don Pompeo, 280, 296-7
Gaeta, Duke of, 124
Gasparri, 113
Gazan, M., 151-2, 180-1
Gerando, Baron de, 17 *et sq.*, 24 n.
Gérard, M., 80
Giorgi, 114, 117
Giuliano, Castel, 86
Giustiniani, Chevalier Don Lorenzo, 74, 93, 138, 140-1, 148, 151, 155 *et sq.*, 177, 201, 206, 226, 231, 234, 268, 274, 278, 280-1, 309
Giusti Tommato, 157, 173-4, 182, 187-8, 194
"Golden Levy," 59, 60, 176, 302

INDEX 323

Gregorio, Monsignor de, 247
Gregory XVI, 168
Guglielmi, Signor Giulio, 105 *et sq.*, 116, 125-6
Guidi, Abbé, 196
Guillot, 39

H

Henri IV, 5
Henri V (Emperor), 252
Henry VIII of England, 252
Herbin, General, 8, 10, 54
Hobbes, Thomas, 17
Hompesch, Ferdinand von, 167

I

If, Château d', 211 *et sq.*, 226 *et sq.*, 255, 259 *et sq.*

J

Janet, Baron, 16 *et sq.*
Jena, Battle of, 5
Jolielen, Madame, 221
Joseph of Saxony, Prince, 35 *et sq.*, 40
Josephine, Empress, 163, 174
Julius Cæsar, 224

K

Kant, Immanuel, 17

L

Lafayette Marquis de, 16
La Flèche, Prytanée de, 63, 66, 122, 144 *et sq.*, 185, 209, 232 *et sq.*, 261, 266, 269, 270, 272 *et sq.*
Lagorse, Cardinal, 250, 253
Lante, Don Giulio, 280
Lante, Pippo, 176, 185
Lavaggi, Marchese, 303
Lehara, Chevalier, 282-3
Leipzig, 23-4
Lemarrois, General, 14, 17
Leo XII, 168
Ligne, Don Joseph de, 265

Louis XIV, 5
Louis XV, 5
Louis XVI, 14, 36, 296
Louis XVII, 38
Louis XVIII, 284, 287 *et sq.*, 296, 304

M

Madelin, M. Louis, 61 n., 131 n.
Maghella, 25, 28-9, 31
Mancini, Canon, 201
Marchisio, Cardinal, 299
Marengo, 2
Mariano, 119, 137, 155
Marie Antoinette, 38
Marini, Monsignor, 231
Marino, Don, 256
Marseilles, 213, 219 *et sq.*, 284 *et sq.*, 305
Martin, M., 234
Massimo, Marchesa, 138, 154, 163
Massimo, Marchese, 48, 58, 138, 154
Metastasio, 37
Milan, 14, 183, 193, 195 *et sq.*, 208
Miollis, General Sextus de, 7 *et sq.*, 13 *et sq.*, 54, 59, 65, 80, 87, 96, 121 *et sq.*, 318
Montbreton (Director of Police), 178, 186
Monterone, 99, 100
Monticelli, Rev. Stephano, 93
Moreau, 283
Murat, Joachim (King of Naples), 12 *et sq.*, 186

N

Naples, King of. *See* Ferdinand and Bonaparte
Naples, 6 *et sq.*, 187, 189, 190
Napoleon :
And the "Concordat," 1 *et sq.*, 52 *et sq.*, 247 *et sq.*
Institutes the Golden Levy, 58 *et sq.*
Summons Xavier and Filippo to La Flèche, 66 *et sq.*
Petition from Giovanni Patrizi to, 76 *et sq.*

INDEX

Napoleon (*continued*):
Defied by Patrizi, 84 *et sq.*
Sequesters the Patrizi revenues, 121 *et sq.*, 161, 186, 246
His personal hatred to the Patrizi family, 178 *et sq.*, 199, 210 *et sq.*, 275
His abdication, 284 *et sq.*
Napoleon III, 5, 303
Naro, Monsignor, 45, 125, 128
National Convention, 12
Nesselrode, Comte de, 305
Nicolai, Abbé, 177
Norvins, 161
Notre Dame, 53

O

Oblates of Tor de' Specchi, Convent of, 41
Occhiobello, 31
Odescalchi, Monsignor, 194
— Don Mommo, 280
Orville, Senator, 185

P

Pacca, Cardinal, 11, 21-2, 46, 55, 61 n., 136, 166, 173, 177, 210, 247, 250, 252, 255 *et sq.*, 317 *et sq.*
Palestrina, Prince and Princess of, 191
Parisani, Signor, 93, 116, 140, 151, 177
Pascal II, 252
Paterson, Elizabeth. *See* Bonaparte
Patrizi, Constantine, 48, 73, 119, 140, 151-2, 178, 183-4, 302, 313
Patrizi, Filippo, 48, 63, 66 *et sq.*, 108 *et sq.*, 119, 121 *et sq.*, 140 *et sq.*, 153 *et sq.*, 164 *et sq.*, 185, 195 *et sq.*, 219, 224 *et sq.*, 245 *et sq.*, 268, 272 *et sq.*, 293, 303, 305, 309, 315 ; his diary, 157 *et sq.*, 234 *et sq.*
Patrizi, Marchesa Cunegonda :
Her betrothal, 35
Her birth and parentage, 36 *et sq.*

Patrizi, Marchesa Cunegonda (*continued*):
Her early life, 38 *et sq.*
Her marriage, 41 *et sq.*
Birth of her children, 48
Her grief at her children being summoned to La Flèche, 72 *et sq.*
Encourages her husband to resist Napoleon's commands, 90
Told of her husband's arrest, 97
First letter to the Marchese, 107 *et sq.*
Ordered to escort her children to La Flèche, 109 *et sq.*
And her husband's removal to Fenestrelle, 138 *et sq.*
Attempts to procure her husband's release, 138 *et sq.*, 267 *et sq.*, 230, 257
Prepares for her journey to Paris, 141
Receives instructions from her husband regarding her journey, 144 *et sq.*
Describes her departure from Rome, 152 *et sq.*
Describes family affairs, 163, 174 *et sq.*, 268 *et sq*
Her stay in Siena prolonged, 164 *et sq.*
Her correspondence censored, 178 *et sq.*, 210 *et sq.*, 223, 228 *et sq.*, 242 *et sq.*, 259, 260, 271
Her doings in Siena, 182, 186 *et sq.*
On Costantino, 184
Leaves Siena, 190
Her journey to Paris described, 191 *et sq.*
Arrives at Turin, 196
Futile attempts to see her husband, 196 *et sq.*, 214, 126
Resumes her journey, 202 *et sq.*
Arrives in Paris, 224
Attempts to see the Duc de Rovigo, 228

INDEX

Patrizi, Marchesa Cunegonda
  (*continued*):
Describes her daily life, 230
  et sq., 238, 268 *et sq.*
Her children ordered to La
  Flèche, 232 *et sq.*, 239
And the "New Concordat,"
  247
Letter to Cardinal Pacca, 255–
  6, 258
And the death of Marchese
  Francesco Patrizi, 266
Anxiety about her children's
  health, 272–3
Her curious dream, 274
Her love of reading, 276–7
Her sweet disposition, 277–8
Her joy at reunion, 205, 304–
  5, 310
Her children returned to her,
  292–3
Starts for Italy, 309
Her death, 315
Patrizi, Marchesa Porzia, 43 *et
  sq.*, 74, 78, 93, 97, 121, 128,
  141, 151, 153, 162, 223, 265–6,
  275, 301
Patrizi, Marchese, Francesco, 43
  et sq., 58 *et sq.*, 68 *et sq.*, 78–9,
  84, 93, 97, 116–17, 119, 121 *et
  sq.*, 140–1, 151, 223, 240–1,
  262 *et sq.*
Patrizi, Marchese Giovanni Naro:
Historical introduction, 32–3
His betrothal to Princess
  Cunegonda of Saxony, 35
  et sq.
His marriage, 44–5
Birth of his children, 48
Invited to serve in the Imperial Guard in Paris, 59,
  60
His grief at the summons of
  his sons to La Flèche, 67 *et
  sq.*
Petitions Napoleon, 76 *et sq.*
Interview with Count Tournon, 80 *et sq.*
Definitely refuses to allow his
  sons to proceed to France,
  87 *et sq.*
His arrest, 94 *et sq.*

Patrizi, Marchese Giovanni Naro
  (*continued*):
His journey to Civita Vecchia,
  97 *et sq.*
Impressions of his new dwelling-place, 102 *et sq.*
Cheered by the arrival of new
  inmates, 112 *et sq.*
Ordered to leave Civita Vecchia, 117 *et sq.*
Napoleon's animosity against,
  121 *et sq.*, 210 *et sq.*
Family revenues sequestered
  by Napoleon, 121 *et sq.*,
  161
His journey to Fenestrelle described, 125 *et sq.*
Arrives at Fenestrelle, 134
His fellow prisoners, 135 *et sq.*,
  196
Prince Altieri intervenes on
  his behalf, 142 *et sq.*
His characteristics, 146–7
His correspondence tampered
  with, 178 *et sq.*, 205, 223,
  242 *et sq.*, 259, 271–2
Compromised by a letter, 207
  et sq.
Napoleon orders his removal
  from Fenestrelle, 211 *et sq.*
Describes his journey from
  Fenestrelle to Château d'If,
  216 *et sq.*
His ignorance of the welfare of
  his wife and children, 223,
  228 *et sq.*
Vain hopes of release, 246–7,
  254 *et sq.*, 284
His father's pathetic letters to,
  262 *et sq.*
His father's death, 266–7
Allowed to celebrate his
  mother's birthday, 275
His liberation, 285 *et sq.*
Celebrates the restoration of
  Louis XVIII, 286 *et sq.*
Describes a Masonic festival,
  295–6
His journey from Marseilles to
  Rome described, 296 *et sq.*
Arrives home, 301–2
Future of his sons, 302–3

INDEX

Patrizi, Marchese Giovanni Naro (*continued*):
  Reunited to the Marchesa, 310
  Private audience with Pius VII, 313-14
  Honoured by Pius VII, 314
  His death, 315
  Translator's note on, 317 *et sq.*
Patrizi, Maria Agnese, 69, 301
Patrizi, Mariuccia, 140
Patrizi, Palazzo, 38
Patrizi, Xavier, 48, 63, 66 *et sq.*, 108 *et sq.*, 119, 121 *et sq.*, 140 *et sq.*, 153 *et sq.*, 163 *et sq.*, 178, 185 *et sq.*, 195 *et sq.*, 219, 224 *et sq.*, 245 *et sq.*, 268, 274 *et sq.*, 293, 302, 305, 309, 315
Paul I of Russia, 167
Pelucchi, Signor, 89, 90
Pepe, Commissary, 154
Pepe, General, 17, 109 *et sq.*, 154
Pernon, 221
Pesme, Monsieur, 225
Pez, Maestro, 175
Pichegru, General, 283
Pignatelli, Cardinal, 251, 299
Pignatelli, Prince, 21, 30
Pignerolle, 207
Pius VII, 3 *et sq.*, 31, 52 *et sq.*, 85, 136, 160, 203, 246 *et sq.*, 310 *et sq.*
Pius IX, 57, 302
Poland, King of. *See* Frederick
Pollastri, 157, 174
Pont-sur-Seine, 224-5

R

Racine, 259
Radet, General, 17, 20-1, 30, 56-7
Riario, Duca, 48
Ricci, Don Girolamo, 300
Rochelle, M., 282
Roederer (French Prefect), 63 *et sq.*, 78, 232 *et sq.*, 238
Rolla, Signor, 217 *et sq.*
Rome :
  Appian Way, 15
  Campagna, 7, 23

Rome (*continued*) :
  Palazzo della Consulta, 35, 44 *et sq.*
  Palazzo Doria, 29, 30, 96
  Palazzo Farnese, 15, 17, 25, 29, 30
  Piazza di Spagna, 16, 24, 28, 30
  Porta d'Anzio, 25
  Porta Pia, 22
  Porta del Popolo, 16, 301, 312
  Porta San Giovanni, 15, 21
  Quirinal Palace, 7, 8, 11, 22, 54, 313
  Sant' Angelo, 29, 30, 54-5, 94, 97, 113, 177
  St. Maria Maggiore, 315
  St. Philip Neri, 44
Rospiglioso, 58
Rousillon, Major, 283
Rovigo, Duc de, 60, 62, 78 *et sq.*, 87, 91, 109 *et sq.*, 145, 154, 165, 180, 199, 210 *et sq.*, 218 *et sq.*, 223, 227-8, 232, 244, 246
Ruffo, Cardinal, 248, 300
Ruspoli, Bailli (Grand Master of Malta), 167 *et sq.*, 194, 240-1, 269, 270, 300
Ruspoli, Don Camillo, 280

S

St. Cloud, 124, 186
Sala, Abbé Domenico, 134-5, 143
Salicetti, Count, 12 *et sq.*, 18, 20, 22
Santo Spirito, Arch-hospital of, 125-6
Sasso, Castel, 86
Saxony, Princess Cunegonda of. *See* Patrizi, Marchesa
— Princes of. *See* Xavier, Joseph
— King of. *See* Frederick
— Queen of, 39
Scotti, Count Francesco, 194, 207 *et sq.*
Serrey, Bishop of, 158
Siena, 48 *et sq.*, 123, 126-7, 150 *et sq.*, 155, 161 *et sq.*, 174, 180 *et sq.*, 195, 300

Somunaglia, Giovanna dei Conti (1st wife of Filippo Patrizi), 303
Spada, Alessandro, 176
— Benedetto, 192
— Clementino, 192
— Donna Prudenzia, 130, 300

T

Thibeaudeau, Count, 260
Tournon, Count de, 24–5, 61–2, 64, 80 *et sq.*
Troyes, 39
Turin, 118 *et sq.*, 130 *et sq.*, 139, 150–1, 155, 181, 194 *et sq.*, 213 *et sq.*, 297
Tuscany, Elisa Baciocchi, Grand Duchess of, 182–3

V

Vandouvre, M. de, 281
Vaudal, 2
Vauguyon, Comte de, 28, 30
Venere, Don Giuseppe, 290, 295 *et sq.*, 301
Versailles, 235
Viscardi, C., 177
Viterbo, 96, 125–6, 129, 158–9

X

Xavier of Saxony, Prince, 35 *et sq.*, 47, 224, 270, 294
Xavier of Saxony, Princess, 37, *et sq.*, 294

Z

Zondadari, Very Rev. Archbishop, 127, 166, 187, 300
Zuccari, 20 *et sq.*

PRINTED BY
HAZELL, WATSON AND VINEY, LD.,
LONDON AND AYLESBURY.

www.ingramcontent.com/pod-product-compliance
Lightning Source LLC
Chambersburg PA
CBHW022048160426
43198CB00008B/156